The Rough (Chronicle

India

Rough Guides online

www.roughguides.com

credits

Text editors: Orla Duane, Andrew Dickson
Rough Guides series editor: Mark Ellingham
Production: Julia Bovis, Michelle Draycott, Katie Pringle
Design: Henry Iles
Proofreading: Jo Mead
Picture research: Eleanor Hill

publishing information

This edition published October 2002 by
Rough Guides Ltd, 80 Strand, London WC2R ORL

distributed by the Penguin group

Penguin Books Ltd, 80 Strand, London WC2R ORL.
Penguin Putnam, Inc. 375 Hudson Street, New York 10014, USA
Penguin Books Australia Ltd, 487 Maroondah Highway, PO Box
257, Ringwood, Victoria 3134, Australia
Penguin Books Canada Ltd, 10 Alcorn Avenue,
Toronto, Ontario, Canada M4V 1E4
Penguin Books (NZ) Ltd, 182–190 Wairau Road,
Auckland 10, New Zealand

Typeset to an original design by Henry Iles

Printed in Spain by Graphy Cems

© Dilip Hiro, 2002
400 pages includes index

A catalogue record for this book is
available from the British Library.
ISBN 1-85828-842-8

The Rough Guide
Chronicle

India

by
Dilip Hiro

series editor
Justin Wintle

notes and acknowledgements

The following references provide full publication details for quotations used (page references indicate where each citation occurs in this book).

p.26 Vyasa, *Mahabharata* (trans. Romesh C. Dutta), Jaico Publishing House, Bombay, 1944; p.40 *The Dhammapada: The Sacred Books of the East Series*, vol. X (trans. Max Fredrich Muller), Clarendon Press, Oxford, 1881; p.49 Chankaya Kautilya, *The Arthasastra* (ed. L.N. Rangarajan), Penguin India, Delhi, 1992; p.53 Romila Thapar, *Ashoka and the Decline of the Mauryas*, Oxford University Press, Oxford, 1961; p.55 *Manu Smriti: Sacred Books of the East Series*, vol. XXV (trans. G. Buhler), Clarendon Press, Oxford, 1886; p.64 *The Bhagvad Gita* (trans. Juan Mascaro), Penguin, Harmondsworth, 1962; p.66 Tiru Valluvar, *The Kural, or The Maxims of Tiru Valluvar* (trans.V.V.S. Aiyar), Woriur, Tiruchirapalli, 1915; p.72 Vatsyayana, *Kama Sutra*, Castle Books, New York, 1963; p.92 A.L. Basham, *The Wonder That Was India: A Survey of the History and Culture of the Indian Subcontinent Before the Coming of the Muslims*, Fontana/Collins, London, 1971; p.121 Albiruni/beruni, *Tahqiq-i-Hind* , cited in E.C. Sachau, *E. C. Alberuni's India*, London, 1914; p.132 Minjahu as Siraj, *Tabakat-i Nasiri* (trans. G. H. Raverty), Trubner & Co., London, 1881; p.137 Milton Rugoff (ed.), *The Travels of Marco Polo*, Pocket Books, New York, 1961; p.180 and p.184 Waldemar Hansen, *The Peacock Throne: The drama of Mogul India,* Holt, Rhinehart and Winston, New York, 1968; p.185 Thomas Roe, *The Embassy of Sir Thomas Roe to India, 1615–19* (ed. W. Foster), Hakluyt Society, London, 1926; p.197 Niccolao Manucci, *Storio do mogor /Story of the Moghul* (trans. W. Irvine), 3 vols, London, 1907–08; p.235 Bipan Chandra *et al.*, *India's Struggle for Independence*, Penguin, New Delhi, 1989; p.245 Eugene Kamenka (ed.), *The Portable Karl Marx*, Penguin, Harmondsworth, 1983; p.253 M. J. Akbar, *Nehru: The Making of India*, Viking-Penguin, London, 1988.

contents

Introduction

The word 'India' derives from **Sindhu**, the Sanskrit name of the great river – known in English as the Indus – that flows into the Arabian Sea from its source in the snowy peaks of the Himalayas. The ancient Persians, unable to pronounce the initial 'S', used the word *Hindu* to denote both the land and the people beyond the river's eastern bank. The term then passed to the Greeks and into Europe generally, resulting in the word *Indu*, which in turn became 'India' in English. Muslim invaders from Afghanistan and beyond adopted the term *Hindustan* (meaning 'Place of Hindus') – a sobriquet sometimes applied by British and other European interlopers in the 18th and 19th centuries.

It is appropriate that India's modern name should derive from the Sindhu/Indus, for it was in the fertile watershed of that river that an agrarian civilization, the **Indus Valley Civilization**, developed in prehistoric times – in much the same way as other such civilizations germinated along the banks of the Nile in Egypt, the Euphrates in Mesopotamia and the Yellow River in China. On modern atlases, of course, the Indus flows through Pakistan, which came into existence in 1947. Before that year, however, 'India' – or what is meant by 'India' in most of this book – was a vast subcontinent, bounded by the jungles and hills of Myanmar (Burma) in the east, the Himalayas to the north, Persia and other central Asian empires to the northwest and west, and by the apron of the Indian Ocean to the south. Within this frame, a rich diversity of peoples and cultures, empires, kingdoms and republics, have flourished – not just in the luxuriant northern plains, but also in the peninsular southern plateau.

Even in prehistoric times India's population was ethnically diverse, ranging from **Negritos** (dwarfish negroid peoples

PHYSICAL GEOGRAPHY

Metres
6000
5000
4000
3000
2000
1000
500
200
0

CHINA

AFGHANISTAN

Hindu Kush

Karakoram

Kunlun Shan

Tibetan Plateau

TIBET AUTONOMOUS REGION

NEPAL

Mt Everest

HIMALAYAS

BHUTAN

Brahmaputra

BANGLADESH

MYANMAR (BURMA)

BENGAL

Ganges

Ghangara

Ganges

DOAB

Jamuna

Chambal

Betwa

Son

INDO-GANGETIC PLAIN

VINDHYA RANGE

Narmada

SATPURA RANGE

Indus

Jhelum

Chenab

Ravi

Satlej

PANJAB

Sutlej

Thar Desert

SULAIMAN RANGE

KIRTHAR RANGE

PAKISTAN

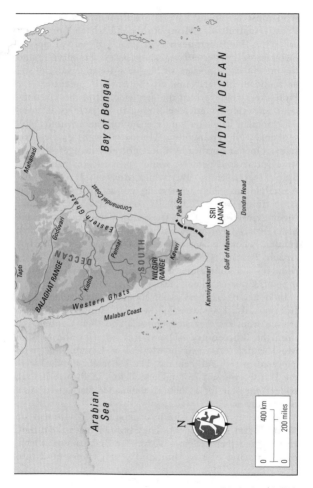

who must originally have come from Africa by sea) to **Proto–Australoids**, **Mongoloids** and what is sometimes called the **'Mediterranean type'**. Each of these groups, all members of the species *homo sapiens sapiens*, has survived into the present day – pockets of Negritos, for instance, can still be found in the far south. At the dawn of prehistory, the Proto-Australoids formed the core element in the subcontinent, speaking tongues belonging to the widely diffused Austronesian language family – among them Munda, still spoken by the eponymous Munda tribes of east-central India. On the northeastern and northern fringes of India were Mongoloid peoples, whose speech forms part of the Sino-Tibetan group. But while Mongoloids and Proto-Australoids are likely to have arrived at approximately the same time – from 70,000 BC onwards – it is the later Mediterranean type that is most closely associated with the Indus Valley Civilization and the subcontinent's Dravidian culture. Following later conquests these races were joined by Aryans, Persians, Greeks, Scythians, Huns, Afghans, Turks, Mongols and some modern Europeans. The result is a melting-pot of unrivalled complexity.

Indo-Aryans achieved major conquests from around 1500 BC onwards. They were followed by Muslim tribes, who arrived from the Arabian peninsula and then Central Asia from the 8th century AD onwards; then by the Muslim Mughals (the term used for Mongols in Central Asia), who appeared in the 16th century. The last major invaders were the British, whose 1757 military victory at Plassey, Bengal, opened the way for a political dominance that lasted nearly two centuries.

The Aryans were decisive in shaping the religious makeup of the Indian subcontinent. They brought with them their customs and their religion, Vedism or Brahmanism, which, over a period of two thousand years, transmuted into

Hinduism. This transformation occurred against the background of the emergence of two major religions, **Buddhism** and **Jainism**, around the turn of the 6th and 5th centuries BC. Under **Emperor Ashoka** (r. 273–232 BC) – India's first great ruler, whose domains included modern Afghanistan as well as most of the subcontinent – Buddhism became the state religion. Facing the rising popularity of Buddhism, Vedic brahmins (priests) simplified and reformed their elaborate rituals – if only for their political survival. In the end they were so successful that while Buddhism spread successfully to China and other parts of Asia, it became a minority faith in India and remains so; some four-fifths of Indians are Hindu.

While this first recorded wave of invaders resulted in an amalgamation of beliefs, no such synthesis occurred in the case of the next ones – the Muslim Arabs from the Arabian peninsula, and later Muslim tribes from Afghanistan and beyond. Pantheistic Hinduism and monotheistic Islam were antithetical, and remain so. Nonetheless, cultural amalgamation occurred – most notably in architecture, painting, music and dance. This reached a high point in the 16th and 17th centuries during the reign of Mughal emperors **Akbar**, **Jahangir** and **Shah Jahan**.

The intrusion of **Europeans**, which started with sea trade in the early 16th century, opened a new chapter in the history of South Asia. The involvement of Britain proved particularly long-lasting. England's earliest traders sailed to India and destinations further east in search of spices (used for preserving meat) and fine textiles. By 1830, the East India Company was transporting shiploads of unprocessed Indian cotton to textile factories in Lancashire – much of it to be shipped back to India as finished cloth. In due course, Britain developed India as its major supplier of indigo, jute, tea and opium. This burgeoning maritime empire, geared towards maximum economic exploitation of the colonies, required a new administrative system: relays of European soldiers and civil servants travelled to the colonies, served for a fixed period and returned home. Out of this arose an unprecedented pattern of relationship between British masters and non-British subjects. In South Asia, this divergence became sharply defined after the failure of the **Great Indian Uprising** of 1857. The British set up a segregated system in India, living in separate neighbourhoods from Indians and distancing themselves socially.

During the second half of the 19th century, the **industrial revolution** – which generated railways, electricity, the telegraph, the telephone and radiotelephony – set the technological foundation for a political revolution, both in Britain and its colonies. These inventions, and the spread of anti-imperialist ideas in the wake of World War I, set the stage for the downfall of the British Empire in India and elsewhere. The **Indian National Congress**, founded by upper-class Indians towards the end of the 19th century, steadily became a powerful vehicle of Indian nationalism. It achieved its aim of full independence in 1947 – but only after agreeing, reluctantly, to the partition of the erstwhile Indian empire into Hindu-majority **India** and Muslim-majority **Pakistan**, whose eastern wing would emerge as **Bangladesh** in 1971.

Today the Republic of India has more than a billion inhabitants spread across some three million square kilometres. Containing a wide variety of races, languages and religions, it is the world's most complex political-administrative entity. Wherever there is diversity, there is tension – latent or overt. In the Indian subcontinent, the north-south divide is sustained partly by the Vindhya-Maikal mountain range, which runs west to east. Then there is the continual refrain of Hindu-Muslim tensions within India itself, despite the formation of the Muslim-majority states of Pakistan and

Bangladesh. Most recently, the territorial dispute between India and Pakistan over **Kashmir** has threatened to escalate into nuclear war. Seen in the longer perspective, however, India's history seems more like one of absorption and amalgamation rather than exclusion and rejection. Invaded and conquered by successive waves of outsiders, those cultures have enriched the subcontinent's indigenous society, resulting in a pan-Indian identity.

Note on spellings

There is as yet no satisfactorily standardized transliteration of Indian words into English. For Sanskrit terms the original terminal 'a' has been retained – 'Mahabharata' rather than 'Mahabharat'; 'Rama' instead of 'Ram'. For the original 's' and 'c', 'sh' and 'ch' respectively have been used – 'Shiva' and 'Vishnu', not 'Siva' and 'Visnu'; 'Chola', not 'Cola'. To distinguish 'Brahmanas' (prayers), part of the Vedic scriptures, from the plural of 'brahman' (priest), the latter is spelt as 'brahmin'. Instead of the more recent 'Mumbai' for 'Bombay', 'Kolkota' for 'Calcutta' and 'Chenai' for 'Madras', traditional Anglicizations have been adhered to – chiefly because they were also the names of the three principal presidencies under British rule. The Ganges River, now called 'Ganga', also retains its Anglicized name because of the related Gangetic plain. Elsewhere, changes have been embraced – 'Varanasi' rather than 'Benares', 'Pune' rather than 'Poona' and 'Panjab' rather than 'Punjab'. But in every case, at the first mention of a place name, the alternative is also offered, and variants are included in the index. Finally, 'Persia' means 'Iran' and vice versa.

1

Prehistory, the Indus Valley Civilization and the Aryan colonization

c.3000 BC–c.800 BC

Two hundred million years ago, today's continents formed a single landmass surrounded by one great ocean. The landmass split into different parts, as determined by the techtonic plates it rested on. The Americas drifted westward, while the subsequently named Africa, Antartica and Australia moved southward. Then, a large segment of this secondary landmass broke off and began drifting northward until, some thirty million years ago, it collided with the underbelly of Eurasia, pushing up a long range of mountains we call the **Himalayas**.

Thus was the **Indian subcontinent** born, its northern plains watered by the mighty **Indus** and **Ganges** river systems – both originating in the Himalayas – as though those mountains, also containing the wellsprings of the Yellow, Yangzi and Mekong rivers, had been designed to serve as a perennial, life-sustaining water tank for South and East Asia.

Other, smaller rivers crisscross the Indian peninsula. Except for a few of these that flow westward – originating in the mountain ranges separating the sub-tropical north from the tropical south, called the **Deccan** – they are watered by the mountains along the westen coast, known as the

Western Ghats, and run eastward. It is likely that the peninsula was inhabited, albeit sparsely, by man's hominid precursors, who were followed by *homo sapiens sapiens* from around 50,000 years ago.

The precise order and means of settlement remain obscure. Around 3000 BC an advanced human culture arose in the **Indus Valley**, an agrarian civilization known to us chiefly through the archeological sites at **Moen-jo-Daro** and **Harappa**, comparable to civilizations that emerged along the banks of the mighty rivers in Mesopotamia, Egypt and northern China. The absence of such archeological sites in the Deccan – the homeland of the **Dravidian culture** dating back to a pre-Indus Valley Civilization era – implies a continuity in the peninsula that is absent in the north.

Given the physical difference between the mainly flat north and the plateau of the south, their histories have evolved differently. Since overland access proved difficult, the Deccan was approached chiefly by sea, with the result that its foreign contacts were mainly maritime – with Sri Lanka and Indonesia. By contrast, the north was accessible overland through the Khyber, Gomal and Bolan passes in the north-western mountain ranges of the Hindu Kush, Suleiman and Kirthar through which occurred a series of incursions by the peoples from the Eurasian landmass and beyond.

This explains the linguistic and racial differences between the north and the south. The racial origin of southerners is **Dravidian**, a hybrid of proto-Australoids with black skins, flat noses and thick lips – the predominant inhabitants of the subcontinent after the Negrito settlers – and the **'Mediterranean type'**, originating in the lands around the sea of the same name, who arrived later. By contrast, north-erners, descended chiefly from the tribes from Eurasia, have thin lips and narrow noses. Whereas the languages of the north (eg Sanskrit, Pali, Hindi and Bengali) belong to the large, complex Indo-European family, the four major languages of the south form a small family of their own, with Tamil its pre-eminent member.

A critical problem confronting the chroniclers of India's early history is the absence of even vaguely reliable dates. Though the Indus Valley Civilization had a writing system, as evidenced by its **soft stone seals**, this has not yet been deciphered despite high-tech computer analysis. After a few centuries, following the disintegration of this civilization around 1900 BC, came the **Indo-Aryans**, who were illiterate. Because they gradually switched from burial to cremation to dispose of the dead, they left no treasure trove of tomb materials that informs our knowledge of ancient Egypt and China. It was only after they came into contact with such literate civilizations as Persian, Greek, Chinese and Sri Lankan that a reliable chronology can be teased out.

In the centuries that followed the decline of Moen-jo-Daro and Harappa, the foundations of much of the spiritual culture of India were laid. The Aryan colonization of the northern plains that started around 1500 BC brought with it **Vedism**, a polytheistic religion, that later evolved into **Hinduism**. Like Europe's Celtic bards and other practitioners of oral poetry (Homer among them perhaps), Vedic priests memorized long verse cycles, so that when writing re-appeared in India in the 6th century BC, there was plenty to transcribe and record afresh.

The extent to which Vedic lore synthesized with the existing beliefs when the Aryans arrived in India remains conjectural. So too does the degree to which the Indus Valley culture had been affected by the earlier Dravidian civilization. The key to both seems to lie with the deciphering of the soft stone seals of the Indus Valley. Until that happens, precise answers to these and other related questions will continue to elude us.

c.30m BC The **Indian peninsula** is formed when an island landmass moving northward through the waters of the southern hemisphere begins colliding with the southern shores of the much larger Eurasian landmass. Over an extended period of time, this phenomenon creates the **Himalayan mountain system**. As rainwater and alluvial sediment flow southward from the Himalayas, the large, fertile plains of the northern subcontinent – extending over today's India, Pakistan and Bangladesh – are formed. So too are two great river systems: the **Indus**, flowing southwestward into the Arabian Sea, and the **Ganges**, running southeastwardly, into the Bay of Bengal.

c.35,000 BC By approximately this time, *homo sapiens sapiens*, having evolved in Africa around 100,000 BC, has replaced all previous species of hominid worldwide, including *homo sapiens*. With the third and the last great Ice Age at its peak, Upper Palaeolithic Man – also known as **Advanced Hunter** – uses thin, parallel-sided blades of flint or other firestone as blanks for shaping into various implements.

c.16,000 BC A drop in sea levels during the last great Ice Age stimulates human migration to previously uninhabited regions.

c.9000 BC First evidence emerges that Advanced Hunters have colonized central India. They possess small flints (microliths) and live in caves sometimes decorated with paintings.

c.8200 BC In adjoining Iran, Advanced Hunters begin domesticating goats.

c.8000–5000 BC As the last Ice Age recedes and warmer climates prevail, beginning in the Black Sea and Caspian region, humans turn to agriculture as well as animal husbandry, heralding the Neolithic Age, sometimes called the **Neolithic Revolution**. From 7000 BC onward, there is evidence of houses made of dried mud bricks. There are also signs of animal cults and worship of a **Mother Goddess**. In the Indian subcontinent food-gathering and hunting with small flint implements continue.

c.5000–4000 BC Agriculture spreads from (modern) Iran into the northwestern Indian subcontinent. Settled communities living in mud-brick houses emerge in the forested foothills and mountains of Baluchistan, Makran and Sind. Stone remains the dominant technology, but now **copper** is used in the manufacture of some utensils.

c.4000 BC The inhabitants of the northwestern subcontinent, already in possession of the **wheel**, produce pottery and bricks baked in **kilns**. The painted pottery, usually black on bright red, depicts animals, birds and plants.

c.3500 BC Across the subcontinent, evidence suggests increasing numbers of inhabitants are living in dwellings made of kiln-baked brick and mortar. The matriarchal **Dravidian culture** that emerges is characterized by fortified villages, sometimes linked together to form a confederation or principality, and by the worship of the Mother Goddess. **Phallus worship** is also prevalent. There is no evidence yet of larger towns.

In southern India, many of the original, sparse Negrito settlers have been supplanted by the **Tamils** (identified by the **Tamil language** they speak) and kindred groups whose mother tongues – Kannada, Malayalam, Telugu and Tulu – belong to the same family as Tamil.

c.3200 BC Carbon-dating and other archeological techniques indicate the emergence of the **Indus Valley Civilization**, also known as **Harappa Civilization** – after a major urban site discovered in the 1920s by British and Indian archeologists on the eastern bank of the Ravi River, one of five Indus River tributaries that collectively make up the **Panjab** region.

Terracotta figure of the Mother Goddess from Moen-jo-Daro

A second equally important site from the same period, and containing similar artefacts, has been excavated at **Moen-jo-Daro** in Sind on the western bank of the Indus, while a third, called **Port Lothal**, has been found in northern Gujarat, with fine dock works on the Gulf of Cambay. The

Indus Valley Civilization is characterized by the presence of **soft stone seals** inscribed with pictographs. While these have yet to be deciphered, they were most probably used by merchants as way-bills, indicating the existence of an advanced economy.

Seals and other artefacts of the Indus Valley Civilization will be found at some 2000 sites spread over 1.2 million sq. kms, a territory larger than the contemporaneous Nile Valley and Mesopotamian civilizations.

Evidence also reveals that Harappa and Moen-jo-Daro are major settlements – perhaps the northern and southern capitals of a single state – and are maintained by the surplus produce and labour of hundreds of surrounding villages, and that together they form a nation sharing a common culture.

c.2500 BC Around this time, the Indus Valley Civilization reaches its zenith. In Harappa and Moen-jo-Daro, the buildings and artefacts are so uniform – down to, and including, the size of bricks – that we can assume both belong to a single empire.

Weights and measures are also standardized. **Urban planning**, as evidenced at Moen-jo-Daro, requires straight streets, three to ten metres wide, to accommodate wheeled transport. Houses, often ten metres square, are built at regular intervals and have broad stairways. The two-metre thick walls have windows on all sides except facing the street. Made of baked brick and mortar, these dwellings have their own wells, bathrooms and drains, which flow into sewers under the main streets. These in turn lead to man-holed soak-pits.

Also unearthed at Moen-jo-Daro is a public bathing hall, measuring 54 x 33 metres, with a 12 x 12 x 2.5-metre pool, made watertight with bitumen, and surrounded by rooms and galleries. The presence of relics of gold, silver,

Indus Valley (Harappan) Culture

The populations of **Harappa** and **Moen-jo-Daro** have been estimated at 50,000 each, implying well-developed land and river transport, a rural foodgrain surplus, reliable labour force, and facilities for storing food. An **ox-driven wagon** with solid wooden wheels – reproduced as toy carts in bronze and terracotta and discovered at many sites – was the chief means of land transport, a feature of daily life in the subcontinent that remains unchanged to this day. Meat, fish, milk and vegetables comprised the Harappan diet. Crops included wheat, barley and peas. Pigs, sheep, goats, camels, buffaloes, bulls and cows were domesticated.

The single most important commercial crop was **cotton**. As spinners and weavers of cotton, Harappans were unrivalled by their contemporaries. Harappan men covered themselves with two pieces of cotton textile, one worn round the waist, the other passing under the right arm and thrown over the left shoulder, toga-style. Women used one piece as a short skirt, and another to cover their breasts. Both sexes wore long hair and jewellery.

There is no sign of communal worhsip in public. Worship appears to have been private, centred on symbols of fertility: the **Mother Goddess**, and a male god wearing a horned headdress, seated in the lotus position, and sometimes accompanied by an elephant, tiger, rhinoceros or buffalo. Presence of several cone-shaped objects indicate **phallus worship**. On the female side, the

copper, tin and lead, as well as conch shells, turquoise, lapiz lazuli and jade indicate widespread trading links not only with the adjoining Rajasthan and Gujarat in the subcontinent, but also Afghanistan, Iran, Central Asia and China. There is further evidence to suggest that Harappans have established trading colonies in Bahrain, and in Ur and other Mesopotamian cities.

statuette of a bronze dancing girl found at Moen-jo-Daro shows a naked figure wearing bangles, earrings and a necklace. A slender female with parted legs, she delights in her sexuality in a casual way. Her thick lips and broad nose mark her as proto-Australoid. But the bearded soft stone head, possibly of a royal personage, also found in Moen-jo-Daro, shows both proto-Australoid and Mediterranean features.

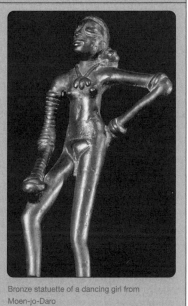

Bronze statuette of a dancing girl from Moen-jo-Daro

c.2000 BC Having flourished for a thousand years, the Indus Valley Civilization goes into sharp decline, as does the Egyptian Old Kingdom on the Nile. In all probability, a famine-inducing mini-Ice Age is responsible for the collapse of both empires.

In the subcontinent, where contemporary political events remain unknown, over-extraction of timber from forests for housing and land and river transport leads to **defor-estation**. This in turn reduces rainfall, turning most of modern Baluchistan into desert and much of Sind into an arid zone. Over the centuries, annual flooding of the Indus Valley, including Panjab, results in cumulative silting and salination. The skills developed by earlier Harappans to irrigate their agriculture and generate the surplus required to fund crafts and commerce, now prove inadequate. Archeologically, this manifests itself in a steady decline in the quality of housing.

c.1900 BC The decay of the Indus Valley Civilization is hastened by **cataclysmic flood** in and around Moen-jo-Daro. In the outlying areas of Gujarat and Panjab, deterioration appears less dramatic.

In the distant Ukrainian and south Russian steppes, and/or the Caspian Sea basin, the **Aryan tribes** – fair, fine-featured, tall and long-headed – begin emerging as nomadic pastoralists. Crucially, they have learned how to tame the swift and terror-striking beast of the steppes – the **horse** – and use it for drawing **chariots** with spoked wheels. Over the next several centuries, an increase in their numbers and/or climatic variations, resulting in lack of pastures, compel the Aryans to seek new pastures. They spread westward into Europe, southward into Anatolia, and southeastward into Iran and Afghanistan.

c.1800 BC Without evidence of any further building in brick, or production of Harappan artefacts, northern India becomes an archeological vaccum. It is assumed that the now politically fragmented peoples of the Indus Valley (Sind and Panjab) revert to constructing their dwellings out of such perishable material as wood and reed.

c.1500 BC Now, if not before, the Aryans begin penetrating the Indian subcontinent. Riding horse-drawn chariots and possessing superior bronze weapons, they easily overpower

Indus Valley Soft Stone Seals

Every Harappan merchant had a square or rectangular **seal**, the size of a large postage stamp, made of steatite, and engraved with **five pictographs** and the image of an animal in reverse. He used it to create an image by pressing the seal upon soft clay, and the subsequent tablet was then attached to a consignment of goods, either identifying their

Seal depicting a bull

origin, content, owner or destination – or all of these – thus serving as a **way-bill**. The most common animal was a variant of the **unicorn**, possessing the body of a bull and the head of a zebra, its single horn curving upward and forward. Other quadrupeds included elephants, rhinos, tigers and humped bulls with fatty dewlaps.

Altogether, over 1800 seals have been recovered, most of them of local origin, but some of them cylindrical in shape, originating in **Mesopotamia**. This leads to the conclusion that the **Indus Valley Civilization** was part of a wider trading region, just as figurines of the Mother Goddess common to both cultures suggest exchanges beyond commerce. More intriguingly, one Harappan

Seal depicting an elephant

seal depicts a hero fighting two tigers, uncannily similar to the Mesopotamian motif that has Gilgamesh, the legendary Sumerian king of Uruk, grappling with two lions. But while the distribution of Harappan seals has helped establish a broad time-frame for the Indus Valley Civilization, historians have been hampered by the failure so far to unravel them.

the inhabitants of **Baluchistan** and **Sind**, describing them in their hymns as dark, bull-lipped, snub-nosed worshippers of the phallus. Later, the Indian indigenes will be called *dasas* ('destroyers'), a term that eventually becomes synonymous with slaves. At first the Aryans, organized into tribes, seize cattle during their raids and return to their base outside the subcontinent.

c.1400 BC Drawn by the warm sub-tropical climate, and the fertility of the alluvial Indo-Gangetic plains, the Aryans begin establishing **fortified communities** in the northern subcontinent. Each Aryan tribe has a *sabha* (council of elders) and a *samiti* (larger assembly) – a political administrative system sometimes called an **oligarchical republic**, since tribal leadership is elective, not hereditary. In the absence of money, Aryans use cattle and horses as currency and to reward priests, called brahmins.

At celebratory occasions, such as weddings, Aryans **sacrifice animals**, eating the cooked flesh. They also maintain slaves. Their weapons include bows-and-arrows, spears and bronze battle-axes. In battle, they deploy **chariots** to carry an armour-clad warrior as well as a driver. Rival Aryan tribes fight among themselves, but combine against Indian indigenes in order to establish territorial control.

Having subjugated the native *dasas*, the Aryans press-gang them to clear forests to create new and rich pasture land for their cattle and sheep. This, coupled with the monsoons of summer that make migration onerous, alter the Aryans' nomadic way of life. They slowly take to cultivating food crops which they harvest in winter.

c.1300 BC Despite the steady influx of the Aryans into northern India, they continue to be outnumbered by the indigenes. Because of this, and the easy access that a victor has over the females of the vanquished, there is **interbreeding**.

Surrounded by the locals, the Aryans gradually adopt indigenous cults, technology and vocabulary, which results in the appearance in their language (ancient Sanskrit) of such cerebral consonants as 'ksh', absent in other Indo-European tongues.

During this period, the four **Vedas** (literally 'knowledge'), composed orally in ancient Sanskrit, and transmitted from one generation of priests to the next, come into existence. Of these the earliest, and the greatest, is the **Rig Veda** ('Knowledge in Verse'), a cycle of 1028 hymns addressed primarily to the pantheon of Aryan gods, and containing speculation on the origins of the universe. Eventually

> ❝ In the sky's border hath she shone in splendour:
> The goddess hath thrown off the veil of darkness;
> Awakening the world with purple horses,
> On her well-harnessed chariot Dawn approaches....
> Give us treasure of cattle, or horses, O Dawn,
> Treasure of horses that nourishes many. ❞
>
> from the hymn 'To Ushas (Goddess of Dawn)', *Rig Veda*, I. 133, trans.
> Ralph T.H. Griffith

> ❝ One plies his constant task reciting verses:
> One sings the holy psalm in Sakvari measures;
> One more, the Brahman, tells the lore of being,
> And one lays down the rules of sacrificing. ❞
>
> from the hymn 'To Jnanam (Knowledge) – of the Supreme Reality', *Rig Veda*,
> X.71, trans. Ralph T.H. Griffith

The *Vedas* and the Aryan Gods

Classed among the great scriptures of the ancient world, the four surviving *Vedas*, along with the *Brahamanas* (prayers) and *Upanishads* (treatises, see p.29) together constitute **Vedism** (aka Brahminism), the religion of the early Indo-Aryans. They and their descendants, later called **Hindus**, regard the *Vedas* as 'inspired revelation' (*sruti*, in Sanskrit), and not traditional learning (*smriti*).

At the heart of the *Rig Veda*'s over 1000 hymns – some of which are recited at weddings and funerals – is a belief in the divinity of natural phenomena. As pastoralists, Aryans were at the mercy of the elements, and therefore attributed divine powers to the sun, moon, earth, wind, thunder, sky, fire, rivers and oceans. Thus, in the Aryan pantheon, **Indra** represents weather/rain/atmosphere, **Agni** fire, **Varuna** rivers and seas, **Vayu** wind, and **Ushas** dawn. These and other deities were propitiated through complex rituals, involving incantation and animal sacrifice, and conducted by trained priests, brahmins.

Significantly, many of the Vedic gods and goddesses have equivalents in other ancient Indo-European cultures. **Dyaus-Pita**, for example, the Sky-Father, corresponds to the Greek Zeus, and the later Roman Jupiter. And it was out of Dyaus-Pita's union with **Prithvi**, Goddess of the Earth, that Indra, Agni (cognate with Latin *ignis*) and Varuna were born. Each deity – called *deva* for male or *devi* for female (from *div*, to shine) in Sanskrit – had its own devotees. Constantly battling with evil, a deity was disposed to be munificent to its devotees if they, assisted by priests, sought his/her goodwill through prayers and sacrifices.

arranged in ten books, the *Rig Veda* is longer than Homer's *Iliad* and *Odyssey* combined, and is the oldest literature in any Indo–European language.

c.1300–1000 BC The *Soma Veda*, or Knowledge of Soma, is composed during this period, consisting of stanzas added to the *Rig Veda* that deal specifically with the use of **soma**, a powerful hallucinogenic in Vedic rituals. The fermented juice of *Asclepias acida*, a climbing, milky plant, soma is both offered to gods as a libation, and imbibed by worshippers together with the flesh of sacrificed animals that include sheep, goats, cows, bulls, pigs and, on important occasions, horses. Known also to the Persians and other peoples of Western Asia, soma is regarded by some as providing the underlying inspiration of certain forms of ecstatic mysticism.

c.1200–800 BC Composition of the *Yajur Veda* begins, an anthology of verse and prose formulas for recitation by priests when performing sacrifices. Unlike the *Rig Veda*, which refers only to the Indus River basin, the *Yajur Veda* alludes to an area between the Satlej and the Jamuna tributaries of the Ganges, thereby indicating eastward expansion of the Aryan tribes across India's northern plains. It also

An early example of Sanskrit calligraphy

Varna, Caste and Sub-caste

One of the most widely known features of the Indian life is its **caste system**. Like Hinduism, it can be traced back to the **Aryan colonization**. The early hymns of the *Rig Veda* indicate that the Aryans distinguished between *rajanya* (later *kshtra*, meaning nobility) and *vish* (later *vaishya*, common tribesmen). Thus, along with brahmins (priests), the Aryan society initially consisted of three *varnas* (literally colour; figuratively, class). But as colonization spread, the Indo-Aryans distinguished between themselves and non-Aryans. A hymn in the last book of the *Rig Veda* specified a four-*varna* society, with *dasas*, now called *shudras* (serfs), serving the three Aryan classes. Indo-Aryans obliged *shudras* to live outside their settlements, excluding them from their socio-religious life. Brahmins foreclosed the *shudras'* chance of being absorbed into the Aryan society by denying them the rite of the sacred thread at puberty – signifying the second birth, into one's *varna* – thus separating the 'twice-born' (*dvijas*) *varnas* from the rest. Though technically twice-born, *vaishyas* were socially excluded by brahmins and *Kshatriyas*. Below *shudras* were *panchama* (fifth class) or *panch-janah* (fifth people), a term applied to those aboriginal tribes, especially Chandals, who engaged in hunting and in handling corpses or animal carcasses. Indo-Aryans so despised the 'fifth people' they turned them into outcastes.

This formalization of a four-*varna* social order is mistakenly described in Western literature as a four-caste system. 'Caste', derived from the Latin *castus* through the Portuguese *casta*, signifies breed or race. But caste in India is an amalgam of race and class. The correct term for caste in Sanskrit is *jati* (birth). We should therefore think of *varna* as caste and *jati* as sub-caste (of which there are about 3000). The Indo-Aryans' descendants, called **Hindus**, are born into their sub-caste. A Hindu surname/sub-caste often tells the trade or profession of its bearer. Examples in north India are Kumbhar (potter), Nai (barber), Sonar (goldsmith) and Teli (oil presser). In south India, Reddi is the commonest surname of landowners in Andhra Pradesh; a Chetty is a trader or money-lender in Tamil Nadu; and a Mukkava a fisherman in Kerala.

reflects the increased ritualism of Vedism and – with brahmins becoming more specialized – the emergence of the Aryan **varna-caste** system.

c.900–600 BC The last of the four *Vedas*, the **Atharva Veda** is composed. Consisting largely of popular magic spells, songs and incantations, it contains many non-Aryan elements.

c.800 BC Indo-Aryans begin penetrating the south and this accelerates the synthesis between the cultures of plebeian Aryans and indigenous *dasas/shudras*. This results in the absorption of pre-Aryan animism and magical incantation into mainstream Aryan practices. As a consequence of this

> Like wild winds, the draughts have raised me up
> Have I been drinking soma?
> The draughts have borne me up as swift steeds a chariot
> Have I been drinking soma?
> Frenzy has come upon me as a cow to her dead calf
> Have I been drinking soma?
> As a carpenter bends the seat of a chariot, I bend this frenzy round my heart.
> Have I been drinking soma?
> Not even in the mote of my eye do the five tribes count with me
> Have I been drinking soma?
> The heavens above do not equal one half of me
> Have I been drinking soma?
> In my glory I have passed beyond the sky and the great earth
> Have I been drinking soma?
> I will pick up the earth, and put it here or put it there
> Have I been drinking soma?

from the *Rig Veda*, 10.119.2–9, trans. A.L. Basham

fusion – or perhaps independently – invocations to Indo-Aryan nature gods and nature worship give way to allusions to such new deities as **Vishnu** and **Shiva**. In due course they, together with **Brahma**, will form the *Trimurthi* (Three Images), encapsulating the overarching natural order: creation (birth), preservation (life) and destruction (death). Given the almost total absence of followers of Brahma, present-day Hindus are either Vishnuite or Shivaite.

The image of Shiva Nataraja ('Lord of the Dance') is one of the most powerful in Hindu Art. Shiva's Dance of Bliss symbolizes the cosmic cycle of creation and destruction.

The *Trimurthi*

Brahma

The early hymns of the *Rig Veda* make no reference to a demiurge, (distinguished from the Supreme God). Book 10, however, refers to **Prajapati** (Lord of Creatures) possibly another name for Purush (the Primordial Person) mentioned earlier. It was his sacrifice by other gods which resulted in the creation of the universe. By then, sacrificial ritual had become a celestial mystery, and the priest performing it was called **brahmin**, the neuter of masculine *Brahmin*, now regarded as the creator-god. In the subsequent Indo-Aryan literature, Prajapati/Brahma and **Indra** (see p.14) were treated as great gods.

Figuratively, Brahma is portrayed with four faces, probably signifying the four directions of the universe. According to tradition, Vishnu and Shiva are the two perceptible aspects of Brahma. His consort is **Saraswati**, originally the deity of rivers, later the goddess of learning and speech, often depicted as a young woman carrying a lute and a book, and attended by a swan. Worshipped by writers and artists, tradition credits her with the invention of both the Sanskrit language and the Devnagari script.

Brahma suffered a steady decline in popularity, and today only one temple devoted to him survives near Ajmer.

Vishnu

Originally a Vedic sun-deity associated with Indra, **Vishnu** (derived from *vish*, 'to prevail') is the god of mercy and health, and his consort, **Lakshmi**, the goddess of good fortune. Tradition has him cross the universe in three steps: sunrise, noon and sunset. According to a later myth, he sleeps on a thousand-headed snake, resting on the floor of the primeval ocean. From his navel rises a lotus upon which sits Brahma. Vishnu awakes, and rises to the highest heaven astride **Garuda**, a gigantic eagle with a half-human face. From there, Vishnu – portrayed as a crowned, enthroned, dark-blue, half-naked, four-armed man, holding a conch, discus, mace and lotus – observes the universe. When evil threatens to destroy it, he intervenes by turning himself into a mortal form.

continued overleaf

The *Trimurthi* (continued)

He has done so nine times. As a fish, he saved Manu (the Vedic amalgam of Adam and Noah) and his family from the Great Flood. As a tortoise diving into cosmic ocean, he supported the elephant who held up the world. As a boar, he killed the demon Hiranyaksha and raised the world on his tusk. As a man-lion, he destroyed Hiranyakashipu. As a dwarf, he tricked the demon Bali and left him hanging in the infernal region of the universe. As Parasurama (Man with Axe), he avenged the injustice suffered by his brahmin father. In his seventh form, Vishnu appeared as Rama in the *Ramayana* (see p.28). In the *Mahabharata* (see p.24), he is Krishna. His latest appearance, prompted by his love for animals, was as the Buddha (see p.32). In his forthcoming, and final, incarnation, as Kalki, he is predicted to appear on a white horse, wielding a flaming sword.

Shiva

Shiva (meaning 'propitious') is an amalgam of the Aryan deity Rudra and of the Tamil god Murugan. His probable antecedent was the horned, ithyphallic deity of Moen-jo-Daro. He has five manifestations. He is worshipped as **lingam** (penis), in the form of a short cylindrical pillar, a practice dating back to pre-Aryan times. In his second manifestation he is **Maha-kala** (Great Time), destroyer of everything. In his third, he is the ascetic, seated half-naked on a tiger skin, meditating on Mount Kailash. From his long hair flows the sacred Ganges and in the middle of his brow is the third eye, emblem of his unrivalled wisdom. His neck and arms are encircled by serpents, of which he, as **Pushupati** (Lord of Animals), is master. Beside him is his wife Parvati (Daughter of Mountains), by whom he has **Ganesha**, as a trident, and his mount, the bull Nandi, a fertility symbol. His followers believe the universe is maintained not by periodic sacrifices, as Indo-Aryans argued, but by Shiva's penance. In his fourth form, Shiva is **Nataraja**, King of Dance, whether on Kailash Mountain in the north, or in the southern temple of Chidambaram. Finally, in his role as Pushupati, he is depicted in south India as a four-armed man, one hand blessing, one bestowing a boon, one holding an axe, and the last sprouting deer from its fingers. His consort is Meenakshi, daughter of the king of Madurai.

2

The age of the epics, the birth of Buddhism and the rise of monarchy

c.800–400 BC

The fertile alluvial river basins of northern India would sooner rather than later bring forth a society to surpass the Indus Valley Civilization. The **Aryan colonization**, proceeding steadily eastwards along the Ganges towards its delta in the Bay of Bengal, blossomed into a thriving, wealthy culture that, by the 8th and 7th centuries BC, rivalled any other in the world. Yet sketching a coherent chronology of events during this period eludes historians. On the one hand, they have access to a masterpiece of world literature, the **Mahabharata ('Great Bharata Dynasty')**, the encyclopedic epic of ancient Indians; on the other, they face an absence of coeval written records.

Like the preceding *Vedas*, the *Mahabharata*, the *Ramayana* ('Rama's Story') and other important works were composed and transmitted orally. It was much later – centuries after writing reappeared in the subcontinent – that they came to be transcribed. From these works we may infer many details of the Indo-Aryan lifestyle, and their concerns and aspirations, from the 8th century BC onwards.

But there are caveats. The *Mahabharata* was not only continually revised, but the events it described were embellished and mythologized, and suffused with passages on theology, morals and statecraft by many priests over a long period of time, thus transforming it into a scripture. The religious outlook it conveyed was therefore neither purely Vedic nor exactingly consistent. Vedism itself was metamorphozing into Hinduism as a result of interaction between the Aryan and non-Aryan cultures. Nonetheless, the epics of the *Mahabharata* and the *Ramayana* – centred around a conflict over royal succession – illuminate the existence and importance of **monarchical social order**.

Undoubtedly, this was an epoch of creative flux with many facets. The subcontinent was divided into numerous **political-administrative units**, some of them ruled by leaders chosen by tribal elders and lesser representatives, and others by hereditary kings. During peacetime they traded; during war they fought.

In the *Mahabharata*, the central conflict is between two dynastic families – **Pandavas** and **Kauravas** – for a royal throne in the Gangetic basin. This indicates that the traditional method of governance through tribal councils and assemblies was giving way to monarchy. Indeed, kingdoms were predominant in the populous Gangetic plain, with republics limited largely to their north and the foothills of the Himalayas, and in Panjab.

Such a theory is borne out by actual political events in northern India. Circa 542 BC, the ambitious ruler of **Magdha** (South Bihar), **Bimbisara**, initiated a programme of **territorial expansion** partly through force and partly through marital alliances. He was the first to entertain the idea of establishing an **imperial order** founded on an essentially agrarian economy. He was no doubt inspired by the emergence of a **Persian empire** under the Achaeminids (558–330 BC), which had by then extended its boundaries into the Indian subcontinent.

To the north of the expanded Magdha kingdom were principalities governed by ruling families of the Mongolian stock like **Gurkhas**, **Bhutias** and **Tibetans**. The racial difference between these inhabitants and their Indo-Aryan brahmin teachers encouraged independent thinking on religion and philosophy in an environment where they and many others found the Vedic practice of animal sacrifice repugnant, and Vedisim overburdened with ceremonies. As a result, many heterodox sects emerged.

Little wonder that serious challenges to Vedic orthodoxy came from **Gautama Buddha** of the Shakya tribe in the Himalayan foothills and **Vardhaman Mahavira** of the Jnatrika clan in southern Nepal. The former founded **Buddhism** and the latter **Jainism**. In due course, Buddhism produced a further tranche of material which would serve historians well. Most of it was transmitted orally before being penned.

Around the time of the birth of **the Buddha** (c.563 BC), the **Persian empire** under Cyrus the Great expanded – westward toward the Mediterranean world of the Greeks, and southeastward toward the Indus. Unlike the Indo-Aryans – whose high culture was dominated by illiterate priests lacking aptitude or training for recording political and military events – the Persians and Greeks paid much attention to compiling politico-military chronicles.

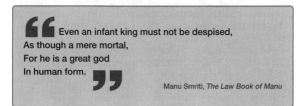

Even an infant king must not be despised,
As though a mere mortal,
For he is a great god
In human form.

Manu Smriti, *The Law Book of Manu*

c.800 BC As the Aryan colonization of the north matures and expands eastward and southward, important changes occur among the Aryans. Their Vedic religion is tempered by contact with indigenous beliefs, and there is a gradual replacement of the tribal administrative institutions of the Council of Elders (*Sabha*) and Assembly (*Samiti*) by **hereditary monarchy**.

At first, the elected tribal leader acquires monarchic powers, and is called *raja* (cognate with the Latin *rex*, king), and then the office becomes hereditary. Brahmins play a crucial role in this development. A legend popularized by

The *Mahabharata*

It took more than a thousand years of accretion and gestation before the *Mahabharata* was eventually transcribed around 400 AD. Its **Great War** verses – covering a protracted struggle between two royal families of the Bharata tribe in the region of modern Delhi – are generally ascribed to the poet **Krishna Dwaipayana Vyasa**.

In the Bharata kingdom of Kuru, power is contested between the **Kauravas** (the hundred sons of Dhritrashtra) and the five sons of his younger brother, **Pandu**. Declaring himself incapable of rule due to blindness, Dhritrashtra abdicates in favour of Pandu. Succumbing to a curse, Pandu renounces the throne (which reverts to Dhritrashtra) and retires to the Himalayas. On his death, his sons, including the eldest Yudhishtra, are taken to the capital Hastinapur to be educated alongside their Kaurava cousins.

When, on coming of age, Yudhishtra is consecrated heir-apparent, the Kauravas, led by the eldest Duryodhana, conspire to oust the Pandu brothers. Forced to flee, the Pandus travel from court to court. During their many adventures they forge a friendship with **Lord Krishna**, chief of the Yadava tribe (see p.41). After a time, the elder Dhritrashtra, the nominal king, recalls the

them has it that, facing an imminent defeat in their battle with demons, gods assembled and chose **Manu** (see p.55) as their raja from among themselves, who led them to victory – followed by another legend that the elected king of gods had certain distinctive qualities.

As intermediaries between gods and humans, brahmins arrogate themselves the right to confer divine attributes on a temporal ruler through specially devised sacrifices. This becomes the basis for a long-lasting nexus between a king and his chief priest (*purohita*), and leads to the downgrading of the Council and the Assembly. It also results in monarchy

Pandus to Kuru. Announcing his final decison to abdicate, he divides his realm between the two factions. The Pandus construct their capital at Indraprastha (near modern Delhi) but the fragile peace between them is undermined by Duryodhana's intrigue. The Pandus find themselves exiled for a period of thirteen years but are denied the restoration of their kingdom on their return. Raising a vast army from numerous kingdoms and republics of the subcontinent, they unleash an eighteen-day war at Kurukshetra (field of the Kurus). Aided by the sagacious Lord Krishna, the Pandus defeat the equally large Kauravas army and rule the unified kingdom for a lengthy period thereafter. Following Krishna's death, however, they choose to abdicate, and set out for the City of Gods in the Himalayas. But only Yudhishtra, being the noblest, reaches it.

The Great War verses account for only one-fifth of of the *Mahabharata*. It also contains the *Ramayana* (see p.28), the *Bhagvad Gita* (see p.63) and an appendix, entitled *Harivamsha*, which recounts the legend of Lord Krishna. Each of these originated independently, well before being incorporated into the *Mahabharata*.

becoming hereditary, with the raja's immediate entourage including not only the chief priest and the military commander (*senani*), but also the treasurer, charioteer, steward and supervisor of dicing, with gambling with dice becoming a popular pastime.

The Indo-Aryan tribes' colonized world now comprises a series of **contending states**, with each domain consisting of fortified villages and towns. The social nucleus of the village community remains unchanged: the family headed by the father whose authority is final. Marriage remains monogamous and indissoluble.

c.800–600 BC Oral composition of the *Brahmanas* – a collection of metrical hymns, prayers and spells, interspersed with prose passages – provide theological explanations of the *Vedas*, and are regarded as appendices to them.

> " Ushas with her crimson fingers opened the portals of the day,
> Nations armed for mortal combat in the field of battle lay,
> Beat of drum and blare of trumpet and the holy conch's lofty sound,
> By the answering clouds repeated, shook the hills and tented ground,
> And the voice of sounding weapons which the warlike archers drew,
> And the neigh of battle chargers as the armed horseman flew,
> Mingled with the rolling thunder of each swiftly speeding [chariot] car,
> And with peeling bells proclaiming mighty elephants of war! "
>
> from the *Mahabharata*, trans. Romesh C. Dutta

c.800–500 BC The central events of the *Mahabharata* are believed to have occurred during this period. An encyclopedic work of literature originally composed orally by numerous royal bards, it consists of nearly 100,000 double octosyllabic couplets (called *shlokas*). Eventually transcribed into Sanskrit and accorded scriptural status by Hindus, the **Great War** verses of the *Mahabharata* indicate that contemporary Indo-Aryan politics are dominated by rivalries between different courts and royal families.

c.700–300 BC If the events described in the *Ramayana* – a poem of some 24,000 *shlokas* reputedly composed by the sage Valmiki – have any basis in reality, then they occur in this period. Consisting of seven books, the *Ramayana* will be transcribed around c.200 AD – that is, two centuries before the transcription of the *Mahabharata*.

Rama Charita Mansa ('Rama's Life Story'), a free translation of the epic by the 17th-century poet Tulsi Das will become the most popular book ever published in north India. Representing the victory of light over darkness, it describes the battle between **Rama**, a virtuous Aryan hero, and his adversary **Ravana**, a demon king of Sri Lanka. Hindus will celebrate Rama's victory with a ten-day festival known as Daserra (Tenth Day), when effigies of Ravana, filled with firecrackers, are burned. Just before Daserra, scenes from the *Ramayana* will be performed in public in many cities and towns. Rama's triumphant return to his kingdom will be celebrated at Dipavali (row of lamps), popularly called Divali, the Festival of Lights. Versions of the *Ramayana* will also become embedded in Thai, Indonesian and other Asian cultures through the spread of Hinduism and Buddhism.

c.642 BC The kingdom of **Magdha** (South Bihar) is founded by **Sisunaga**, a chieftain of Varanasi (Benares), with its capital at Rajagriha in the hills of the Gaya district, 100km southeast of modern Patna. Over the next two centuries

The *Ramayana*

As a story of the life and times of Rama, the **Ramayana** is different from the encyclopedic *Mahabharata*. While the *Ramayana*'s tone and pious intentions resemble Virgil's *Aeneid*, its romantic themes are closer to Homer's *Odyssey*. Rama, married to **Sita**, daughter of King Janak of Videha, is the son and heir of King Dasaratha of Kosala (capital, Ayodhya). But Rama's stepmother Kaikeyi, intent on her own son acceding the throne, redeems Dasaratha's promise to fulfil any wish she expressed when she had saved his life. She demands Rama's banishment for fourteen years.

Sita and her brother Lakshmana insist on joining him. Their exile takes them to the Dandaka forest in the south, where they live as hermits. By destroying many demons, who are troubling villagers, Rama angers Ravana, the demonic king of Sri Lanka. Dressed as an ascetic, Ravana abducts Sita while Rama and Lakshmana are absent and returns home with her in a flying chariot. Rama enlists the support of Sugriva, king of monkeys, whose monkey-army is led by Hanuman, a simian general. Aided by them, Rama builds a causeway across the sea, defeats Ravana, and rescues Sita. But as Sita has lived under another man's roof, the Sacred Law requires that Rama reject her. When Sita throws herself on a funeral pyre and remains unharmed, her chastity is proven and

Magdha becomes the most powerful kingdom in the Gangetic plain.

c.600 BC Iron is mined and used for making implements in Magdha, an important element that contributes to the kingdom's steady ascendancy over its neighbours.

Different tongues begin to develop from classical **Sanskrit** – the language of priests and the intellectual elite, official proclamations and Vedic ceremonies – as common people find its sounds and grammar much too difficult. They take to speaking a simpler version of Sanskrit, called **Prakrit**,

Rama accepts her back. They return to Ayodhya to administer Kosala as a Utopian state.

Responding to public opinion still sceptical of Sita's virtue, however, the last book of the *Ramayana* sees Rama banish her. Taking refuge in a hermitage, she gives birth to Kusha and Lava, whom Rama acknowledges as his sons years later. Still traumatized by her rejection, Sita (meaning 'furrow') calls on Mother Earth to swallow her up. Rama returns to heaven and reverts to being the god Vishnu.

A scene from the *Ramayana* showing Rama (left) and Hanuman (right)

which has several dialects. Most popular of these are **Shauraseni**, spoken in the western Gangetic plain, and **Magdhi** in the eastern. **Pali**, based on Sanskrit, is also widely spoken. In the northwest of the southern peninsula, **Maharashtri**, a derivative of Sanskrit, is the popular language.

c.600–300 BC Composition of the *Upanishads* (*upa* means supplementary, and *nishad*, sitting next to the guru). Consisting of metrical hymns, prayers or spells, interspersed with prose passages, the 150 *Upanishads* – varying in length from a few verses to many pages – are speculative theological and philosophical treatises on the *Vedas* and their appendices, the *Brahmanas*. Together with the *Vedas* and the *Brahmanas*, they form the scriptures of Vedism/Brahmanism. They identify the power that sustains the cosmos with the unchanging essence of life that permeates both the Universal or Absolute Soul (**Brahman**) and the individual Human Soul (**Atman**). Human salvation, or release from the eternal cycle of birth and death, depends on the individual soul achieving one-ness with the Universal Soul. The teaching of the *Upanishads* is summarized in the phrase '*tat twam asi*' ('that art thou').

More generally, the *Upanishads* cover the **Vedanta** doctrine, yoga and ascetic life as well as the Vishnuite, Shivaite and other cults. The term **Vedanta** is applied both to the overall philosophy of the *Vedas* and to one of the six doctrines interpreting the *Vedas*, devised from around 550 BC onwards.

c.600–200 BC Composition of the **Dharma Sutra**, a prose manual on the Sacred Law (*dharma*), covering human

> ❝ The Atman, the Self, has four conditions. The first condition is the waking life of outward-moving consciousness, enjoying the seven outer gross elements. The second condition is the dreaming life of inner-moving consciousness, enjoying the seven subtler inner elements in its own light and solitude. The third condition is the sleeping life of silent consciousness when a person has no desires and beholds no dreams. The fourth condition is the Atman in His own pure state: the awakened life of supreme consciousness. ❞
>
> from the *Mandukya Upanishad*, trans. Juan Mascaro

Karma, Transmigration and *Dharma*

The Aryans brought to India their own views on the afterlife. The early hymns of the *Rig Veda* state that the virtuous will go to the World of Fathers, while the wicked will be condemned to dwell indefinitely in the House of Clay. As a result, the concept of being rewarded or punished in afterlife for the deeds done during one's existence was implicit in Indian culture. Later, this became known as the **doctrine of karma** (literally, deed or action), meaning both the deed and its spiritual residue, which determines a human being's future after his or her death.

A hymn in the last book of the *Rig Veda* intriguingly suggests that the dead may pass to the waters or remain in plants. This was an allusion to a belief prevalent among many primitive tribes that the souls of the dead pass to animals, birds, insects or plants before being re-born in human form. In the 7th and 6th centuries BC, the idea of a soul passing from body to body, **transmigration** (*samsara* in Sanskrit), carrying forward a residue of its previous incarnations for eternity or a very long period, became popular among Indo-Aryans.

The twin doctrine of karma and transmigration offered Indo-Aryans a plausible explanation for pain – punishment meted out to a human for bad deeds in previous reincarnations. Parallel to karma is the concept of *dharma*. A derivative of *dhr* – meaning to bear or sustain – dharma means 'bearer', 'law', 'condition' or 'phenomenon'. In religious terms, it implies divine cosmic order; in a legal context, law; in a caste context, the special behaviour or duties of a caste. In general *dharma* means social duty stemming from the position in which one is born. Among deities, **Yama**, the god of death, punishes those who break the *dharma* and rewards those who follow it.

conduct, morals and ethics. Two other sutras, the **Shrauta Sutra** concerning sacrifice, and **Grahiya Sutra** concerning domestic religious ceremonies, are attributed to the same legendary but unnamed sage. The complete set is called the

The Buddha underneath the pipal tree where he attained Enlightenment. His hands are arranged in the mudra of meditation (Dhyana mudra)

Kalpa Sutra. Later, the *Dharma Sutra* will be expanded and versified, and retitled ***Dharma Shastra*** (Instruction in Sacred Law).

c.563 BC Birth of the **Buddha** (Enlightened One), born **Siddhartha** (Aim Achieved), with the clan name **Gautama**, at Kapilasvastu in the Himalayan foothills. Son of Shuddhodhna, the kshatriya chief of the Shakya clan and his consort Mahamaya, Siddharta Gautama is raised in luxury. According to legend, he is carefully isolated from every sign of misery, disease and death.

550 BC **Cyrus the Great** founds the Achaeminid dynasty in **Persia**. Determined to rule a large empire, he conducts military campaigns on all his frontiers, including the mountainous border with the Indian subcontinent.

c.547 BC Siddharta Gautama marries his cousin Yashodhra.

c.542 BC **Bimbisara**, also known as Sreniga, becomes the fifth Sisunaga king of Magdha. The dowry of his chief queen gives him control of adjoining Kashi (contemporary Varanasi/Benares), an important kingdom in its own right. Dynastic inter-marriage with the royal houses of Kosala (North Bihar) and Vaishali further help him in his expansionist policy.

Bimbisara goes on to conquer Anga (modern Bhagalpur and Monghyr districts) and so control trade routes to seaports in the **Ganges delta** which have commercial contacts with Southeast Asia and South India. The linking of domestic with foreign trade enrichs Magdha.

An aspiring emperor, Bimbisara is noted for his careful choice of councillors, whose advice he values. He creates a hierarchy among his officials and builds new roads as a means of administering a realm where the village is the basic unit under a headman charged with collecting taxes. He appoints special officials to measure agricultural land

and assess crop yields, one-sixth of which is paid as a state **tax**.

c.540 BC Probable birthdate of **Vardhamana Mahavira**, the founder of **Jainism**, born to Siddhartha, the kshatriya chief of the Jnatrika clan in south Nepal, and his consort Trishala.

c.536 BC Siddhartha Guatama, straying from his palace quarters, is shaken by his encounters with a geriatric, a sick man, a corpse and finally a peripatetic beggar of serene appearance. He decides immediately to become a beggar himself, only to be inundated with more luxury by his father. On the night when a son, Rahula, is born to his wife Yashodhra, he leaves the royal palace unannounced.

c.530 After six years of wandering and self-mortification, Siddhartha Gautama concludes that penance does not lead to enlightenment, and begins begging for food. While meditating under a pipal tree near **Gaya** (in Bihar), he vows not to leave his seat until he has perceived the root of suffering. On the 49th day, having resisted all temptations, Siddhartha achieves his goal by identifying desire as the cause of sorrow.

Able also to recall his former lives, for the next 49 days Siddhartha reflects on his newfound knowledge. He then delivers his first sermon at **Sarnath**, near Varanasi, usually regarded as the foundation of **Buddhism** (see p.36). In his sermon he advocates a middle way, incorporating the Noble Eightfold Path, to five disciples: Assagi, Bhaddiya, Kondanna, Mahanama and Vappa. Now called Buddha (from *budh*, to perceive or awaken), he assembles a body of monks who, accepting a common discipline, adopt yellow robes. A preacher of non-violence, he averts a battle between the Shakyas and Koliyas by walking between their armies and convincing them of the evils of violence.

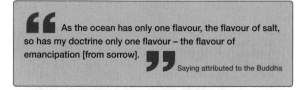

As his reputation grows, so does his **Sangha** (Order), whose membership is not restricted by caste. Siddhartha and his followers divide their time between peripatetic preaching (eight months in the year) and living in huts in parks and forests (four months).

c.533 BC Cyrus the Great of Persia crosses the Hindu Kush and exacts tribute from the kingdoms of Kamboja and Gandhara to the east of the mountains. As a result of the infusion of **Persian influence** into the subcontinent, **Kharoshti**, an Aramaic script, is introduced into northwest India.

It complements the indigenous **Brahmi** script prevalent in most of the subcontinent. Circumstantial evidence points to merchants using a writing script for at least a hundred years, and there are allusions in literary sources – dating from the 6th century BC but transcribed later – to an alphabet. Used for transcribing Sanskrit, the two scripts will be among those found in pillar inscriptions cut during the reign of the **Emperor Ashoka** (see p.50), with Kharoshti only in northwestern India (and Greek and Aramaic in Afghanistan).

Between them, Brahmi will prove more enduring, with Kharoshti becoming extinct in the 3rd century AD. Brahmi will provide the basis for later Indian writing systems. Derived from either Harappan seal script (see p.11), or from a North Semitic script, it is so well adapted to Indian phonetics that it is thought to have been deliberately developed by brahmins, well versed in phonetics.

Buddhism

Among major world religions, **Buddhism** stands out for its agnosticism. It may therefore be described more as a philosophy or way of life than a faith. Despite the Buddha's strict instructions to his followers not to deify him, he is revered as a godlike figure by them. His disciples summarized their master's teaching as the **Three Refuges**, which a Buddhist recites daily: 'I seek refuge in the Buddha; I seek refuge in the *Dharma* (Doctrine); I seek refuge in the *Sangha* (Order).'

According to the Buddhist creed, all phonemenona of the universe, material or mental, are transient, lack any enduring soul (*atman*), and are prone to suffering and sorrow (*dukkha*, in Pali). The five components of a human – body, feeling, perception, state of mind and awareness – exist before him. On his death, they separate and may re-combine in a different form. It is from this cycle of death and re-birth that we should try to escape and achieve **nirvana** – literally 'non-existence', but figuratively 'emancipation'. To do this, we must overcome desire, which is the cause of suffering, by following the **'Noble Eightfold Path'**: Right Views, Right Resolve (to refrain from harming living creatures, stealing, lying etc), Right Speech, Right Action, Right Livelihood, Right Effort, Right Mindfulness and Right Contemplation.

In his sermons, transcribed posthumously, Buddha maintains that faith in him can secure a human being's rebirth in the heavens – a prospect more comprehensible to common folk than the indescribable nirvana. He led a proselytizing fraternity of monks and nuns who observed an exemplary code of conduct, including celibacy and vegetarianism. His popularity owed much to his repudiation of animal sacrifice and the oppressive caste system. Following his death, his disciples worshipped him by circumambulating a stupa or a pipal tree, then focusing on his image. With the passing of time Buddhist doctrine evolved from its basic **Hinayana school** to the complex **Mahayana** (see p.74).

521 BC **Darius I** succeeds Cambyses, son of Cyrus the Great, as King of Persia. During his 26-year reign, Persian hegemony is established over Gandhara and most of the Panjab. **Taxila** (Takshashila), the administrative capital of Gandhara, emerges as an important centre of learning for Persian and Vedic scholars, accelerating cultural exchange.

c.510 BC Vardhaman leaves his home, his wife and a daughter, to become a mendicant.

c.497 BC Following twelve years of severe penance, Vardhaman finds enlightenment and becomes known as Mahavira (Great Hero) and Jina (Victor). He delivers his first sermon, the foundation of **Jainism**, and establishes an order of friars and nuns who preach his doctrines in various kingdoms in northern India.

c.494 BC King Bimbasara of Magdha renounces his throne and either voluntarily starves himself to death – not an uncommon practice – or his son and heir **Ajatashatru**, also called Kunika, starves him to death. Ajatashatru continues to expand Magdha to the north and west, taking full control of Kashi. Further expansion is resisted by the tribal confederacy of **Vriji**, against whom Ajatashatru fights a war lasting sixteen years.

486 BC **Xerxes** of Persia succeeds Darius I. He and his successors continue to maintain a Persian presence in Gandhara and the Panjab.

c.483 BC The Buddha dies at Kushinagara, modern Nepal. His last words to his disciples are: 'All composite things decay. Strive diligently.' In his wake will emerge a vast canon of **Buddhist scriptures** in Sanskrit, Pali and other languages, all of them transcribed many generations after his demise. Among these, the best-known and most widely translated will be the *Dhammapada*, purportedly an anthology of the Buddha's aphorisms and sayings.

Jainism

Scarcely practised outside India, **Jainism** is divided between two sects, the **Svetambara** ('white robed') and **Digambara** ('sky-robed', meaning naked) and has around five million followers. According to the Jain doctrine, first propounded by **Vardhaman Mahavira**, the cosmos functions through constant interaction between living creatures and five categories of inanimate objects, and that minerals, air, wind and fire, as well as plants possess souls with varying degrees of consciousness.

Jains practice *ahimsa*, or the non-hurting of any life form. It is therefore a sin to hurt even the smallest insect. Jain monks and nuns wear veils over their mouths and noses to prevent minuscule organisms in the air being inhaled and killed. Jains believe that souls remain conscious of their identity through successive incarnations, which are determined by the cumulative effect of conduct (karma). To achieve release (nirvana) from the cycle of rebirth, the believer should follow the **Three Gems**: Right Faith, Right Cognition and Right Conduct, the last involving a long course of fasting, self-mortification, study and meditation. Since Jains believe that God is only the noblest and fullest manifestation of powers latent in the human soul, they can be described as agnostic.

A 'sky-robed' Jain monk at the feet of the huge statue of Gomateshwara

Buddhism will also inspire fine religious architecture in the form of the **stupa** – a semi-spherical dome derived from pre-Buddhist burial mounds, designed to house either a relic of the Buddha, or the remains of a venerated monk.

c.480 Money appears in the form of silver bars in North India, either minted by royal courts or by guilds of merchants, set up to protect their interests. With trade routes flourishing, the increased wealth of North Indian states is reflected in the production of polished **black pottery** as well as other luxuries.

c.478 BC Ajatashatru of Magdha finally triumphs over the Vriji confederacy. His victory stems primarily from the superiority of a centralized army under a single king over the disparate forces of a tribal confederacy. The secondary factor is the Magadhans' deployment of superior weaponry. They use large catapults to hurl heavy stones, and their chariots – armed with knives and cutting edges attached to the wheel shafts, and driven by charioteers seated under cover – mow down the enemy ranks.

In celebration, Ajatashatru builds the fortified township of **Patali** on the Son River, which later becomes Pataliputra (Son of Patali), modern Patna.

c.468 BC Death of Vardhaman Mahavira.

c.467 BC In Maghda, Darsaka succeeds his father Ajatashatru as king.

c.450 BC The *Nirutka*, India's oldest linguistic text, explaining obsolete Sanskrit words used in the *Vedas*, is composed by the sage Yaska.

c.437 BC In Magdha, Udayin succeeds Darsaka, and builds **Kushumpura** near Pataliputra.

c.413 BC King Nagadasaka of Magdha, having succeeded Kings Anuruddha and Munda, is removed from power. The throne is offered to **Amatya Saisunaga**, a royal viceroy. As monarch, Amatya brings a long conflict with

> **❝** As rain does not break through a well-thatched house, passion will not break through a well-reflecting mind. **14**
>
> If one man conquers in battle a thousand times a thousand men; and if another conquers himself, he is the greatest of conquerors. **103**
>
> Men who have not observed proper discipline, and have not gained wealth in their youth, perish like old herons in a lake without fish. **155**
>
> He who formerly was reckless and afterwards became sober brightens up the world like the moon when freed from clouds. **170**
>
> He who holds back rising anger like a rolling chariot, him I call a real driver; other people are but holding the reins. **222**
>
> Those who are slaves to passions run down the stream of desires as a spider runs down the web he has made himself. When they have cut this, at last, wise people go onwards, free from cares, leaving all pain behind. **347**
>
> The sun is bright by day, the moon shines by night, the warrior is bright in his armour, the brahmin is bright in his meditation; but the Buddha, the Awakened, is bright with splendour day and night. **387** **❞**
>
> from the *Dhammapada*, trans. from the Pali by F. Max Muller

the kingdom of Avanti (capital Ujjani, near Indore) to a victorious conclusion.

c.385 BC Kakavarna, also called Kalashoka, succeeds his father Amatya Saisunaga as king of Magdha.

c.383 BC Kakavarna convenes the **Second Buddhist Gener-**

al Council at Vaishali in order to resolve doctrinal disputes, an event that shows Buddhism enjoying royal patronage.

c.370 BC Either in a palace coup or battle, Mahanandin, the last Saisunaga king of Magdha, is overthrown by **Mahapadma Nanda**, a low-caste upstart who now establishes a new dynasty.

Krishna

A godhead who bestrides and typifies the emergence of **Hinduism** out of Vedism, **Lord Krishna** (literally 'black') is variously portrayed as a pastoral playboy, a valiant warrior and a meditative philosopher. Most probably he is an amalgam of several larger-than-life characters from diverse regions of the subcontinent. He may have originated as Mayon ('the black one'), a Tamil fertility god famed for playing the flute and seducing milkmaids, whose cult probably travelled north through nomadic pastoralists. More traditionally, Krishna was born in Mathura, southeast of Delhi, the son of Vasudeva and Devaki, a cousin of King Kamsa. Responding to a prophecy that he would be killed by Devaki's eighth son, Kamsa resolved to murder all her sons. Through divine intervention, Krishna was spared and raised by a cowherd couple, Nanda and Yashoda.

As a boy Krishna killed many demons. As a young man, his flute-playing lured many women from their husbands. King Kamsa, having traced Krishna's whereabouts, made further attempts on his life. Krishna killed Kamsa and seized his kingdom. But, finding himself sandwiched between Kamsa's father-in-law and a hostile Yavana king, Krishna left Mathura with his followers to establish a new capital in Dwarka, Gujarat. There, blessed with an ability to divide himself into as many men as women desired him, he acquired 16,000 wives and sired 180,000 sons. In the *Mahabharata*'s Great War, he sided with the Pandus against the Kauravas, and preached the sermon of *Bhagvad Gita* (composed in the 1st century BC, see p.63). Eventually, having returned to Dwarka, Krishna was pierced by a huntsman's arrow, whereupon he reverted to being the god **Vishnu**, whose avatar he had all along been.

3
The Nanda and Maurya dynasties

c.370–180 BC

By the 4th century BC the Indo-Aryan heartland had shifted eastwards from the Indus to the Ganges. In the Gangetic plain, **Magdha**, formerly one among many contending kingdoms and states, had emerged pre-eminent, both in size and strength. Under the shortlived **Nanda dynasty**, and then the longer-lasting **Maurya**, Magdha continued to consolidate and expand its power. During the reign of **Emperor Ashoka** (273–232 BC), widely regarded as a just, benevolent ruler, Magdhian authority extended not only to most of the peninsula, but also far into the northwestern territories, to include parts of modern Afghanistan – chiefly because of the collapse of the Achaeminid empire of Persia in 330 BC under the heels of Alexander the Great's army.

Far more than their predecessors, the early Maurya monarchs were adept at establishing the institutions needed to administer what (given the criteria of the times) constituted an empire. Such is the thrust of the text in the *Arthashastra*, a treatise on statecraft compiled by **Chanakya Kautilya**, the chief minister of the first Maurya ruler, Chandragupta.

In it, Chanakya urges a sovereign to appoint a **privy council**, with specific roles for the chief councillor, chief priest, minister of war and peace, treasurer, chief tax collector, army commander, chief justice, and secretary-cum-records-keeper. Government bureaucracy should consist of departments headed by superintendents of royal estates, forests, forest produce, state farms, wastelands, cattle herds, mines, granaries, tolls and customs, gold and goldsmiths, storehouses, commerce, armoury, weights and measures, spinning and weaving workshops, agriculture, slaughterhouses, passports, shipping, and, for good measure, distilleries, gaming and prostitutes.

Such a bureaucratic infrastructure, when combined with a standing army of up to 650,000 men, was costly to maintain. Chanakya, therefore, deals with tax and other revenues at some length. Following his recommendations, the Mauryas expanded their tax base to include levies – payable in either coin or kind – on gaming, prostitution and even water, as well as on more traditional activities such as agriculture, commodity production (including pottery and textiles) and trade, with severe penalties imposed on tax evaders.

General taxes such as these, however, were effective only if the population at large was well off, since overtaxing an impoverished society, warned Chanakya, was a recipe for rebellion. Contemporary evidence indicates unprecedented prosperity. While caste militated against social mobility, it encouraged pride in one's occupation, with each generation building on the skills of its predecessor. In crafts and industry, the localization of occupation, combined with the hereditary nature of the caste, reinforced the **guilds**, which facilitated tax collection.

By now the **Indo-Aryans** had lost their original nomadic pastoral identity. They constituted a settled, agrarian society, with a scattering of urban centres, where literacy was spreading. Evidence of this is to be found in the main archeological remains of the period: a series of rocks and pillars, inscribed with royal proclamations from Emperor Ashoka's reign at sites frequently visited by crowds, containing at least a sprinkling of literates. Some of the inscriptions refer to Ashoka's conversion to Buddhism, which had by now graduated from being a sect to a distinctive religion.

The inscriptions on the Ashokan pillars in Greek, Aramaic or Kharoshti, a derivative of Aramaic, in modern Afghanistan and the adjoining Pakistani provinces reflect the imprint two centuries of Persian rule had left on the northwestern sector of the subcontinent. The Indo-Middle Eastern trade that resulted from the Achaeminid reign benefited both sides.

c.370 BC The son of a barber and his *shudra* wife, **Mahapadma Nanda** becomes the founder of the first non-*kshatriya* ruling dynasty in the north, which lasts half a century. He adds Kalinga (modern Orissa) and parts of Maharashtra in the southwest to his Magdha kingdom, thus qualifying later as India's **first emperor**, or the 'one-umbrella sovereign'.

He commands a standing army of 200,000 infantry, 20,000 cavalry, 2000 four-horse chariots and 3000–6000 elephants. In order to augment his agricultural revenue he builds canals and other irrigation facilities. He reciprocates the hostility that brahmins and *kshatriyas*, who consider him a low-caste upstart, show toward him.

c.358 BC Artaxerxes III succeeds Artaxerxes II as ruler of the **Persian empire**, which extends as far as the Indus and the Panjab.

c.338 BC Murdered, Artaxerxes II is succeeded by Cyrus II.

c.336 BC Cyrus II is ovethrown and **Darius III** ascends the Persian throne.

c.335 BC Following Mahapadma Nanda's death, the succession in Magdha is disputed by his surviving sons.

c.333 BC Alexander of Macedon (aka **Alexander the Great**), the 23-year-old ruler of the Greeks, leads a military expedition into Persia and defeats Darius III on the banks of the **Issus**.

c.331 BC Suffering defeat by Alexander yet again at **Gaugamela**, Darius III flees to neighbouring Bactria, where he is murdered the following year.

c.330 BC Dhanananda Nanda, the youngest of Mahapadma's sons, becomes the king of Magdha.

327 BC In his drive to seize the easternmost parts of the Persian empire, Alexander crosses the Hindu Kush.

326 BC Intent on extending his empire beyond that of the Persians, Alexander fords the Indus and defeats **King Porus**, the ruler of the lands between the Hydaspes (Jhelum) and Akensines (Chenab) Rivers in Panjab. While Alexander loses only 1000 of his men during the **Battle of Hydaspes**, his army reputedly slaughters 12,000 of Porus's 30,000 infantry. When the wounded Porus is asked how he should be treated, he replies, 'As befits a king'. Impressed by his captive's dignity, Alexander makes him an ally.

326–325 BC Subduing several republican and monarchical Indo-Aryan tribes, Alexander crosses the remaining three of the five Panjab rivers. But at the last river (the Bias), his exhausted troops mutiny. Instead of pushing forward into the northern plains, therefore, Alexander leads his army down the Indus to the Arabian Sea. Sending some of his forces by boat to Babylon, he takes the remainder along the Baluchistan coast, appointing **Greek governors** to rule his Indian territories.

323 BC Alexander dies in Babylon, Mesopotamia, after a drinking bout. This leaves his Greek governors of his Indian provinces leaderless and confused.

322 BC The Nanda dynasty comes to an abrupt end with the overthrow of Dhanananda by 24-year-old **Chandragupta Maurya**, a *vaishya* by caste, and a member of the Moriya

This 16th-century Mughal painting depicts Alexander the Great having himself lowered into the sea in a glass diving bell in order to observe the underwater world

tribe. In establishing a new dynasty, Chandragupta is ably assisted by his chief minister **Chanakya Kautilya** (aka Vishnugupta), an exceptionally shrewd, Kerala-born brahmin, partly educated in Taxila (see p.48).

317 BC The last Greek governor, Eudamus, leaves northwest India.

316–14 BC Following the collapse of Greek authority, Chandragupta extends Maurya rule as far as the Indus. Then, turning his attention southward, he conquers the region above the Narmada River in central India.

312 BC The Greek commander **Seleucos Nikotar** recaptures Babylon in Mesopotamia and becomes its governor.

306 BC Having consolidated his hold over Babylon, Nikotar campaigns to recover territories east of the Indus.

305–3 BC Chandragupta defeats Nikotar and acquires provinces far beyond the western bank of the Indus, including a part of (modern) Afghanistan. Unprecedently, therefore, the Mauryan empire includes both the Indus and Ganges basins as well as the land to the far northwest.

302 BC Nikotar's envoy **Magesthenes**, sent to the Mauryan capital at Pataliputra, travels extensively in the north and writes a journal, entitled *Indika*. While the original text is lost, its contents are extracted by such later historians as Arrian and Diodorus. According to Magasthenes, there are 118 kingdoms and republics in India, including those that are vassal states of the Mauryan empire. Of the Mauryan standing army – 600,000 infantry, 30,000 cavalry and 9,000 elephants – he writes: 'When they are not in service they spend their time in idleness and drinking bouts, being maintained at the expense of the royal treasury.'

c.300 BC Chanakya Kautilya compiles the ***Arthashastra***, a political treatise.

The *Arthashastra* of Chanakya Kautilya

The *Arthashastra*, India's oldest treatise on statecraft, is ascribed to **Chanakya Kautilya**, Chandargupta's enterprising and talented chief minister, with some subsequent accretions by interpolators. Its down-to-earth pragmatism has been compared to *The Prince* (1513) by Niccolò Machiavelli of Florence, and its emphasis on the production of wealth (*artha*) as being of primary concern to the state makes it the forerunner of Adam Smith's *Wealth of Nations* (1776).

Its fifteen books and 150 chapters cover almost all aspects of statecraft. At the outset, Chanakya declares that his purpose is to enlighten rulers as to how social forces operate so that they can apply the doctrine of punishment (*danda*) in such a way that deserving subjects, pursuing their occupations in peace, are enriched. In its subsequent books, the *Arthashastra* deals with such subjects as the duties of the government, law as a system of codified custom, marriage and property, and the conduct of war. Chanakya advises rulers to direct battle operations from the rear, and recommends deploying heavy infantry and elephants in the centre with light infantry, chariots and cavalry on the wings. His statement that 'Intrigue, spies, winning over the enemy's people, siege and assault are the five means to capture a fort' neatly illustrates his earthly cunning.

His peacetime advice to kings is to deploy an elaborate system of espionage and intelligence. Householders, merchants, ascetics, students, mendicant women and prostitutes should all be enlisted in the monarch's secret service, and cipher-writing and carrier pigeons used. The duties of a spy should include seeking out sedition, acting as an *agent provocateur*, working as a criminal detective and assessing public opinion by eavesdroping in taverns, brothels and gambling dens.

298 BC Chandragupta, the Mauryan 'one-umbrella sovereign', abdicates in favour of his son **Bindusara Amitraghata** ('killer of foes'), and retires to a Jain monastery at Sravana Belgola, west of contemporary Bangalore. There, at the age of 60, he starves himself to death. Megasthenes is replaced by Deimachos as the Greeks' ambassador to Pataliputra.

c.285 BC Bindusara Amitraghata reputedly conquers 'the land between the eastern and western seas' in the southern peninsula.

273 BC The Magdhan throne passes to Ashokavardhana, better known as **Emperor Ashoka** ('Without Sorrow'), even though he is not Bindusara's eldest son.

269 BC During his coronation Ashoka acquires the royal name of Priyadarshi ('Of Gracious Mien'), and the title *Devanampiya* ('Beloved of Gods'). While he will be ranked among the most outstanding rulers of India, his reign is also significant for its **inscriptions on twenty rocks and twelve pillars**, the first of their kind in India.

261–60 BC Winning a war that claims 100,000 lives and 150,000 prisoners, Ashoka conquers **Kalinga**.

259 BC Ashoka elevates **Buddhism**, still one sect among many, on a par with Vedism/Brahmanism. He dispatches

> ❝ Just as it is impossible not to taste the honey or the poison that finds itself at the tip of the tongue, so it is impossible for a government servant not to eat up at least a bit of the king's revenue. Just as with fish moving under water it cannot possibly be discerned whether they are drinking water or not, so it is impossible to detect government servants employed on official duties when helping themselves to money. ❞
>
> from the *Arthashastra*

Buddhist missionaries to (modern) Burma/Myanmar and Sri Lanka, and at home initiates a programme of building Buddhist *viharas*, which combine the functions of temples and monasteries.

258–257 BC Ashoka's edicts are inscribed on rocks in four scripts: Greek and Aramaic in Afghanistan, Kharoshti in present-day Pakistan, and Brahmi elsewhere. Rock XIII stresses inter-faith tolerance, reflecting the emperor's policy of patronizing Buddhism while studiously refraining from attacking Brahmanism.

256–255 BC Further rock inscriptions contain the **Kalinga Edicts**, summarizing Ashoka's conversion to Buddhism in the wake of the Kalinga war as well as promulgating his

Emperor Ashoka r. 273–232 BC

Combining military genius with humanitarian vision, **Ashoka** was the first Indian ruler to govern both the north and the south. He revealed a touch of naïveté and a large measure of pomposity, but he was also domineering and strong-willed. His practice of inscribing rocks and specially erected stone pillars (see p.52) with public proclamations, moral and ethical exhortations, expressions of royal duty and remembrances of his pilgrimages to Buddhist holy sites provides the earliest reliable written records in the subcontinent's annals.

As his **Kalinga Edicts** indicate, Ashoka's bitterly fought conquest of that province altered his way of thinking, and made him receptive to Buddhist doctrine. However, his conversion to Buddhism did not mean abandoning imperial ambition, only its modification to meet his new faith's precepts. Ashoka's authoritarianism, summarized in the statement, 'All men are my children', remained intact. To maintain security in his far-flung empire he maintained an efficient intelligence apparatus, which also kept him abreast of popular opinion. And for the same purpose, he frequently toured his territories.

imperial wishes such as 'safety, self-control, justice and happiness for all [living] beings'.

250 BC Mahendra, a son of Ashoka who has become a Buddhist monk, embarks on a mission to **Sri Lanka**, when he carries with him a branch of the pipal tree under which Buddha achieved enlightenment (see p.32).

249 BC Ashoka makes a pilgrimage to the places of the Buddha's birth and death (Kapilavastu and Kushinagara), enlightenment (Gaya), and first sermon (Sarnath). Breaking with tradition, his tour is not interspersed with royal hunts.

243–242 BC Seven major pillars, inscribed with imperial edicts dictated by Emperor Ashoka, are erected throughout the empire.

c.240 BC Under Ashoka's patronage the **Third General Buddhist Council** is held in Pataliputra. The canon of Buddhist scriptures in the Pali language is codified and fresh missions are dispatched around the Indian subcontinent and to foreign lands. Ashoka's increasing intervention in Buddhist affairs coincides with a loss of grip over his sprawling empire.

240–32 BC Five minor pillars, carrying edicts dictated by Ashoka, condemn differences among Buddhist monks regarding the nature of Buddhism and its founder. The capital of one such pillar, discovered at Sarnath (modern Gujarat) – consisting of four lions resting over a round base containing the Buddhist wheel of *dharma* – will become the official emblem of the Republic of India in 1950.

232 BC Ashoka's death heralds the disintegration of his empire. As his succession is disputed by his three sons – Kunala, Tivara and Jalauka – the viceroys of some large provinces, often themselves members of the Maurya dynasty, assume power locally.

Rock and Pillar Inscriptions

Rocks and pillars inscribed with **Emperor Ashoka's edicts** and proclamations have been found across his subcontinental empire, except in the sub-Karnataka region, southern Nepal and eastern Afghanistan. The inscriptions themselves, beautifully carved, are in Greek or Aramaic in Afghanistan; in Kharoshti near Peshawar (modern Pakistan); and in Brahmi elsewhere. Their purpose was to propagate and expound Ashoka's understanding of *dharma* (see p.31), and to engender social responsibility and mutual tolerance among citizens amid tensions created by the vastness and diversity of his empire. They stress non-violence, renunciation of war as a means of conquest, and restraint in animal slaughter.

Yet Ashoka also recognizes that force may sometimes be unavoidable, for example in combating rebellious minorities: 'The Beloved of Gods reasons with the forest tribes in his empire, and seeks to reform them. But the Beloved of Gods is not only compassionate, he is also powerful, and he tells them to repent lest they be slain.' Overlooking his own pleas for tolerance, Ashoka appointed officers to enforce *dharma* with extensive powers of interference in the private lives of his subjects. Yet even these measures proved inadequate to contain social and sectarian divisions.

CLIVE FRIEND

Rock inscriptions of the Emperor Ashoka's edicts

c.230–181 BC Accession of Dasaratha, a grandson of Ashoka, in the eastern provinces of the Maurya empire; and probable accession of Samprati, another grandson, in the western provinces. They are followed by Salisuka, Devavarman and Satadhanvan.

221 BC In China, the First Emperor Qin Shihuangdi orders the construction of the **Great Wall** along the northern frontier of his territories. Excluded from their traditional pasturages, the nomadic Yueji (Kushana) and other tribes are forced to turn westwards, creating knock-on migrations that, over the coming century and a half, will impact on the Indian subcontinent.

c.206 BC Demetrios I, the Greek king of Bactria, crosses the Hindu Kush into India and defeats Subhagasena, a local ruler.

c.200 BC Classical **Sanskrit** replaces ancient (archaic) Sanskrit.

> ❝ [Show] consideration towards slaves and servants, obedience to mother and father, generosity towards friends, acquaintances and relatives, and towards priests and monks ... But the Beloved of the Gods does not consider gifts of honour to be as important as the essential advancement of all sects ... [O]ne should honour another man's sect, for by doing so one increases the influence of one's own sect and benefits that of the other man while, by doing otherwise, one diminishes the influence of one's own sect and harms the other man's ... therefore concord is to be recommended so that men may hear one another's principles. ❞
>
> Rock Edict XII, cited by Romila Thapar in *Ashoka and the Decline of the Mauryas* (1961)

Sanskrit and the Prakrits

Sanskrit (literally 'cultivated') is the mother of all North Indian languages. Archaic Sanskrit, used in the *Vedas*, prevailed until around 200 BC, when Sanskrit assumed its classical form – an evolution hastened by the efforts of early scholars to standardize grammar. In the 5th century BC Yaska's *Nirutka* explained Vedic words that were already obsolete, and in the 4th century BC Panini's *Astadhyayi* ('Eight Chapters') extrapolated 4000 rules for spoken Sanskrit.

In order to maintain the purity of the *Vedas* – transmitted orally from generation to generation by highly trained memorizers – it became necessary to develop phonetics. This led to a Sanskrit alphabet, which began with vowels and progressed to consonants, grouped together according to the manner in which they were read aloud through the use of the tongue, lips, teeth and throat. While this alphabet was easy to master, the inflection-driven Sanskrit was not. Depending on its inflection, a single word denotes person, gender, number, tense and case, and word-compounding is common. Unable to master these complexities, common folk made less and less use of Sanskrit, and replaced inflections with prepositions.

Out of this arose simplified derivatives of Sanskrit, known as **Prakrits**, the earliest being Magdhi and Pali (the preferred language of Buddhists). Other important Prakrits were Shaurseni and Maharashtri. By the 5th century AD, the Prakrits too would become standardized, with the written language diverging from the spoken. Later, they would spawn the regional languages of the north and west: Hindi, Panjabi, Sindhi, Gujarati, Marathi and Bengali. However, classical Sanskrit, as the language of learning, literature, religion and – later – royal records, remained supreme.

Its flowering during the Gupta (250–500 AD) and post-Gupta periods coincided with a brahminical renaissance fuelled by resistance to Buddhism. Indophile rulers in Southeast Asia chose Sanskrit for their names and inscriptions, believing it bestowed authority and distinction on their non-Indian dynasties.

c.200 BC The *Yoga Sutra* is composed by Patanjali, a grammarian. Also composed around the same time is Vishnu Sherman's ***Panchtantra*** ('five books'), a collection of fables, in which animals and birds are endowed with human qualities.

The *Manu Smriti*

Comprising 2684 couplets in twelve chapters in classical Sanskrit, the ***Manu Smriti*** (literally 'remembered Manu') is the first law book in verse. By tradition, Manu, an ancient folk god, is a hermaphrodite whose son (Ikshvaku) and daughter (Ilaa) become the respective progenitors of the solar (*Suryavamisha*) and lunar (*Chandravamisha*) royal dynasties. *Manu Smriti* codifies many prevailing customs, principal among them the caste system. Caste consideration permeates even commercial transactions. For unsecured loans it specifies annual interest of 24 percent for brahmins, 36 percent for *kshatriyas*, 48 percent for *vaishyas*, and 60 percent for *shudras*. Conversely, while a convicted *shudra* thief is required to pay eight times the value of the stolen goods, the penalty for a *vaishya*, *kshatriya* or brahmin thief is 16, 32 and 64 times the value. Reflecting a growing practice among higher castes, the *Manu Smriti* rules that 'Nowhere is a second husband permitted to respectable women' – a departure from early Indo-Aryan custom. In modern times the *Manu Smriti* became the foundation of Hindu Law covering personal and family matters.

> ❝ Duty of the brahmin is to study and teach, to sacrifice, and to give and receive gifts;
> The kshatriya must protect the people, sacrifice, and study;
> The vaishya also sacrifices and studies, but his chief function is to breed cattle, to till the earth, to pursue trade and to lend money;
> and the shudra's duty is only to serve the three higher classes. ❞
>
> *Manu Smriti*, I.88, trans. G. Buhler

Yoga

Yoga has been an integral part of Indian life for almost 3000 years. While Patanjali's *Yoga Sutra*, composed around 200 BC, is the first surviving manual, there are references to yogic practices in earlier works. Related etymologically to the word 'yoke', its ultimate purpose is to enable the practitioner – yogi – to achieve oneness with the Universal Soul.

Patanjali's work contains 200 aphorisms arranged in four sections: *samadhi*, the nature of mental concentration; *sadhana*, the pathway to it; *vibhuti*, supernatural powers attainable through yoga; and *kaivalya*, detachment of the self. Among yoga's main schools, *Hath Yoga* ('Yoga of Force') focuses on difficult body postures, enabling the yogi to maximize physical self-control; *Mantra Yoga* prescribes repetition of certain syllables or phrases as a means of achieving *samadhi*; and *Raj Yoga* ('Royal Yoga'), which is the highest form.

Its eight stages are divided into outer and inner ones. The outer stages are *yama*, self-control, exercised through non-violence and chastity; *niyama*, observance of purity, austerity and study of the *Vedas*; *asana*, posture, sitting in certain positions, the best known being *Padmasama* (Lotus Position); and *pranayama*, breathing control, when respiration is directed into unusual rhythms – a preamble to the first of the four inner stages, *pratyahara*, withdrawal of senses, when sense organs are trained to ignore their perceptions.

Then follow *dharna*, steadying the mind, by concentrating on a single object or a sacred symbol; *dhyan*, meditation, when the object of concentration fills the mind; and finally *samadhi*, super-consciousness, when the practitioner loses contact with the world and achieves union with the Universal Soul. That is how an advanced yogi can hold his breath for long periods without any ill-effect, control the rhythm of his heartbeat and endure extreme heat or cold.

An illustration from a Mughal manuscript of the *Bahr al hayat* ('The Ocean of Life'), a text outlining various yogic asanas or postures

c.200–100 BC The *Manu Smriti* ('Remembered Manu'), the popular term for *Manava Dharma Shastra* ('Text of Manu's laws'), is composed in classical Sanskrit by the sage Bhrigu (see p.55).

c.190 BC **Tamils** attack and occupy northern **Sri Lanka**.

c.181 BC Brihadratha, the last ruler of the Maurya dynasty, is killed by **Pushyamitra Shunga**, a brahmin general, who founds the Shunga dynasty.

4
Era of the Shakas and Kushans

c.180 BC–250 AD

Amidst the break-up of the Mauryan empire, new kingdoms arose and old ones revived. In particular, the **Shatavahana dynasty** established a powerful dominion in the Deccan. And, as before, the prolonged internal disarray besetting the subcontinent encouraged encroachments by foreigners into the northwest. Underlying such incursions was a pattern that had shaped Eurasian history for at least three millennia. Settled, agrarian communities evolved on the warmer riverine edges of the Eurasian landmass. In the semi-arid Central Asian interior, however, society remained peripatetic. Nomadic tribal peoples driving herds of cattle and sheep on horseback moved across the Steppes, stretching from the Black Sea to the Gobi desert, according to the season. This lifestyle was dependent on climate, with the right amount of rainfall bringing prosperity and population growth, and drought causing misery and migration to faraway places in search of pasture. This in turn led to battles between nomadic tribes competing for the scarce pastures, or between them and the surrounding sedentary communities.

To what extent the **Great Wall of China** – running mainly along the edge of the Mongolian plateau – shaped the migratory pattern is speculative. What is certain, though, is that from about the time of its construction at the end of the 3rd century BC, there was increased westward migration in Central Asia as a result of the best pasture lands being enclosed behind the Great Wall. In the course of such migration, a Mongoloid tribe – called **Yueji** by the Chinese and **Shakas** by Indians – came across the **Scythians**, inhabiting the area east of the inland Caspian Sea on the northern border of Bactria (modern North Afghanistan), adjoining Parthia (modern Eastern Iran), a remnant of the earlier Achaeminid empire. When expelled from their territory by the Yuejis, the Scythians attacked Bactria, then the few surviving Indo-Greek principalities, and finally the Indus Valley and the Panjab.

Out of this welter emerged **Kushan**, an empire founded by **Kanishka**, a Central Asian of mixed Yueji and Turkic blood. The boundaries of Kushan – dwarfed later only by the Mongol and Tsarist empires – stretched from Khotan in the present-day Chinese province of Xinjiang to Parthia, and from the Aral Sea to Mathura in northern India and Sanchi in central India.

The upshot of the Shaka and Kushan invasions was that the northern subcontinent became sharply divided into two main zones: one extending over the **Indus basin** and the highlands of Afghanistan and beyond; the other covering the **Gangetic plain**, with **Magdha** still the dominant kingdom. The southern peninsular plateau was now roughly divided between northwestern Deccan (modern Maharashtra), Kalinga (present-day Orissa), and the far south, where the kingdoms of Chola, Pandya and Chera vied for supremacy.

Despite political-military turmoil, cultural activity remained undiminished, both in the north and the south. Among the literary jewels of this period were the *Bhagvad Gita* and the *Tiru Kural* by Tiru Valluvar, a Tamil poet. In painting and sculpture, this era witnessed the emergence of the **Gandhara school**, named after a province in eastern Afghanistan. Part Indian, part Graeco-Roman, this furnished the template for **Buddha images** throughout the Far East and Central Asia.

Those regions experienced an accelerated spread of Buddhism of the **Mahayana school**, originating in the Indian subcontinent, which at this time also proved a fertile ground for the diffusion of a religion that stressed good deeds and piety. In the spreading of Buddhism to the north and east of India an important role was played by **Khotan** – a city on the edge of the Taklamakan desert – which had become a meeting point for Greek, Iranian, Indian and Chinese concepts.

The diverse influences at work can be gauged from the titles given to Kanishka, a native of Khotan, on coins discovered at Peshawar and Taxila: 'Great Raja of Rajas' (*Maharajatiraja*), an Indian title; 'Son of Heaven', in imitation of China's emperors; 'King of Kings' (*Shah-en-shah*), from the Persian Achaeminids via the Shakas; 'Saviour', from the Greeks; and 'Caesar' from the Romans.

c.180 BC Pushyamitra Shunga of Magdha begins persecuting Buddhists, burning many of their monasteries. Around this time Demetrius II, son of Demetrius I, an Indo-Greek king, captures parts of northwestern India. The rule of Indo-Greeks, called Yavanas (derivative of Ionians), becomes such an established fact that they are described as degenerate *kshatriya* in the *Manu Smriti* (see p.55), and thus given a place in the caste system.

c.174–160 BC Besides the Great Wall, the westerly expansion by the Chinese Han empire accentuates population and migratory pressures in the Mongolian steppes, the Tarim basin and other parts of Central Asia. Consequently, the Yueji and other nomadic tribes migrate westward in search of fresh pastures, and clash with the Scythians (known in India as Shakas) – a people of Turkic origin, speaking an Iranian language and living around the Aral Sea north of the Oxus River. As Yueji and other hordes prevail, the defeated Shakas start migrating, some toward the Caspian and Black seas, others southward toward Bactria, present-day north Afghanistan, and eventually the subcontinent.

c.165 BC Death of Demetrius II.

c.155 BC **Menander**, another Indo-Greek king, rules over Bactria with his capital at modern Kabul. Setting out to conquer northern India, he captures Panjab and the land beyond, as far as Mathura. Next, he takes the Indus delta, including north Gujarat. He attempts to seize the Gangetic plain but is repulsed by Agnimitra, the Shunga ruler of Magdha.

Menander converts to Buddhism, assuming the name 'Milinda'. During long discussions with the monk-philosopher Nagasena, preserved in the Pali text *Malindapana* ('Questions of Milinda'), he seeks and receives clarification on Buddhist doctrines.

With the easing of the Shunga dynasty's persecution of Buddhists, the faith continues to spread in India, with existing stupas being expanded and embellished with carved railings, terraces and gateways. Of these the best-known surviving example is at Sanchi, near Bhopal in modern Madhya Pradesh, with a domed hemisphere 40 metres in diameter. Elsewhere, rulers, merchants and craftsmen are equally generous in their donations to the Buddhist Sangha.

c.140 BC Dutthagamini, the Sinhalese king of Sri Lanka ends the Tamil occupation of the island.

130 BC Death of Menander (King Milinda).

c.120 BC Around this time the ***Bhagvad Gita*** ('Song of the Lord') is composed, a religious verse dialogue later incorporated into the *Mahabharata*.

Bhagvad Gita

Bhagvad Gita is the scripture used by Hindus in Indian law courts when swearing an oath. Consisting of 606 couplets, arranged in eighteen cantos, it is one of numerous interpolations by brahmins to the *Mahabharata* (see p.24). A work of many minds, it is a philosophical treatise in a literary style, presented as dialogue between **Arjun**, the most skilled Pandu archer, and his charioteer on the eve of the climactic war between the Pandus and the Kauravas.

Dejected by the sight of his cousins and teachers among the enemy, Arjun turns to his charioteer, and wonders aloud if it is morally right to kill someone. Revealing himself as Lord Krishna (see p.41), the charioteer argues that as a warrior by birth, Arjun is required by *dharma (*Sacred Law) to fight, and is therefore exempt from the sin of killing resulting from war. He must battle regardless of the outcome, victory or defeat. What ultimately matters is that the individual should strive so that his soul (*atman*) achieves oneness with the Universal Soul – and with it salvation. The means to salvation are knowledge, yoga (see p.56) or *bhakti* (devotion). Krishna's sermon dispels Arjun's doubts, and he fights.

By mandating that right actions – specified by the traditions of caste, and sanctified by the Sacred Law – must be taken irrespective of the results, the *Bhagvad Gita* defends the status quo. It also encapsulates the beliefs in karma and transmigration (see p.31) which had taken root in the Indo-Aryan psyche by the time of its composition.

c.128 BC A Chinese traveller, Zhang Qian, notes that the land around the Aral Sea, previously inhabited by the Shakas, is occupied by the Yueji. The Shakas now rule adjoining Bactria, their administration modelled on the Achaeminid practice of dividing their kingdom into provinces, each under a military governor called Great Satrap.

> **❝** Think thou also of thy duty and do not waver. There is no greater good for a warrior than to fight in a righteous war. 2.31
>
> Set thy heart upon thy work, but never on its reward. Work not for a reward; but never cease to do thy work. 2.47
>
> Action is greater than inaction: perform therefore thy task in life. Even the life of the body could not be if there were no action. 3.8
>
> The visible forms of my nature are eight: earth, water, fire, air, ether; the mind, reason, and the sense of 'I'. But beyond my physical nature is my invisible Spirit. This is the fountain of life whereby this universe has its being. 7.4–5
>
> Brahman is the Supreme, the Eternal. Atman is his Spirit in man. Karma is the force of creation, wherefrom all things have their life. Matter is the Kingdom of the Earth, which in time passes away; but the Spirit is the Kingdom of Light. 8.3–4 **❞**
>
> From the *Bhagvad Gita*, trans. Juan Mascaro

c.100 The Buddhist Sangha, funded largely by rich merchants and craftsmen's guilds, begins creating **cave temples**, particularly in the Deccan, from Ajanta and Aurangabad in the east to present-day Bombay (Mumbai) and Kalyan in the west.

Buddhist Cave Temples

India's ancient **cave temples** are awe-inspiring works of religious devotion, later copied in Central and Southeast Asia and in China. Supervised by the Buddhist Sangha, their construction continued until late in the 2nd century AD, and extended to nearly one thousand sites. Skilled craftsmen, assisted by labourers, carved pillars, arches, facades and stupas out of solid rock. Initially, they merely refurbished caves into hill sides which Buddhist monks used as shrines or temples. Later on, however, such undertakings, sponsored by merchants and other wealthy patrons, became more ambitious, resulting in entire temple complexes, including barrell-vaulted prayer-halls and free-standing stupas on the cave-floor.

Among the most elaborately rendered is the cave temple at **Karle, Maharashtra**. Typically, a rectangular entrance leads to a large worshipping hall – a rectangle surmounted by a semi-circle – with an apse at the circular end containing a miniature stupa often containing a relic of the Buddha. A series of cells, cut into the rock on both sides of the main complex, provided accommodation for resident monks.

The Chaitya, or prayer-hall, of the cave temple at Karle, Maharashtra

c.100 BC Tiru Valluvar, a Tamil sage-poet, composes the vivid ***Tiru Kural*** ('Tiru's Sacred Couplets'). Consisting of 133 chapters of ten couplets each, and dwelling upon the conduct and character of princes, councillors, ambassadors, government officials, businessmen, citizens, householders, ascetics and lovers, it is divided into three parts: Righteousness or *dharma* (*Aram*); Wealth of mind, body, family and goods (*Porul*); and Love, or Kama (*Inham*).

> " Behold the man whose strong will controls his five senses even as the goading hook controls the elephant; he is a seed for the fields of heaven. Introduction, 24
>
> The flute is sweet and the guitar dulcet, so say those who have not heard the babbling speech of their little ones. I. 26
>
> Behold the businessman that looks after the interests of others as his own; his business will expand. I. 120
>
> He is a lion among princes who is well endowed in respect of five things – to wit, troops, population, council, alliances and fortifications. II. 381
>
> Two are the eyes of the living kind: the one is called Numbers and the other, Letters. II. 392
>
> Wine gives joy, but only to him that tastes it; it can never delight at the mere sight as does love. III, 1090 "

from the *Tiru Kural*, trans. V.V. Aiyar

c.90 BC Parthian kings, chiefly Pahalavas, briefly occupy the northwest of the subcontinent.

c.88 BC The Shakas (Scythians) attack Parthia, then pour through the Bolan Pass (near modern Quetta) and overcome the Indo-Greek rulers of the Indus Valley. They penetrate as far as Mathura to the east and Gandhara (eastern Afghanistan) to the north. Still harassed by the Yueji, the Shakas subsequently move southward into the Indian peninsula.

c.80 BC Maues, the first Shaka king of Gandhara, also rules the western Panjab.

c.73 BC In the eastern kingdom of Magdha, the Shunga monarch Devbhuti is murdered by the daughter of one of his concubines at the behest of his brahmin minister **Vasudeva Kanva**, who seizes the throne. The Shunga dynasty ends. The Kanva dynasty lasts 45 years.

c.60 BC Having destroyed the last vestiges of Shunga power, the Shatavahanas in the Deccan – erstwhile administrators during the Maurya period, and led by Satakarni Shatavahana – set up their own realm. A strict adherent of Brahminism, Satakarni consolidates his control of the Deccan before crossing the Narmada and taking control of the Sanchi region.

58 BC The start of the **'Vikrama era'** – incorrectly named after Vikramaditya, the title of Chandra Gupta II who reigns four centuries later – which Hindus in north India continue to use.

c.50 BC King Kharavela of Kalinga, a Jain, embarks on a dramatic war of conquest. He first captures Pataliputra, the capital of Magdha, then defeats the 'three crowned kings' in the south, the rulers of Chola, north Tamil Nadu; Pandya, south Tamil Nadu; and Chera, Kerala. In addition, he establishes trade links with the Pandya kingdom. Exactly when Kharavela died remains uncertain, as does the identity of his successor(s).

28 BC The last of the Kanva monarchs is overpowered by King Simuka of the Shatavahana (aka Andhara) dynasty, with its capital first at Nasik and then Paithan in modern Maharashtra.

c.25 BC The monarch of Pandya sends a mission of men and animals (tigers, pheasants and tortoises) to the first Roman emperor, Augustus Caesar. Their arrival in Rome signals an expansion of maritime trade between western India and the Roman empire.

c.1 AD Composed some time between 200 BC and 100 AD are the two great verse epics of the Tamils: the *Shilappadikaram* ('Ankle Bracelet') by Ilango Adikal, and its sequel *Manimekhalai* by Kulavanigam Cattatnar, which together incorporate inherited Dravidian knowledge, stories and songs within the framework of legend.

c.40 In the far northwest, the Kushanas – one of the five septs of the Yueji horde – become predominant when Kushana Kadphises I unites all the septs under his command.

41 Mastering the monsoon winds, Roman merchants sail from the Red Sea to the southern Indian port of Muziris (modern Cranganore, north of Cochin in Kerala) in forty days during July and August. In December and January they make the return voyage safely.

c.48 Kadphises I succeeds Gondophares as the Kushana king of Taxila. He leads his unified tribe into adjoining Gandhara and Kashmir and establishes a Kushana foothold in the subcontinent, pushing the defeated Shakas southward into the peninsula.

The *Shilappadikaram* and *Manimekhalai*

These two great epics of the Tamils celebrate the era when Dravidian monarchs reputedly carved the boundary of their northern expeditions in the Himalayan rocks. Unlike the royal contests that inform the *Mahabharata* and the *Ramayana*, however, the story of *Shilappadikaram* – centred on a young, commoner couple, **Kovalan** and **Kannaki** – is distinctly domestic.

An inhabitant of a coastal town in the Chola kingdom (modern Tamil Nadu), Kovalan abandons Kannaki for courtesan Madhavi, but returns to his wife after losing his family assets. The reconciled couple decide to move southwards to Madurai, in the plains of the kingdom of Pandya. Short of funds, Kannaki gives Kovalan her golden anklet to sell in the bazaar, where it is suspected by a royal goldsmith to be stolen property rightfully belonging to the queen. The king decrees Kovalan's death – a poetically fitting punishment for Kovalan's erstwhile infidelity. Grief-stricken, Kannaki disfigures herself and departs for Vanji in the mountains of Chera (modern Kerala).

There her story turns into legend. Determined to carve Kannaki's image from a rock in the Himalayas and bathe it in the Ganges, Chera's king, Shenguttavan, leads a successful expedition to the north. Thus Kannaki, the Lady of the Ankle Bracelet, is honoured as the Goddess of Faithfulness, and the monarch is granted a beatific vision.

By taking his main characters on a journey through the coastline, plains and mountains, the poet portrays the cultural, economic and political lives of the peoples of different regions, with their varied occupations and attitudes. In much the same vein, the *Manimekhalai* continues the earlier epic, with the central part played by Kovalan's daughter Manimekhalai (by Madhavi) who adopts Buddhism.

As a result of interbreeding with non-Chinese tribes in central Asia during their two centuries of migration, the Kushana leaders look more Turkic than Mongoloid. They are large, pink-faced men, speak an Iranian language, and follow a modified version of Zoroastrianism. They wear long coats and soft leather boots and, like Europeans, sit in chairs.

52 According to the annals of the Christian Church of Edessa, **St Thomas the Apostle** comes to Kerala and sets up several Syrian churches along the coast. He then journeys to the east coast of India to a settlement near

---

Kama Sutra

In many parts of the world *Kama Sutra* conjures up images of exotic sexual activity. But, in reality, it is a useful manual on sex, reflecting the erotic preoccupations of Indo-Aryans – well captured in sculpture by the broad-hipped, thick-thighed, slender-waisted woman with ample breasts, an ideal partner for man's sexual satisfaction.

Written in Sanskrit prose with occasional verses, it consists of seven parts, including Sexual Intercourse, the Acquisition of a Wife, the Wife, the Wives of Others, Courtesans and Prostitutes, and Seduction and Aphrodisiacs. Aimed at sophisticated townsmen, it describes their daily life, duties, amusements and companions in Part I. 'A social gathering is an assembly where men of the same age, education and disposition, who enjoy the same things meet and invite some courtesans to a public hall or to the home of one of the assembly, and spend the evening in pleasant conversation ... composing poems and completing verses begun by others, and testing each other's knowledge in various arts and sciences.' In the chapters on foreplay, the author lists four kinds of embrace, eight types of love scratch ('tiger's claw', 'leaf of the blue lotus' etc), eight types of love-bite and sixteen ways of kissing. Thirty-seven different positions of coitus are given such names as 'bamboo cleft', 'lotus', 'crab', 'cow', 'packet', and 'chasing the sparrow'– and include those where a woman mounts a man. There is a separate chapter on oral sex.

present-day Madras (Chenai) where he meets strong opposition to his missionary activity.

62 St Thomas the Apostle is martyred by King Misdeos at Mylapore, a suburb of Madras. Even though Misedos has never been identified as an historical figure – since the Syrian Orthodox church survives in Kerala to this day – in this repect the annals of the Church of Edessa are credible.

The *Kama Sutra* shows a remarkable understanding of the differences between male and female sexuality. It urges the male to be tender to his female partner and regard her sexual satisfaction as his own, and stresses foreplay and variety. 'If a man rubs his penis with a mixture of the powder of cactus, black pepper and honey, and then indulges in sexual intercourse, his partner will submit completely to his will, and will never desire union with another,' states the chapter on aphrodisiacs.

FITZWILLIAM MUSEUM

In this image of love-making, the man adopts the Ashva (stallion) posture, the woman the Hastini (cow-elephant) posture

c.65 The first recorded Buddhist missionaries to China depart India to establish a monastery at Luoyang. Taking the 'Silk Road' through the Tarim basin (Taklamakan desert), they spread Buddhism among oasis townships at Yarkand, Khotan, Kashgar, Tashkent, Turfan, Miran, Kuchi and Kara Shahr, and also at Dunhuang, at the head of the Gansu steppe corridor leading into China proper.

78 According to tradition, the **Shaka era** begins when a Shaka king annexes Ujjaini in central India, 137 years after the Vikrama era. Today, along with the Gregorian Christian calendar, the Indian government uses the Shaka calendar.

c.78 Wima Kadphises, known as **Kadphises II**, succeeds his father Kadphises I as the ruler of Gandhara. He conquers northwest India, reaching as far as Mathura. A devotee of Lord Shiva, his extensive issues of mainly gold coinage is evidence of a long reign. He administers his Indian provinces through governors.

c.86 In the Deccan, Gautamiputra Satakarni of the Shatavahana dynasty rules the peninsula below the Narmada River from coast to coast.

> **"** An ingenious and sensual lover
> Should multiply the act of love by a million;
> Initiate the ways and cries of birds and beasts,
> For imagination, lightly bound by custom and tradition,
> Which varies the delight of love each time,
> Opens a woman's heart and engenders there
> Love, respect, friendship and submission. **"**
>
> *Kama Sutra*, Book II, chapter 6

c.110 Death of Kadphises II.

c.114 Vasishthiputra accedes to the Shatavahana throne.

c.120 The *Kama Sutra* ('Manual on Love/Sex') is composed by Vatsyayana.

c 121 King Vasishthiputra of the Shatavahana dynasty dies.

c.128 Kanishka, son of Vajheshka of Khotan in the Tarim Basin, accedes to the throne of the Kushana kingdom of Gandhara with its capital at Purushapura, present-day Peshawar. He rules for more than forty years. He annexes Kashmir, consolidates his domains in the Indus and western Gangetic plains, and sets up a subsidiary capital at Mathura.

According to Buddhist sources, which hail Kanishka as the Second Ashoka, he captures Magdha. He fights the Parthians, subdues potentates in Khotan, Yarkand and Kashgar, and maintains contacts with the adjoining Chinese empire. In his coinage he honours an eclectic mixture of Zoroastrian, Greek, Mithraic, and Brahmanical gods.

During the latter part of his reign Kanishka becomes a Buddhist and a patron of the Sangha. In Peshawar he builds a monumental stupa, 100 metres in diamater and 200 metres high. Largely as a result of his sponsorship of missionary activity, **Mahayana (Great Vehicle) Buddhism** becomes the dominant Buddhist sect in Central Asia and China, from where it later spreads to Japan.

c.140 Rudradaman of the Shaka dynasty, now known as the Western Satraps, controls Gujarat and Malwa in central India. He is noted for a long encomium, inscribed in perfect Sanskrit on a rock, retailing *inter alia* his triumphs over Gautamiputra Satakarni south of Narmada River and the ruling tribe in Rajasthan.

Hinayana and Mahayana Buddhism

Like all major religions, Buddhism split into sects, **Hinayana** and **Mahayana**.

Respecting the Buddha's wish not to deify him, his early followers indicated his person by such symbols as a horse, an empty throne (Gautama's renunciation of a princely life), the pipal tree (enlightenment), a wheel (first sermon), or a stupa (his death and nirvana). Focusing on his ethical teachings, they argued that nirvana could be achieved only through self-discipline and meditation. But this failed to appeal to the masses in India and abroad who were given to worshipping images.

At the philosophic level, Buddhist thinkers had to contend with myriad Brahmanical theories rooted in the *Upanishads*. Out of this challenge arose the Buddhist concept of the *bodhisattva* (literally Buddha-to-be), one who is prepared to forego nirvana until such time as his mission of furthering human welfare has been accomplished. The orthodox school, now called **Hinayana** (Small Vehicle), applied the term only to **Gautama Buddha** and his previous incarnations. But rival **Mahayana** Buddhists applied it to many spiritual beings with mythical names inhabiting a complicated system of heavens. This pantheon included the compassionate **Padmapani** (Lotus Bearer); **Manjushri**, who stimulates understanding; **Maitreya**, the future Buddha, full of gentleness; and **Vajrapani** (Thunderbolt Bearer), a destroyer of evil and vice.

The Buddha and *bodhisattva* were then transformed into deities to be worshipped, with the Buddha at the apex, to be propitiated by the intercession of *bodhisattvas*, all now provided with female consorts, or *taras*, in human form. Out of this arose **devotional Buddhism**. Some two centuries after the first stirrings of the Mahayanan thinking in the 1st century BC, came the first stone image of Buddha, carved in **Mathura**. While Mahayana thrived, Hinyana withered in India, disappearing altogether by the 7th century AD. It persisted, however, in Sri Lanka, from where it spread to present-day Burma (Myanmar), Thailand and Laos.

c.150 Emperor Kanishka presides over the Fourth General Buddhist Council, convened in Kashmir, to debate extraneous influences impinging on Buddhism due to missionary work undertaken outside India since Ashoka's (see p.50) reign. These include the concept of the coming of Maitreya, future Buddha, whose suffering will save mankind. The acceptance of this idea advances the cause of Mahayana Buddhism.

c.160 Charak compiles the ***Charak Samhita***, a compendium on *Ayurveda* (literally 'Knowledge of Life'), which covers medicine.

> [He] who by the right rising of his hand has caused the strong attachment of Dharma, who has attained wide fame by studying and remembering, by the knowledge and practice of grammar, music, logic and other great sciences, who [is proficient in] the management of horses, elephants, and chariots, the wielding of sword and shield, pugilistic combat, and other ... acts of quickness and skill in opposing forces, who day by day is in the habit of bestowing presents and honours and eschewing disrespectful treatment, who is bountiful, whose treasury by the tribute, tolls and shares [of crops] rightfully obtained overflows with gold, silver, diamonds, beryl stones and precious things; who [composes] prose and verse which are clear, agreeable, sweet, charming, beautiful, excelling by the proper use of words, and adorned; whose beautiful frame owns the most excellent marks and signs such as auspicious height and dimension, voice, gait, colour, vigour and strength, who himself has acquired the name of *Mahakshatrapa* [Great Satrap].

The Junagadh Rock Inscription of Rudradaman Shaka

Ayurveda: Indian Medicine

According to *Ayurveda*, the traditional medicine of India, life is a combination of body, mind, senses and soul. *Ayurveda* uses herbs, foods, aromas, gems, colours, yoga, mantras, lifestyle changes and surgery to cure illness. Health is maintained by balancing **three humours**, each linked to a particular state of being: air (virtue), bile (passion) and phlegm (dullness); and illness results when this balance is disturbed. Bodily functions are maintained by **five winds**: *udan*, emanating from the throat and creating speech; *prana*, in the heart, breathing and swallowing of food; *samana*, fanning the fire in the stomach to process food, dividing it into digestible and indigestible parts; *apana*, in the abdomen, for excretion and procreation; and *vyana*, diffused wind which circulates the blood and moves the body. Representing the Atreya school of physicians, Charak in his *Charak Samhita* discusses anatomy and physiology as well as symptoms and causes of illness, pathogenesis and diagnosis. He also covers diet, herbal cures, doctor-patient relations and the doctor's professional conduct.

A later work by **Sushrut**, dealing with surgery, and reflecting contacts with Greek physicians, completed Indian medical science. In its early development anatomical knowledge owed much to animal and sometimes human sacrifices by Indo-Aryans. Later, cremation and a taboo against handling corpses retarded research. On the other hand, interest in physiology, originating from a study of meditation and yoga, continued unabated. During the initial phase of educational reforms by the (English) East India Company, an ayurvedic college was established in Calcutta in 1824. After World War II, the World Health Organization recognized *Ayurveda* as a science of healing.

c.170 Kanishka is succeeded by his son **Huvishka** (aka Hush-ka), already experienced at administering the Indian provinces of the Kushana empire. His artistically designed coinage, minted with the profile of a burly, middle-aged or elderly man with a large nose, is more varied than his father's.

Like his father, Huvishka patronizes the **Gandhara School of art** – named after the Gandhara region in the lower Kabul and upper Indus valleys – which combines Indian motifs with Graeco-Roman forms in sculpture, painting and architecture.

The emergence of this school, prompted by greater trading with the Mediterranean world, the eastwards penetration of Rome's legions, and the availability of craftsmen from Syria and Alexandria, coincides with the growth of Mahayana Buddhism, which requires images of the Buddha and *bodhisattvas* in large numbers. The Gandhara artists succeed in producing images of the Buddha that capture the Indianness of his facial features, gestures and body postures while giving his expression Grecian serenity and clothing him in Roman robes.

They also produce votive plaques depicting scenes from the life of Gautama Buddha and his previous reincarnations. With Mahayana Buddhism spreading to Central Asia and China, the Gandhara School provides the foundation of subsequent Buddhist art in the Far East.

c.175 Economic recession in the Roman empire leads to a curtailment of its trade with India.

c.188 Vasudeva I, bearing a distinctly Indian name, succeeds Huvishka. During his reign, the Kushana empire begins to disintegrate.

c.220 Vasudeva II succeeeds his father Vasudeva I and presides over a disintegrating empire which largely falls into the the hands of the Sassanians of Persia.

226 Artaxerxes I (aka Ardeshir I) founds the the Sassanid dynasty of Persia.

c.240 Shapur I succeeds Artaxerxes to the Persian throne. He defeats Vasudeva II and brings the northwestern subcontinent under his control.

5
The Guptas, the Huns and Harsha Vardhana

c.250–680

From the end of the 3rd century, under **Gupta** rule, **Magdha** again became the dominant kingdom in the north. Like the earlier Mauryas, the Gupta dynasty vastly expanded its realm, consolidating the enlarged dominion as an empire that lasted until 480. Five generations later, **Harsha Vardhana**, king of Pushyabuti, carved out an empire almost as large as the Guptas'. But his death without an heir resulted in northern India relapsing into a medley of warring kingdoms. In central and southern India too, conflict between competing states became the norm, with the **Chelukya** and **Pallava** dynasties in Tamil Nad engaged in an extraordinarily long-lasting feud.

During the Gupta era India was again threatened by invaders marching through the mountain passes in the northwest – this time the **Huns**, a confederation of warrior tribes who surged rapidly from their base in the Central Asian steppes, wreaking havoc on China to the east and the Roman empire to the west. Black Huns, called **Hunas** by Indians, staged repeated assaults on the Panjab and the Indus Valley further south. Although they failed to establish a lasting foothold on the subcontinent, their brief occupation of the northwest had profound consequences. Notorious for their ferocity, they triggered a steady flood of refugees.

Those fleeing eastward and southward into the peninsula took with them their Prakrit dialects – simplified derivatives of Sanskrit – so that a **Sanskrit vernacular**, called Apabhramsha (literally 'falling away'), took root in the affected territories, ultimately producing modern Marathi and Gujarati.

The Hunas also brought with them several Central Asian tribes, some of whom stayed even after the Hunas had been expelled. Among these were the **Gurjara**, who would acquire pre-eminence as the **Gurjara-Pratihara** dynasty in the 9th century; while those allies of the Hunas who remained in what is modern Rajasthan spawned the **Rajput** ruling families of later times.

Repeated attacks by the Hunas accelerated the break-up of the Gupta empire, damaging its political-administrative system. Yet enough survived to suggest that at a time when the Roman empire was collapsing, and the Chinese empire was fragmented, Gupta India, with its advanced mathematics and astronomy, its art and architecture, and its paintings and sculpture, was one of the most civilized in the world. In the Indian annals, the Gupta period is known as the golden era.

Most of the court chronicles have been lost due partly to pillage or vermin, and partly to a lack of care and veneration reserved almost exclusively for scriptural writings. For historians, an important witness is **Fa Xian** (Fa-hsien), a Chinese monk who kept a detailed record of his travels to and from India as well as in the subcontinent in search of Buddhist manuscripts. That Fa Xian and other Chinese, including **Xuan Zhang** (Hsuan-tsang), made the arduous journeys to and from India during the rule of Harsha Vardhana was itself significant. For once, Chinese rulers were willing to open their empire's gates. The Gupta period thus coincided with the growth of Buddhism in China as a major faith to rival Daoism and Confucianism.

By contrast, Buddhism fared poorly in its homeland. This was due partly to the failure of Buddhists to gain the consistent patronage of Indian rulers, and partly to the transmutation of Brahminism into **Hinduism** during the Gupta era which was shaped by two disparate influences – Buddhism and the *bhakti* (literally 'devotion') movement originating in Tamil Nad, the home of pre-Aryan beliefs and customs.

Facing the Buddhist challenge, the brahminical establishment abandoned animal sacrifice, which common folk found repugnant, took to vegetarianism and, imitating the Buddhist practice of worshipping the images of the Buddha and *bodhisattvas*, transformed the hitherto distant, transcendental gods into benevolent deities. Brahmins also incorporated the concept of *bhakti*, which emphasized personal devotion at the expense of priestly mediation, thus enabling the adherents of their faith to get closer to the gods. That is how they reclaimed the following they had lost earlier to Buddhists whose creed had now declined.

Under its politically fractured surface, the subcontinent groped towards a shared identity of emerging Hinduism, which remained pantheistic at its root. But any such homogeneity was not destined to last long. It would be assailed by the monotheistic creed of **Islam**, first by the Muslim Arabs from Arabia arriving by ship, and later by the invading Muslim tribes through the mountain passes of the northwest.

c.270 Sri Gupta, probably already the ruler of **Magdha**, builds a place of worship for visiting Chinese and other Buddhist pilgrims at Nalanda. The **Guptas** are most likely wealthy landlords in Magdha who gradually gain political control.

c.290 Ghatotkacha Gupta succeeds Sri Gupta.

311 As the **Huns** – a martial Turkic-Mongoloid nomadic confederacy – gain size and strength in the Central Asian steppes, the Xiongnu (sometimes called the Eastern Huns) breach the Great Wall of China and sack the imperial city of Luoyang. The Western Huns (also known as White Huns) migrate toward the Caspian and Black seas area and further west, ultimately causing the downfall of the Roman empire.

Their close affiliates, called the **Black Huns**, will turn southward toward the Indus Valley where they will be called **Hunas**.

320 On 26 February **Chandra Gupta I** ascends the Magdha throne in Pataliputra, acquires the title 'Great Raja of Raja' (*maharajadhiraja*), and inaugurates the Gupta era. Through his marriage to Princess **Kumara Devi** of the Lichchavi tribe of Vasaili, a powerful independent republic, he gains control of adjoining Kosala, Saketa (capital, Ayodhya) and Prayag. He unprecedently strikes gold coins in the names of himself, Queen Kumara and the Lichchavi nation, with the legend in Sanskrit.

335 Succeeding his father Chandra Gupta I, **Samudra Gupta** describes himself as 'the son of the Daughter of the Lichchavi', implying that his royal authority is derived from his mother. He is also called *kaviraja*, 'king of poetry'. His skill in song and music is captured in gold coins and medals which show him seated on a couch playing the Indian lute (*veena*).

c.336–345 Under Samudra, **Pataliputra** becomes the centre of an empire extending in the north to the foothills of the Himalayas (but excluding Kashmir); in the east to the Brahmaputra River; in the south to the Narmada; and in the west to the Jamuna and Chambal. Tribal republics in Malwa (in central India) and the Panjab also accept Samudra Gupta's suzerainty.

350 The *Vayu Purana*, one of the earliest *Puranas* ('Old Documents'), is composed in its final literary form. It sets out

Ajanta Cave Temples

A complex of thirty **Buddhist cave temples**, hollowed out of the rocky cliff at **Ajanta**, overlooking the Waghora River, is the single most impressive ensemble of figurative arts in India. It was constructed by resident monks and artisans between the 2nd century and *circa* 755. The temples consists of **sanctuaries** (rectangular halls with columned aisles and an apse) and **monasteries** (central prayer halls with residential cells on three sides). About half of them are decorated with frescoes and sculptured friezes.

Of particular note are depictions of the *Jatakas* ('folk tales') – scenes from the Buddha's life and his previous existences. Some walls show different events occurring in the same place over long stretches of time. These include not only the Buddha's reincarnations, but also the worldy life of courts, with stress on harmony and serenity. Processions of men and women on horseback or foot combine with elephants as they march through city gates. Richly clad princes resting languorously in pavilions held up by red or blue lacquered columns observe nubile female dancers whilst listening to music.

In Cave 1, a painted ceiling depicts themes taken from the plant and animal kingdoms. To create such frescoes, a thick coat of plaster – made of sand, lime, clay or powdered brick mixed with rice husk and gum – was applied to the levelled rock-face. Once hardened, the plaster was washed with more lime, then polished with an elephant tusk. Black and white sketches followed. Colours – derived from plants and minerals, some still retaining their original brilliance – were applied by brush, and the final work burnished.

numerous, often muddled, real and imagined royal genealogies – all derived from Manu (see p.55), the mythical progenitor of humans – through the heroes of the *Mahabharata* and the *Ramayana*, and then to the dynasties of the historical period.

c.351 Samudra Gupta defeats Vishnugopa, the Pallava king of Kanchipuram in the south, and begins receiving annual

The entrance to Cave 19 contains several exquisitely carved standing and seated Buddhas

tribute from Nepal, Assam, East Bengal and the Braham-putra delta. But he fails to subdue the **Shakas**, with their capital in the central Indian city of Ujjain.

357 A Buddhist mission is dispatched to China, the first in a series of ten.

c.360 The northwestern **Deccan** is ruled by a member of the **Vakataka** dynasty, successors to the Shatavahanas. During the Vatakata period, extending into the early 5th century, many Buddhist cave temples are added to the **Ajanta** complex in modern Maharashtra.

The Allahabad and Mahrauli Pillars

Of ancient India's inscribed pillars, those found at Allahabad and Mahrauli, a Delhi suburb, are the most important. The **Allahabad pillar**, discovered in 1937 by the British antiquarian **James Princep**, is adorned with the edicts of the **Emperor Ashoka** (see p.50), an encomium to **Samudra Gupta** in classical Sanskrit incised in the Gupta Brahmi script, and an inscription in Persian by the Mughal emperor **Jahangir** (see p.178). It was moved from Kaushambi to the fort at Allahabad by the Mughal emperor Akbar (r. 1556–1605) to raise the citadel's status. With Jahangir's adornment, it became the only pillar in South Asia to carry inscriptions from the three pre-eminent dynasties of the north: the Mauryas, Guptas and Mughals.

Samudra Gupta's inscription, dating from the early 370s, lists those territories annexed or subdued by 'the prowess of his arm in battle': four northern kingdoms around Delhi and western Uttar Pradesh; nine kingdoms of the Gangetic plain's central region, and nine republics in Rajasthan. The tribal chiefs of central India and the Deccan were forced to pay tribute, as were the Kushanas, ruling beyond the Indus, Meghavarman of Sri Lanka, and the kings of Assam and Bengal.

In contrast to the Allahabad pillar, the structure at **Mahrauli** is monolingual. It declares that **Chandra Gupta II** defeated 'a confederacy of hostile chiefs in Vanga [eastern Bengal]', dispatched his army up to 'the seven mouths of the Indus', and conquered Valhika, bordering present-day Kashmir. Probably erected in Mathura before being moved to Mahrauli in the 11th century, it is a metallurgical wonder. Measuring 7.5 metres in length, weighing six tonnes, and made of wrought iron or steel, it has weathered sixteen centuries of monsoon rains without rusting.

c.370 Samudra Gupta caps his conquests with the horse sacrifice ritual, a Vedic practice long in abeyance. He presents 100,000 cows to the brahmins in the congregation and strikes commemorative gold medals. Judging by his coinage, Samudra is a devotee of Lord Vishnu (see p.19). He has his military victories inscribed in prose and verse on a **pillar** at Kaushambi on the Ganges, later transferred to Allahabad.

c.375 Samudra Gupta is succeeded by his son Rama Gupta, who reigns briefly. Rama's younger brother **Chandra Gupta II** ascends the throne with the title *Vikramaditya* (Sun of Valour), and rules for four decades. A devotee of Lord Vishnu, he is tolerant of his ministers who worship Lord Shiva (see p.20) or follow Buddhism. An energetic sovereign, he portrays himself in his coinage fighting a ferocious lion. He is a patron of the arts; his courtiers include **Kalidasa** (see p.88), an outstanding poet and dramatist.

c.383 The Indian Buddhist monk **Kumarajiva**, son of a high-ranking official, arrives in China, where he will set new standards in the translation of Buddhist scriptures into Chinese.

390 King Rudrasena II of Vatakata, married to Chandra Gupta II's daughter **Prabhavati**, dies young, and Prabhavati becomes regent for the next twenty years. As a result, northern Deccan virtually becomes part of the Gupta empire, and Vakataka's capital, **Ujjain**, one of the seven holy cities of the Brahmanism, becomes the centre where most inland trade routes converge.

c.395 By defeating the Shakas in western India, Chandra Gupta II gains full control of the north, an accomplishment he commemorates by issuing special silver coins. His victory gives him access to Baroch, Cambay and other seaports, long engaged in trade with the Arabian peninsula and countries beyond. Their custom duties help fill the royal coffers.

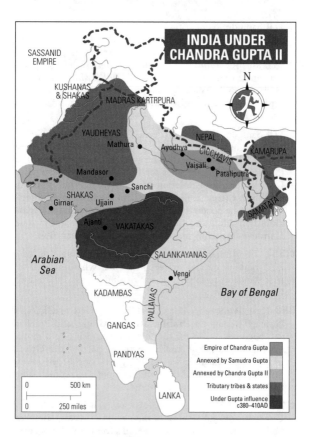

INDIA UNDER CHANDRA GUPTA II

SASSANID EMPIRE

KUSHANAS & SHAKAS

MADRAS KARTRPURA

YAUDHEYAS

Mathura

NEPAL

Ayodhya

CICCHAVIS

KAMARUPA

Vaisali

Mandasor

Pataliputra

SHAKAS

Sanchi

SAMATATA

Girnar

Ujjain

Ajanti

VAKATAKAS

Arabian Sea

SALANKAYANAS

Vengi

Bay of Bengal

KADAMBAS

PALLAVAS

GANGAS

PANDYAS

	Empire of Chandra Gupta
	Annexed by Samudra Gupta
	Annexed by Chandra Gupta II
	Tributary tribes & states
	Under Gupta influence c380–410AD

0 ____ 500 km
0 ____ 250 miles

LANKA

c.400 Having been transmitted orally down many centuries, the *Mahabharata* is transcribed in Sanskrit.

401 Fa Xian (Fa-hsien), a Chinese monk, arrives in India in search of Buddhist texts, a quest that lasts a decade. His journal, *Fuguoji* 'Record of the Buddhist Kingdoms'), containing valuable historical material on the subcontinent, describes the people of **Magdha** as rich and prosperous, who support numerous charitable institutions, including free hospitals. He notices rest-houses for travellers on highways. He refers to the monasteries in the capital, Pataliputra, for the Hinyana and Mahayana Buddhist sects, each housing up to 700 monks. Between the Indus and Mathura, he passes many more Buddhist monasteries housing thousands of monks.

Elsewhere, however, Brahminism is widespread. Fa Xian observes that, unlike Maurya times, people are at liberty to travel where they please without passports or registration. Offenders are more often fined than jailed, and capital punishment is unknown. State revenue is derived chiefly from renting crown lands. He notices the absence of butchers' shops and distilleries, again in contrast to the Maurya era. Outcastes are obliged to live outside villages and towns. When entering a settlement or market, they are required to strike the ground with a wooden stick as a warning of their approach, so that those within the caste system are not polluted by touching them.

c.415 Kumara Gupta I succeeds his father Chandra Gupta II in Pataliputra, and also reigns for four decades. He undertakes the Vedic horse sacrifice ritual, a privilege exercised only by an outstanding conqueror.

During his rule, **Shudraka** writes *Mrichchha Katika* ('The Little Clay Cart'), a play more frequently performed in the West than Kalidasa's *Shakuntala*.

c.431 Having converted many Javans to Buddhism, Gunavarman, Crown Prince of Kashmir, dies in Nanjing, China.

Kalidasa c.376–410

Kalidasa is regarded as the pre-eminent Sanskrit poet and dramatist. A native of Mandasor (aka Dasapura), he grew up in close contact with the Gupta court. His finest poems are *Meghaduta* ('Cloud Messenger'), in which a cloud acts as an intermediary between separated lovers, and *Kumarasambhava*, a re-telling of Shiva's courtship. Kalidasa's most significant work, however, is his drama *Shakuntala*, still widely performed. It tells the story of Shakuntala, the orphaned daughter of a sage (Vishvamitra) and a nymph (Menaka), who is raised by Kanwa, a forest hermit. While Kanwa is away, King Dushyanta encounters Shakuntala while out hunting and falls in love with her. He presents her with a ring and takes her for his bride, but is then recalled to the capital. When the sage Durvass visits the Kanwa hermitage, the distracted Shakuntala is inhospitable. He puts her under a curse, declaring that her husband will forget all about her until he sees the wedding ring again.

When Kanwa returns, he sends the pregnant Shakuntala to Dushyanta's court, but because she has dropped her ring in a river the king fails to recognize her. She calls on the earth to open up and swallow her, but a divine shape lifts her to heaven instead where she is consoled by her mother Menaka. Later a fisherman who has found the ring in the maw of a fish is brought before Dushyanta's throne, and is accused of theft. When Dushyanta sees the ring, he remembers his wife but it is too late. Several years later, the king sees a small boy wrestling with a lion cub. The child is revealed to be Shakuntala's son. The lovers are symbolically re-united.

As in Shakespeare's late romances, court and rustic scenes alternate, and Kalidasa skilfully differentiates even his most minor characters. Though *Shakuntala* is unrealistic, its dialogue is vibrant, articulating conflicts of feeling forcefully.

432 The **White Huns**, under the leadership of **Attila**, force the Roman emperor Theodosius, among other European rulers, to pay annual tribute.

448 The **Black Huns**, known in India as the **Hunas**, occupy Bactria. With a dominion consisting of forty provinces, stretching from Khotan to Parthia, they establish their capital at **Bamiyan** in modern Afghanistan

451 Attila is defeated in Gaul.

453 Attila dies and the White Huns withdraw from central Europe.

455 **Skanda Gupta** accedes to the Magdhan throne. Emulating his grandfather Chandra Gupta II, he assumes the title 'Vikramaditya'. He repulses the Bamiyan-based Hunas when they cross the Hindu Kush, but cannot prevent their subsequent raids on the borders or interior of his empire. With some of his feudatories breaking away, Skanda orders the minting of debased coinage to contain an economic crisis wrought by the loss of royal revenues.

460 Skanda Gupta rallies his forces and temporarily saves the empire from further disintegration.

467 On Skanda Gupta's death, local governors declare themselves **feudatory kings** with hereditary rights.

c.480–490 As the Gupta empire fragments, Magdha becomes just one northern kingdom among many.

484 The Hunas kill King Firoz of Parthia (later, Persia), easing their entry into South Asia.

490 The **Maitraka dynasty** of Persian origin, founds a kingdom in **Gujarat** with its capital at Vallabhi, a place of learning.

499 The latest recorded date for **Bhanu Gupta**, the last Gupta ruler. With the collapse of the Gupta empire, the main dynasties to emerge in the north are the Maukharis of Kanuj (western Uttar Pradesh); the Pushyabhutis of Thanesar (north of Delhi); the Guptas of Magdha, unrelated to the earlier Gupta dynasty; and the Maitrakas of Gujurat.

Aryabhata (b. 476), an astronomy and mathematics teacher at the Pataliputra University, writes the *Aryabhatiya*. By identifying fundamental problems in astronomy, it helps establish **astronomy** as a discipline in its own right.

500 Toramana, chief of the **Hunas**, conquers western India as far as Airikina, north of Sanchi.

520 Mihiragula (literally Sunflower) succeeds his father Toramana. Ruling from Sakala (modern Sialkot, Pakistan), he expands the Huna dominions in the subcontinent, at the expense of the Guptas. A Chinese pilgrim, travelling in India, describes him as uncouth in manner and an iconoclast who persecutes Buddhists.

528 Mihiragula is expelled from the Gangetic plain by the king of Magdha, **Narasimha Gupta** – unrelated to the now extinct Gupta dynasty.

530 King **Yashodharman** of the central Indian region of Malwa expels Mihiragula from western India.

542 Mihiragula dies in Kashmir.

c.543 Pulakesin I, a Jain, founds the **Chalukya dynasty** in western Deccan, with its capital at Vatapi. Natives of modern Karnataka, the Jain Chalukyas celebrate their military triumphs by building **temples**, both rock-cut and free standing. During their reign, temple building becomes a paradigm of royal authority.

c.553 The mathematician and polymath **Varahamihira** (505–87) writes the *Panchsiddhantika* ('Five Systems') – an account of five current mathematical schools, including *Romaka Siddhanata*, originating in Rome, and *Paulisha Siddhanta*, named after the astronomer Paul of Alexandria. Taking his cue from **Greek science**, Varahamihira further divides **astronomy** into three branches: mathematical astronomy, horoscopy and astrology.

The Bhakti Movement

Arguably the single most important factor that transformed **Vedism/Brahminism** – the congregational religion of the Indo-Aryans – into **Hinduism**, a faith to be practised by individuals at home, was the idea of *bhakti*, personal devotion. It grew out of the concept of a compassionate deity, developed in the mid-6th century in **Tamil Nad**, which owed its origin to the Buddhist idea of the compassionate *bodhisattva*. It was allied to another Buddhist concept – of sin and human inadequacy. *Guide to Lord Murugan*, a pre-7th-century Tamil poem, expounded the concept in verse by exhorting the devotee to visit Lord Murugan's shrines. In this poem, the god, initially portrayed as wild and primitive, turns out to be the opposite when the worshipper finally encounters him.

The devotional cult spread quickly among Tamils who saw in it a welcome opportunity to resist Aryanization. The hymns and sermons in Tamil delivered by Shivaite Nayanars and Vishnavite Alvars (most of them farmers and artisans, not priests) played a crucial role in this process. They overlooked or denied Vedic gods, and instead of stressing the object of devotion, emphasized the relationship between humans and the supreme god – Vishnu or Shiva. Unlike brahmins, these Tamil saints did not exclude anyone from their cult on caste grounds.

The cult seriously rivalled Buddhism as a refuge from caste prejudice and the unquestioned authority of brahmins, and so took root in diverse regions of the subcontinent. As had happened before in the religious history of India, a synthesis occurred between the old and the new, the Brahminical doctrine and the devotional, at the level of the local temple. The result was the emergence of **Hinduism** in a form that has endured.

c.555 With northern and western India fragmented into many kingdoms, the southern Kanchipuram-based **Pallava** ruler **Simhavishnu Avnisimha** expands his dominions to the banks of the Kaveri at the expense of the **Pandya** and **Malava** dynasties.

According to some historians, Pallavas are Pahlavas (Parthians) who, during the Shaka-Shatavahanas wars of the 2nd century, migrated to the east coast of the southern peninsula from western India. Others describe them as an indigenous clan from Vengi, modern Andhra Pradesh. Through a concocted genealogy, the Pallavas claim to be direct descendants of Brahma.

c.556 The concept of *bhakti* **(devotion)** takes root in Tamil Nad and becomes a cult. Over the coming decades *bhakti* cults will spring up in different parts of the subcontinent. It impacts on Brahminism and transmutes it into Hinduism. Although *Bhagvad Gita* refers to religious devotion as one way of achieving release from the eternal reincarnation cycle, the concept is restrained in its expression as the divine, then perceived as a distant and mighty sovereign, inspired as much awe as love.

c.560 Further Hun incursions are curtailed when the Huna kingdom on the Oxus is overrun by **Turks**.

> ❝ When you see his face praise him with joy,
> worship him with joined palms, bow before him,
> so that his feet touch your head,
> Holy and mighty will be his form
> rising to heaven, but his sterner face
> will be hidden, and he will show you
> the form of a young man, fragrant and beautiful
> and his words will be loving and gracious –
> "Don't be afraid – I knew you were coming!". ❞
>
> Pattuppattu, *Tirumuruganarrupadi*, 285–90, in *The Wonder that was India*,
> 1971, p.337.

Mahendra Varman c.562–630

Mahendra Varman is principally notable for three things – the founding of the first important royal dynasty in Tamil Nad, the **Pallavas**; his accomplished poetry and drama in Tamil; and his temple-building. Raised as a Jain, he became a devotee of Lord Shiva (see p.19). Of his literary compositions, the best remembered is *Mattavilasaprahasana* ('Delight of Drunkards'), a comedy. But his most enduring, visually dramatic legacy is the **Hindu rock temple** complex at **Mahabalipuram**, begun during his reign. Inspired by Buddhist cave shrines, these show traces of the barrel-vaults and archways associated with Buddhist religious sites. Seventeen temples were sculpted from granite outcrops, with the remarkable **Seven Pagodas** reflecting an earlier Dravidian style. More outstanding still is the relief of the descent of the Ganges, covering a 26 by 10 metre rock-face. A natural cleft is used to portray the holy river, watched on both banks by deities, demigods, sages and elephants, as it descends, according to tradition, from Lord Shiva's head.

WERNER FORMAN ARCHIVE

Relief from the temple complex at Mahabalipuram, depicting 'The penance of Arjuna' from the *Mahabarata*

The ***Panchtantra***, a collection of Indian folk tales and fables with human, animal and bird characters, is translated from Sanskrit into Pahlavi, the language of Iran/Persia, and then into Arabic, and from it into Latin, Spanish, Italian and other European languages – and becomes the foundation for *One Thousand and One Nights*.

c.566 Pulakesin I of the Chelukya dynasty in the Deccan is succeeded by Kirti Varman.

578 Brahma Gupta, a leading astronomer and mathematician, is born. One of the first to distinguish between positive and negative values, he will calculate the circumference of the earth at 36,000km, the closest approximation yet to the actual 40,075km.

c.590 Mahendra Varman I succeeds Simhavishnu Avnisimha, and establishes the **Pallava dynasty** in **Tamil Nad**. However, the long-running feud between the Pallavas and the Chelukyas continues.

595 An Indian inscription is the earliest known example of the use of modern **numerals**, that is, 0–9.

c.597 Mangalesa occupies the Chalukya throne in Vatapi.

604 Prabhakara Vardhana, the **Pushyabhuti** king, with the honorific of 'Great Raja of Rajas', dies while his eldest son and heir **Rajya** is fighting the Hunas. **Bana**, a Brahmin courtier-chronicler, describes Prabhakara Vardhana as 'a lion to the Huna deer, a burning fever to the king of the Indus land, a troubler of the sleep of Gujarat, a bilious plague to that scent-elephant the Lord of Gandhara, a looter to the lawlessness of the Latas, an axe to the creeper of Malwa's glory.'

606 Rajya Vardhana, a Buddhist, is treacherously assassinated by **Sasanka**, the anti-Buddhist king of Gauda, central Bengal. Sasanka also captures Magdha.

Mathematics and Astronomy

As the *Aryabhatiya,* compiled in 499, attests, India by the 5th century was well advanced in mathematics and astronomy. Its eponymous author, **Aryabhat**, took for granted a numerical system that incorporated the concept '0' (zero) and the decimal system, as had the anonymous '*Bakshali Manuscript'* of the 4th century. However, the name of the Indian mathematician who devised the simplified system of nine and a zero remains unknown.

An Indian inscription dated 595 is the earliest surviving record of a date using a system of nine digits and a zero, with place notations for the tens and hundreds. Indians were among the first peoples to think of numbers in abstraction rather than a numerical quantity of objects such as human fingers and toes, totalling twenty, or a score. Since Arabs were the first foreigners to adopt India's new numerical system, Westerners who borrowed it from the latter called them Arabic numerals – vastly superior to the cumbersome Roman variety (I, II, III, IV, V etc.).

Among other things Aryabhat calculated pi to 3.1416 – more accurately than the Greeks – and the length of the solar year to 365.358605 days. The Indian calendar had twelve lunar months with the proviso of adding an extra month every third year. Although the solar calendar in use in the West became known from the Gupta period onwards, it did not replace the local lunar-solar calendar. Indian astronomers gained from their Western counterparts the signs of the zodiac, the seven-day week, the hour and several other ideas. On the other hand, Aryabhat believed the earth to be a spheroid rotating on its axis a millennium before Galileo, and explained that lunar eclipses were caused by the shadow of the earth falling across the moon.

In **Kanuj**, urged on by the Pushyabhuti nobility, Rajya's younger brother **Harsha Vardhana**, aged 16, assumes the throne. During his 41-year reign Harsha Vardhana will emerge as an energetic and effective ruler. Early on in his reign, his marriage to a princess of the Maukharis, the sworn enemies of the Guptas, leads to the merger of the Pushyabhuti and Maukhari kingdoms.

607 Deploying 5000 elephants, 20,000 cavalry and 50,000 infantry, Harsha Vardhana launches military campaigns to the east, where he succeeds in expelling King Sasanka from Magdha, and also to the west. Intent on founding an empire, he does not remove the defeated king from his throne, but lets him retain it as a feudatory.

c.608 Mangalesa of the Chalukya dynasty in Vatapi is succeeded by **Pulakesin II**.

c.610 A separate Eastern Chalukya dynasty of Vengi is founded.

612 His infantry having grown to 100,000, Harsha Vardhana concludes his first series of campaigns.

613 Harsha convenes a three-day assembly in **Prayag** (modern Allahabad), which is attended by twenty tributary rajas. He distributes his accumulated wealth to thousands of holy men of Buddhism, Brahminism and Jainism.

c.620 Following an inconclusive battle with Pulakesin II of the Chalukya kingdom, Harsha Vardhana accepts the Narmada River as his southern border.

622 The **population** of the Indian subcontinent is estimated at 100 million.

In Arabia, the migration of **Prophet Muhammad** from Mecca to Medina marks the beginning of the era of **Islam**.

c.630 In Tamil Nad, Mahendra Varman I of the Pallava dynasty is succeeded by Narsimha Varman.

Xuan Zhang (Hsuan-tsang), a visiting Chinese Buddhist monk, is made a courtier by Harsha Vardhana and becomes a royal chronicler.

Harsha Vardhana 590–647

Besides being a powerful and long-lasting ruler, **Harsha Vardhana** is the subject of the first biography in Sanskrit, *Harsha Charita*, written by the brahmin chronicler **Bana**. Starting out as a devotee of Shiva while honouring the Buddha and the Sun, Harsha turned progressively toward Buddhism. At his first imperial assembly in 613 at Prayag, images of the Buddha received great honours on the first day, followed by the effigy of the Sun, and then Shiva with reduced ceremonial. This ritual was repeated every five years, either at Prayag or Kanuj. Between these assemblies – accompanied by a large body of officials, courtiers, brahmins, Buddhist monks and servants – he supervised his vast empire by touring his and his vassals' provinces.

A lover of philosophy and literature, he composed three competent plays, two of them harem comedies and the third, *Naganada* ('Bliss of Serpents'), based on an edifying Buddhist legend. Toward the end of his life, influenced increasingly by Mahayana Buddhism, he banned the slaughter of any living being and forbade the consumption of meat. By then, however, Buddhism was in decline in India, with many monasteries and pilgrimage sites falling into disuse.

640 Harsha forces the Maitrakas of Gujarat to recognize his suzerainty. He also receives homage from the king of Assam.

In **Sind**, the Rai dynasty, belonging to the *shudra* caste, is toppled by **Chach**, a brahmin. Chach enlarges the Rai domain northward to the Panjab, westward to Baluchistan's coastal region of Makran, and southward to the Indus delta.

641 Muslim Arabs conquer Zoroastrian Persia ruled by the Sassanids.

642 Narsimha Varman avenges his father's defeat by Pulakesin II, and captures Vatapi. He establishes dockyards at Mahabalipuram and Nagpattinam, as well as a naval force, which subdues **Sri Lanka**, where he installs his nominee on the throne.

643 Harsha Vardhana conducts his last campaign against Ganjam on the Bay of Bengal and receives an emissary from the court of the Tang Chinese emperor **Taizong**.

Having travelled much of the subcontinent, Xuan Zhang returns to China, laden with Buddhist scriptures, relics and images. In his journals he describes the dense jungles along the Ganges, as well as how Harsha dispenses justice in a makeshift pavilion by the roadside. There is no capital punishment, but serious offenders are left in dungeons to rot.

Xuan also describes **Nalanda**, a centre of Buddhist learning in Magdha established during the Gupta period, now run by the elderly abbot **Shilabhadra**. Besides training Buddhist novices, the monastery teaches the *Vedas*, Brahmanical philosophy, logic, grammar and medicine, to a 1000-strong student body. It is maintained by the feudatory revenues of 100 surrounding villages, donations by patrons and grants from Harsha.

c.644 Trading much-coveted Arab horses for spices, newly converted **Muslim Arab merchants** arrive at India's western ports, giving the subcontinent its first contact with Islam.

647 Harsha Vardhana dies without an heir. His throne is seized by an ambitious minister, **Arunashiva**. When a second emissary from the Chinese emperor Taizong arrives with a thirty-man escort, Arunashiva orders their arrest. The Chinese envoy escapes to Nepal, then a tributary of Tibet, whose king is married to a Chinese princess. A Nepalese and Tibetan force allies with Harsha Vardhana loyalists, and together they defeat Arunashiva and dispatch him to China, where he will die.

Hinduism

Between the Aryan tribes' earliest incursions into the Indian subcontinent and the late Gupta period, the religion of Indo-Aryans changed due to geography, contacts with the natives, and the rise of Buddhism and Jainism. Its intial title of Vedism or Brahminism gave way to **Hinduism**, derived from Hindu, a geographical term tied to the Sindhu (Indus) River. Image worship, undertaken individually or collectively, became central to Hinduism, superceding the brahmin-dominated congregational animal sacrifice. Hindus offered food and flowers to their deities, not flesh.

Emulating the Buddhist practice of presenting the Buddha and *bodhisattvas* as icons and sculptures, Hindus portrayed their hitherto conceptual gods in human form. However, they considered the image as symbolic; hence the convention of multi-headed or multi-armed deities, each arm bearing a symbol of an attribute associated with that god. Initially, these deities were different manifestations of **Vishnu**, dominant in the north, since **Shiva**, popular in the south and worshipped as a phallus, did not offer much iconic or sculptural opportunity. The concept also of representing the divine's productive activity in sexual union – mentioned in the *Rig Veda* – was developed, and led to gods being given wives: Vishnu with Lakshmi, and Shiva with Durga, Kali, Parvati or Meenakshi.

The roots of this cult lay in the pre-Aryan practice of worshipping Mother Goddess. Brahmins regarded it expedient to incorporate it into their religious ritual under the concept of *shakti* (power). *Shakti* followers believed the wives to be the active aspect of their husbands who, being gods, were inaccessible, and could only be approached through their female consorts. Devotional worship (*bhakti*) by the believer, which developed in the second half of the 7th century, almost dispensed with the brahmin as the performer of religious rituals, with his role now limited to conducting birth, death and marriage ceremonies. Finally came the human-made social law, *dharma*, as the sacred canon interpreted and supervised by brahmins, with the caste system at its core – the fourth pillar of Hinduism.

652 Islam spreads to Bukhara (part of modern Uzbekistan) in Central Asia.

661 An Islamic empire is established under **Caliph Muawiya** of the Umayyad clan with its capital at Damascus, Syria. The Caliph is regarded as the fountain-head of all political authority, to whom all Muslim kings and chiefs are subordinate.

663 Having conquered Persia, Arab Muslims cross the **Bolan Pass** near Quetta (modern Pakistan) and briefly penetrate the subcontinent.

668 In Tamil Nad, Narsimha Varman is succeeded by his son Mahendra Varman II.

670 Mahendra Varman II is succeeded by Parmeshwar Varman. He recaptures Vatapi, earlier lost to the Chalukyas, thus reviving Pallava–Chalukya rivalry.

Tamil Nad, the seed bed of the *bhakti* (devotion) cult, is now its bastion. Impacting on Vedism/Brahmanism throughout the subcontinent, the *bhakti* movement has transmuted it into Hinduism.

6
Fragmented governance of the subcontinent and Muslim incursions

8th–12th centuries

I n the wake of **Harsha Vardhana**, endemic warfare erupted between rival dynasties in the north of India. During the 8th and 9th centuries, the powerful **Gurjara-Pratiharas** of Kanuj and the **Pala kings** of Magdha divided up the region between themselves. In the south, the division of the peninsula into the plateau kingdoms of the west and the coastal kingdoms of the east whetted the desire of each to control fully the Godavari and Krishna, flowing from west to east. **Vengi** (present-day Andhra Pradesh), lying between those rivers, was a particular bone of contention.

The western peninsula maintained its historic role as a conduit for traffic of ideas between the north and the south, as evidenced by the sprouting of the *bhakti* movement rooted in the Tamil devotional cult. Overall, however, the result of this exchange of concepts was the gradual assimilation of Aryan ideas into Dravidian culture. Under the **Pallava dynasty** (8–11th centuries) in the far south this process accelerated among the upper strata of society, and caused a reaction among the lower strata who, in their attempt to assert their non-Aryan identity, gave a sharper profile to the

Tamil personality. This held because the institutions of the south were more firmly rooted than those of the north. Indeed, the rise of the mighty empire of the **Chola dynasty** (850–1215) in the south would demonstrate that the centre of gravity of power and influence in the subcontinent was no longer fixed.

As early as the 8th century, the vigour and innovation of the northern kingdoms seems to have run out. By contrast, **the south** displayed more energy and originality – in civil administration, in the mushrooming of devotional cults presaging the emergence of Hinduism, in the monumentalizing of temple architecture, and in the expanding trade with the Persian Gulf, East Africa, Southeast Asia and China. This shift in the internal power structure of the subcontinent was highlighted by the relative ease with which, in the early 11th century, the **Afghan** commander **Muhammad Ghori** established an empire in the northern plains – a departure from both the quiet rule of Arab Muslims in Sind and Multan since the 8th century, and the earlier raids for loot by Mahmoud Ghazni.

Initially, Indians viewed the Muslim invaders as just another set of aliens making inroads into the subcontinent who, over time, would be absorbed into the native society. They failed to comprehend that the latest foreigners were a new breed, representing an insurgent, vital religion with a well-defined worldview and a proselytizing thrust whose basic tenets ran counter to Hinduism. The new invaders, confident of the superiority of their faith, showed scant interest in the life and condition of the Hindus they encountered.

The fragmentation of the north and the unending warfare there made local rajas vulnerable. Even when rival rulers managed to form a coalition against their common foe, they failed to establish a unified command. Moreover, their fighting prowess was compromised by caste differences. While

Afghans – fired by religious zeal and tempted by the prospect of booty and women – fought vigorously, their Indian enemies were often wearied by earlier local campaigns. Moreover, while Afghan officers and ranks regarded war as a matter of life and death, most Indian rajas – used to fighting according to a time-honoured code of conduct – treated warfare as virtual sport with its own chivalric rules. As a result, Indian generalship came out second best.

Such Indian disadvantages were compounded by the deployment of lumbering elephants during battle and the tactic of using sheer numbers to overpower the enemy by fighting in solid phalanxes. By contrast, the lightly armed Afghans – mounted on their finest Central Asian horses and led by commanders given to changing tactics quickly – outwitted the elephants and the slow-moving infantry.

c.708 King Dahir of Sind faces a major **Arab invasion** ordered by **Al Hijjaj ibn Yusuf**, the Baghdad-based viceroy of the eastern sector of the **Islamic empire** under the Umayyads. Al Hijjaj's pretext is the abduction by pirates (ostensibly operating from Debal, present-day Karachi) of maidens bound for Basra, as a gift from the king of Sri Lanka. After losing two sea battles, Al Hijjaj dispatches an amphibious force of 6000 Syrian troops under the command of his cousin **Muhammad bin Qassim**. He captures Debal, and defeats King Dahir near Brahminabad (modern Hyderabad).

710–713 Muhammad bin Qassim advances north and seizes Rohri and Multan. He leaves Hindu and Buddhist temples intact, allowing donations and alms-giving to continue. As elsewhere in the Islamic empire, he imposes *jizya*, a poll tax on non-Muslims exempted from serving in the army.

c.720 Muslim Arab control of Sind weakens.

724 Junaid al Marri, a representative of the Baghdad-based viceroy of the Islamic empire, regains Sind.

c.725 Nagabhata I of the Gurjara tribe, which has entered the subcontinent in the early 7th century from the north-west, founds the **Gurjara dynasty** with its capital at Bhilmal, near modern Mount Abu in Rajasthan.

731 An upstart warrior, **Yashovarman** establishes an empire in **Kanuj** on the upper Ganges, which briefly includes much of the north.

In Kashmir, **Lalitaditya Muktapida** ascends the throne.

c.736 Delhi (Dhillika) is founded by a raja of the Tomara clan.

c.740 Lalitaditya Muktapida of Kashmir defeats and slays Yashovarman of Kanuj.

c.750 Gopala, probably a ruler from northern Bengal, is selected by nobles to govern Vanga, present-day Bangladesh.

751 Control of the Islamic empire passes from the Umayyads in Damascus to the **Abbasids** in **Baghdad**. The Abbasid Caliph retains Sind as part of his dominion.

c.753 Dantidurga Rashtrakuta, a vassal of the **Chalukya** rulers of western Deccan, defeats Chalukya Vikramaditya II and founds the **Rashtrakuta dynasty**. Having expanded his domain, he assumes the title *Prithvi-Vallabha* (Lover of Earth), the name of one of Lord Vishnu's consorts, and adopts as his ceremonial capital **Ellora** (near modern Aurangabad), the site of earlier Buddhist cave temples.

c.756 Krishna I of the Rashtrakuta dynasty seizes the Chalukya capital at Vatapi/Badami and reigns for seventeen years. By overpowering the Eastern Chalukyas and con-queriing **Vengi** (western Andhra Pradesh), he possesses all of the **Deccan**.

Tantrism and Vajrayana Buddhism

Nowadays, **Tantrism** is associated with Tibetan magical spiritualism, yet it originated in the 6th century in northern and northeastern India, where it impacted on Buddhism and Hinduism. Its esoteric texts, called *Tantras*, outline ways – such as the chanting of mantras, the use of a *yantra* (magic symbol), and other mental disciplines – to compel gods and goddesses to confer superhuman powers upon its practitioners and lead them to the highest bliss.

In the Hindu version, the Tantric ritual, centred on prayer and the worship of a particular deity, is led by a guru. It culminates in the partaking of *madya* (wine), *matsya* (fish), *mamsa* (flesh), *mudra* (grain), and *mithuna* (sexual intercourse). In the final stage of the ceremonial, everyone and everything are equal, which implies repudiation of caste, diet and sexual fidelity. By serving as a catharsis to evil propensities of the initiate, often a normal member of society, the occasional debauchery helps him to lead a virtuous life.

Influenced by local cults of eastern India and Tantrism, the mainstream Mahayana Buddhism was transmuted into the **Vajrayana school**. It accorded the *Taras* – female consorts of *bodhisattvas* – exceptional reverence. Overall, by using Tantric techniques an adept might so hypnotize himself as to imagine that through sexual intercourse with his female partner the two would become, temporarily, the Buddha and his consort. Indeed, Vajrayana Buddhism's most popular mantra, celebrating the divine coitus between Buddha and his perfect *Tara* Prajnaparamita, is *'Om Mani Padme Hum'*, meaning 'Behold the Jewel [ie penis] is in the Lotus [vagina]'.

He celebrates his victories by commissioning a temple dedicated to Lord Shiva at Ellora. By calling it **Kaliashnath** (Master of Mount Kailash, the traditional abode of Lord Shiva), he implies that the godhead has relocated, symbolically, from the Himalayas. The temple itself, once finished, will be admired as the most outstanding single work of art in the subcontinent.

c.769 Lalitaditya Muktapida of Kashmir dies.

c.770 In **eastern Bengal**, Dharamapala, the Buddhist son of Gopala, becomes the founder of the **Pala dynasty** and expands his kingdom westward. The dynasty funds Nalanda and other centres of Buddhist learning, with students from Sind, Kashmir, Nepal, Tibet, China, Burma, Cambodia, Sri Lanka and Indonesia.

Pala architecture influences stupas in Burma and Indonesia, while Pala-style bronze and stone images will become the foundation of later Tibetan and Nepalese iconography.

Pala rule also witnesses the flowering of the **Vajrayana** (thunderbolt) school of **Buddhism**, a variant of Mahayana Buddhism influenced by Indian **Tantrism**, with its own monastery at Vikramshila, Bihar.

c.780 Vatsraja of the Pratihara (ie 'gatekeepers' of the holy city of Ayodhya) section of the Gurjara tribe, based in **Ujjani**, rules over much of **Rajasthan** and the central Indian region of Malwa. From now onwards, his dynasty is known as **Gurjara-Pratihara**.

c.780–93 Dhruva accedes to the Rashtrakuta throne.

c.786 Dhruva Rashtrakuta crosses the Narmada and attacks the north, advancing towards Kanuj but not capturing it. Returning to Ellora, he takes with him the holy waters from the Ganges, Jamuna and Sarswati, depositing them at the Kaliashnath Temple, where a shrine is built to carry the images of these sacred rivers. By this time, the **Hindu temple** has aquired its abiding characteristics.

The Hindu temple

The evolution of the **Hindu temple** owed much to **Buddhism**. Portrayal of the Buddha in stone and other materials encouraged Hindus to represent their deities in a similar fashion. They placed such an idol in terracotta, stone, bronze, silver or gold in a shrine room, called *garbhagriha* (literally womb house), which became the nucleus of the Hindu temple. Imitating Buddhists again, Hindus excavated rocks to lodge their idols in shrine rooms, often next to Buddhist rock-cut monasteries. But as the practice of idol worship caught on, there arose a need for spacious assembly halls and enclosed courtyards to accommodate large congregations. This requirement could only be met by building a **free-standing temple** – with the main sanctuary approached through a passageway entered from an assembly hall opening out to a porch – and the whole building surrounded by an enclosed courtyard.

Built of wood or brick, the first free-standing temples were unimpressive structures, but from the **Gupta period** (250–500) onwards, they were constructed increasingly from stone. As a building material, stone offered unprecedented architectural potential. This fired the imagination of Hindu architects and their royal patrons. A richly decorated, monumental style was born, with the main idol now attended by a host of minor divinities. Manuals on temple construction provided detailed instructions. Later, as the *bhakti* movement (see p.91) spread, brahmins considered it expedient to incorporate the gods of numerous devotional cults into reformed Hinduism. Out of this arose a temple complex dotted with minor shrines in an enclosed compound and furnished with pavilions for scriptural recitation before large gatherings. Rulers vied with one another to build ever grander temples to impress their subjects. Once constructed, they were maintained by royal grants and by donations from rich and poor alike.

c.793 **Govinda III** accedes to the Rashtrakuta throne and launches a series of military campaigns from his capital at Manyakheta/Malkhed, situated between the Godavari and Krishna Rivers. In the north he defeats Nagabhata II of the Gurjara-Pratihara dynasty, but does not occupy his kingdom.

c.804 Supported by nine northern kings, **Dharamapala** of the Pala dynasty deposes the Gurjara-Pratihara king of Kanuj, replacing him with his own nominee as ruler.

c.805 Govinda III defeats the rulers of Chera, Panday and Ganga in the far south and occupies Kanchipuram. Instead

Ellora Rock Temples

The carvings found in the **Ellora rock and cave temples** are among the finest in Indian art. Built between the 5th and early 9th centuries, the complex of 34 caves, 50km from the Ajanta rock temples, is predominantly **Hindu**, though some Buddhist and Jain shrines are incorporated. Indeed, the Ellora construction started as a Bhuddist project, but with the ascendancy of the Rashtrakutas in western Deccan, its denomination changed, with the dynasty's founders, **Dantidurga** and his son **Krishna I**, sponsoring the famous **Kailashnath Temple**.

Rather than hollow out yet another cave, they ordered that the exposed rock-face be sculpted. The result was a stunning statue-like temple – with the uncut rock forming its back – almost as large as the Athenian Parthenon in ground measurement and half as high again. It consisted of the hallowed main shrine room, assembly hall, gateway and the enclosed ground, complemented by cloisters, residential cells and minor shrines – with the walls and pillars embellished with deities and mythological scenes, distinguished by balanced design and graceful strength the like of which has not been repeated since. Sculpted as deep bas-reliefs, the carvings appear free-standing. The Kailashnath Temple is often described as the world's most impressive and elaborate rock-cut monument.

of integrating these kingdoms into an empire, however, he contents himself with their nominal allegiance.

c.810–50 In the east, **Devapala** succeeds Dharamapala and emerges as the most powerful Pala king. His general, Lavasena, conquers Kamarupa (modern **Assam**) and Utkala (modern **Orissa**). Well known for building artificial lakes, which remain a feature of present-day Bangladesh and West Bengal, Devapala sends a diplomatic mission to his fellow Buddhist, the Shalendra king of Sumatra (now part of Indonesia).

CLIVE FRIEND

The Kailasnath temple (Cave 16) at Ellora represents the high point of Indian rock-cut architecture. The temple is directly behind the large column in the centre of the photograph

c.814 The Rashtrakuta dynast Govinda III dies without an heir and is succeeded by **Nagabhata II** of the Gurjara-Pratihara dynasty.

c.816 Nagabhata II captures Kanuj, where he transfers his capital from Bhilmal.

Work ends on the **Ellora rock temples**, occupying a 2km rock-face above a tributary of the Godavari River in western Deccan.

819 In Bukhara, Central Asia, the **Samani dynasty** is founded, whose domain includes northeast Iran. Deploying Turkic slave troops, the Samanis – originally governors of the Abbasid Caliphate in Baghdad – contain nomadic Turkic tribes who are pressing on Iran from across the Oxus River.

Muslim conquests in eastern Iran and Central Asia, part of the Silk Route from the Mediterranean to China, have brought many Turkic tribes into the Islamic fold, and Arab influence in the Muslim world wanes.

c.820 Death of the leading Hindu philosopher and theologian **Shankara**.

c.836 Nagabhata II's grandson Mihira, known as **Mihir Bhoja**, elevates the **Gurjara-Pratihara royal house** to imperial heights. To the north, his realm is delineated by the foothills of the Himalayas; to the northwest by the Satlej; to the west by Sind; to the southwest by the Narmada's lower course; and, to the east, by the Pala kingdom of Magdha, having pushed the Palas back into their heartland in Bengal.

According to an Arab traveller, Mihir Bhoja commands 'a powerful army, including the best cavalry in India and a large force of camels'. The same traveller's favourable comments on Mihir Bhoja's wealth and the absence of robbers in his dominions indicate the efficiency of his administration and tax-collecting apparatus. He is a devotee of Lord

Shankara c.788–820

What St Thomas Aquinas is to Christianity **Shankara** (aka Shankaracharya, Shankra the Teacher), a Shivaite brahmin from Kerala, is to Hinduism. His monist theology, called *Advaita* (allowing no second), seeks to resolve the many inconsistencies and paradoxes in Vedic literature by deliberately adopting a double standard of the truth. On a mundane level, the universe, generated by Brahma, undergoes change; but on the highest level, the cosmos, including the gods, is *maya*, illusion. The ultimate and only reality is **Brahman**, the impersonal Universal Soul of the *Upanishads* with which the individual's soul is identical. Salvation is acquired by realizing this identity through knowledge or meditation.

By deploying logic, and by interpreting some key phrases in a highly figurative way, Shankara forged self-contradictory passages in the *Upanishads* into a coherent thesis that has remained the most widely accepted philosophy of Hinduism. Besides being Hinduism's pre-eminent theologian, he was also its most tireless promoter. He travelled throughout the subcontinent, often holding debates with Buddhist theologians. Determined to rid Hindu worship of meaningless rites, he set up Hindu monasteries at **Badrinath** (in the north), **Puri** (east), **Dwarka** (west) and **Shringeri** (south), where simplified worship was practised. Richly endowed, they established branches elsewhere, while missionary members propagated the teachings of Shankara, who also composed fine devotional poems in Sanskrit.

Shankara encapsulated the propensity of Vedism/Hinduism to transform itself when challenged by a rival faith like Buddhism, and assimilate rather than confront or attack. Such a pragmatic approach, however, was at odds with Shankara's declaration that the world is an illusion. If so, why bother to grasp its working or derive empirical knowledge from it? Little wonder that, over time, this attitude led to vacuous intellectualism, characteristic of the monasteries he had established.

Vishnu (see p.19) in his incarnation as a boar, and of his consort Lakshmi. His coins carry the words *Adi Varaha* (Original Boar).

c.846 In the south, Vijayalaya founds the **Chola dynasty** with Tanjore as its capital.

c.850 In the east, Devapala is succeeded by his son.

c.850s The **Shahiyas**, of Turkic origin, rule Gandhara and the Kabul Valley.

c.870 Lalliya, a Brahmin minister of the Shahiyas, usurps the throne and establishes the **Hindu Shahiya dynasty**. Pressed by other Afghan principalities, King Lalliya makes the Attock region the heartland of his territory, and effectively a buffer between Afghanistan and the northern subcontinent.

c.871 In the south, Aditya I, succeeding Vijaylaya, captures Madurai, and enlarges his Chola kingdom at the expense of the Pallavas and the Western Gangas.

c.887 In the north, Mihir Bhoja is succeeded by his son, **Mahendrapala**, who manages to retain most of the empire he inherits. A learned king, Mahendrapala is a student of **Rajashekhara**, a courtier poet from Deccan whose four plays, written in Prakrit, include *Karpura Manjari*, named after the heroine.

c.907 In the south, Aditya I of the Chola dynasty is succeeded by **Parantaka I**. He extends his realm as far south as Nellore at the expense of the Pallavas.

Surviving records show that the **Chola administration** rests on the *kurram*, or **village collective**. Each collective runs local affairs through a *Mahasabha* – Great Assembly – invested with considerable power under the general supervision of a royal official. Assembly members, elected by casting lots, hold office for one year. Each collective has its own treasury, controls village lands, and has committees to oversee gardens, communal water tanks, justice and other departments.

A number of collectives form a district (Nadu), a group of districts a division (Kottam), and several divisions one of six provinces. Land revenue comprises one-sixth of the crop. Roads and other public works are well maintained. The extent of popular participation in local government under the Cholas is without precedent in the north.

c.909 In the north, King Mahendrapala of the Gurjara-Pratihara dynasty is succeeded by his son Mahipala.

c.914 In the Deccan, **Indra III** accedes to the Rashtrakuta throne.

c.916 During an expedition to the north, Indra III defeats King Mahipala and briefly occupies Kanuj. Although he does not attempt to annex the Gurjara-Pratihara kingdom, his incursions enfeeble its power, thus reducing Mahipala's ability to control his western provinces.

In the coming decades, repeated raids from the south divert the attention of Gurjara-Pratihar monarchs away from the northwest where Muslim forces are steadily gaining strength.

c.928 Death of Indra III.

932 In the Islamic world, Baghdad falls into the hands of Ahmad Muizz al Dawla, a Buyid king and follower of the minority **Shia sect**. But neither he nor his descendants attempt to institute Shiaism at the court or abolish the Abbasid Caliphate which is affiliated to the majority **Sunni sect**.

c.940 In the north, King Mahipala of the Gurjara-Pratiharas is succeeded by Bhoja.

c.950 In the Bundelkhand region south of the Jamuna, **Dhanga Chandel**, a vassal to the Gurjara-Pratiharas, rebels. He extends his kingdom to the Jamuna, captures strategic Gwaliar and establishes the **Chandel dynasty**, adopting the **Khajuraho temple complex** as its ceremonial capital, with temple inscriptions describing the accomplishments of Chandel sovereigns.

c.953 Rashtrakuta King Krishna III defeats Chola King Parantaka I, but does not annex his dominion.

c.957 Parantaka II accedes to the Chola throne.

963 Alptigin Samani, a governor of Turkic slave descent under the nominal tutelage of the Abbasid Caliphate in Baghdad, crosses the Hindu Kush from Balkh in Afghanistan and seizes **Ghazni**, a strategic town on the Kabul–Kandahar road. He founds the Samani dynasty in Afghanistan.

c.973 Death of King Parantaka II of Chola.

977 Alptigin is succeeded by his son-in-law **Sabuktigin**, formerly a slave. He annexes adjoining parts of Central Asia, including Khiva, and the trans-Indus regions of the Hindu Shahiya kingdom.

978 In the east, Mahipala is the ninth king of the Buddhist Pala dynasty.

c.980 The Rashtrakuta dynasty ends.

985 In the far south, **Rajaraja Deva I** of Tanjore accedes to the **Chola throne** and turns the dynastic domain into an **empire**. He first overpowers the Pandays as well as the Cheras of Quilon on the Malabar coast, then the eastern Chalukya kingdom of Vengi, Kalinga, Coorg, and other areas of the Deccan. He attacks **Sri Lanka** and sacks Buddhist stupas there. Devotees of Lord Shiva, the Cholas institutionalize various *bhakti* cults in the south, thus reforming Vedism into Hinduism.

The Khajuraho Temples

This complex of twenty **Shivaite Hindu** temples, situated 16km southeast of Jhansi and built between the 10th and early 12th centuries, is renowned for erotic sculptures, displaying an extraordinary blend of energy and grace. A typical Khajuraho temple contains a shrine room, assembly hall and covered ambulatory. The **Vishvanatha Temple**, distinguished by sculptures of Nandi, Shiva's bull, bears an inscription of King Dhanga Chandel. But the largest, finest and most sculpturally impressive is the temple dedicated to **Kandariya-Mahadeva** (literally Great God, being one of the names of Shiva). Built in the first decade of the 11th century, it is 33 metres high and designed to resemble a mountain range. Colonnades and beautifully domed assembly halls are surmounted by gradated towers rising to the highest – directly above the main shrine room. The temples are embellished with the figures of mythological deities and, more strikingly, of uninhibited lovers in various attitudes and postures of foreplay and coitus.

The outer walls of the Kandariya-Mahadeva temple are covered in ornate friezes depicting ritualized sexual postures

986–87 Sabuktigin Samani of Ghazni attacks **Jaipal** of the Hindu Shahiya dynasty, the foremost king in the north-western subcontinent, but the result is inconclusive.

988 King Jaipal counterattacks Sabuktigin, but suffers defeat and is forced to yield lands west of Peshawar, including the Khyber Pass.

991 Fearing a renewed Muslim attack, King Jaipal organizes a coalition of Hindu sovereigns, including Rajyapala, the Gurjara–Pratihara king of Kanuj, and Dhanga, the Chandel king of Bundelkhand. But Sabuktigin defeats the Hindu coalition near the Kurram Valley, and Jaipal is obliged to relinquish Peshawar.

c.996 In the south, Rajaraja Deva I, the Chola king, decrees the building of the Shivaite **Rajarajeshvara Temple** in Tanjore. On completion fifteen years later, it becomes the largest Hindu temple ever constructed.

The Rajarajeshvara Temple

Notable for its size and its architecture, the **Rajarajeshvara** (literally Lord Shiva) **Temple** became a model for temple-building in south India. Instead of a modest tower rising above the main sanctuary – typical of Pallava-financed constructions – this Chola place of worship is distinguished by a vast pyramid, called a *shikara*, resting on a high, upright base, and topped with a domed finial, rising to 65 metres. The passageway between the primary shrine – where Shiva is represented by a giant phallus – and the outer precinct, is decorated with paintings portraying Shiva in his multitudinous forms, as well as the narrative legends in the poems of such Shivaite Tamil saints as Sundramurti and Cerman Perumal.

997 In Ghazni, Sabuktigin is succeeded by his son **Mahmoud**, who adopts the title sultan (ruler). A staunch Sunni Muslim, and famed for his ugliness, Mahmoud decides to expand into the Shia Buyid territory in western Iran, and thus enhance his standing in the Islamic world.

Affirming his loyalty to the Abbasid Caliphate, he raises a large army, maintained by looting the riches of Hindu kings and temples in the Indian subcontinent, and enlarges his empire from the Caspian Sea to the Indus.

Though proud of his Turkic pedigree, he encourages the use of Persian in literature and administration. He is a patron of Sunni theologians, poets and scholars, among them **Alberuni** (see p.121). He beautifies Ghazni, where he builds a huge mosque, a library and a museum.

King Mahipala dies in the eastern subcontinent.

1001 In a battle near Peshawar, Sultan Mahmoud defeats and imprisons Jaipal, the Hindu Shahiya king and his family. After securing a conditional release, Japial abdicates in favour of his son, Anandpal, then jumps onto a funeral pyre, thus expiating the loss of his exalted caste status due to his capture by non-Hindus.

1002 Mahmoud captures the Sistan province of the Buyid kingdom.

1004 Mahmoud crosses the Indus and sacks the town of Bhatia, but loses most of his booty when his army is ambushed by regrouped enemy forces.

1006 Fanatical about his Sunni affiliation, Sultan Mahmoud attacks the Emir of Multan in northern Sind because he is an Ismaili (a sub-sect within Shia Islam), but also because of Multan's strategic value for gaining control of the lower Indus Valley.

1008 To avenge his father's humiliation, Anandapal Shahiya organizes a league of Hindu rajas lead by King Vishala Deva of Ajmer to confront Sultan Mahmoud. The rajas are defeated, and Mahmoud annexes Panjab, then advances to Kangra in the Himalyan foothills and captures a fort holding the accumulated wealth of the Hindu Shahiya kings. Mahmoud takes home 180 kilogrammes of gold, 1800 kilogrammes of silver, and coins worth 70 million dirhams. Since its Central Asian horses are of better stock than its Indian counterparts, Mahmoud's cavalry has greater mobility in combat.

Muslim generalship, uninhibited by ancient Hindu traditions and tactics, is also more innovative, while Mahmoud's troops, fighting infidels, are highly motivated by their comparatively new, vigorous faith. By contrast, Hindus perceive no particular merit, religious or otherwise, in slaughtering *mlechchas*, impure foreigners. They also reckon Muslim incursions will continue regardless of the outcome of individual battles. Further, Mahmoud's meat-eating soldiers, used to living in temperate and mountainous terrain, are heavier and stronger than their enemies, often vegetarian, from the hot plains.

1009 Sultan Mahmoud overpowers the Emir of Ghor, a town situated between Ghazni and Herat.

1012 Mahmoud seizes **Thanesar**, a place of pilgrimage north of Delhi under the control of Anandapala Shahiya, during a campaign that targets temple towns due to their concentrated wealth.

1013 Anandpala's successor Trilochanapala retires to Kashmir, signalling the virtual end of the Hindu Shahiyas dynasty.

c.1014 In the far south, **Rajendra Choladeva I** succeeds his father Rajaraja Deva I.

Sending ships across the Bay of Bengal to occupy Pegu in Burma, he stages the first such Indian naval expedition.

1018 During his twelfth Indian raid (of sixteen) **Sultan Mahmoud** advances as far as the **Ganges**. In December he captures Mathura, a richly endowed place of pilgrimage for the followers of Krishna, with its temples harbouring bejewelled, golden idols of Hindu gods.

He is awed by the intricately structured principal temple of the city, estimating the cost of its construction at 100 million dirhams spent over 100 years. After pillaging it, his troops burn it.

Mahmoud then attacks and loots **Kanuj**, putting King Jayapala Gurjara-Pratihar to flight. His booty from this campaign amounts to 20 million dirhams, 53,000 slaves and 350 elephants.

c.1020–21 Rajendra Choladeva's military commander seizes Vengi, modern Andhra Pradesh. He is then ordered to march further north and fetch holy water from the Ganges with which to sanctify the Chola realm.

1021–22 Sultan Mahmoud reaches Kalinjar in Budelkhand, subdues Ganda Chandel and returns home with 530 elephants and other booty.

c.1023 Rajendra Choladeva I defeats Mahipala of the Pala dynasty in the east. In celebration of this and previous victories, he assumes the title Gangaikonda, Conqueror of the Ganges, and builds a new capital, Gangaikonda-Cholapuram, with an impressive temple which remains intact.

c.1025 When the ruler of **Shrivijaya** – spanning the Malay peninsular and Sumatra – threatens to cut south India's seaborn trade with China so that his own merchants can deliver cargo to Chinese ports, Rajendra Choladeva I dispatches a naval expedition to the region. By occupying strategic positions in the **Straits of Malacca**, his navy ensures safe passage for Indian merchants.

1025–26 Leading 30,000 cavalry and many more volunteer infantry, Sultan Mahmoud attacks Somnath in north Gujarat, the site of a massive fortified temple of Lord Shiva, where a huge stone phallus is enshrined in the inner sanctum. He captures the temple after a bloody battle in which some 50,000 are killed. His booty is put at 20 million dirhams worth of gold, silver and precious stones.

1027 Mahmoud's last raid on the Indian subcontinent is directed against southern Sind.

1030 Sultan Mahmoud dies and is succeeded by **Sultan Masoud**.

1038 Nayapala, Mahipala's successor in Bengal, sends a **Buddhist mission** to **Tibet**, led by the monk Atisa.

1040 With the loss of eastern Iran to an adversary, Sultan Masoud of Ghazni turns his attention to the east. Relations with the Emir of Ghor remain tense.

c.1044 **Rajadhiraja I**, son of Rajendra Choladeva I, accedes to the Chola throne in Tanjore. After suppressing rebellions in Pandya and Chera provinces, he performs the traditional horse sacrifice ritual.

1048 Alberuni, an outstanding Muslim scholar and astronomer, dies.

c.1049 In Bundelkhand, Kirtivarman is the Chandel sovereign.

c.1054 Rajadhiraja I is killed in a battle with the Chalukyas at Koppam. His younger brother **Rajendra II** succeeds him and continues the Cholas' inconclusive war with the Chalukyas.

c.1063 Following Rajendra II's death, his younger brother **Virarajendra** resumes the conflict with the Chalukyas. He also sends a second Chola naval expedition to Southeast Asia.

c.1070 Virarajendra dies without a son. Following a contested succession, a grandson of Rajendra Choladeva I and

Alberuni 973–1048

Born Abu Rihan Muhammad ibn Ahmad in Khiva (in modern Uzbekistan), **Alberuni** was the first known Muslim scholar to learn Sanskrit and so gain access to the vast knowledge available in that language. Brought to his court at Ghazni by Sultan Mahmoud, he was transferred to Panjab in the early 11th century after its annexation.

During his ten-year stay there, he studied Indian contributions to mathematics, astronomy, physics, chemistry and mineralogy – as well as works of Hindu philosophy and history, including the *Bhagvad Gita* and the *Puranas*. In his book *Tahqiq-i-Hind* ('Description of India'), he made astute observations on the character, customs and history of Hindus. Described by a leading Indologist as 'a magic island of quiet impartial research in the midst of a world of clashing swords, burning towns and plundered temples', Alberuni's classic mentions the reluctance of Indians to share their scientific knowledge with non-Indians. Yet despite such strictures, Alberuni gathered sufficient knowledge of Indian sciences to seal his reputation as one of the leading scientific intelligences of the medieval period.

> **"** The Indians believe that there is no country but theirs, no nation like theirs, no king like theirs, no religion like theirs, no science like theirs... They are by nature niggardly in communicating what they know, and they take the greatest care to withhold it from men of another caste from among their own people, still more of course from any foreigner. **"**

Alberuni, *Tahqiq-i-Hind*

Princess Ammangadevi of the East Chalukyan dynasty, ascends the Chola throne under the name of **Kulottunga I**. During his reign the Cholas are expelled from Sri Lanka.

c.1077 Kulottunga I sends a diplomatic mission to China.

c.1090 The Gurjara-Partihara dynasty of Kanuj is supplanted by the **Gaharwar dynasty**, which is related to the Chandels. The only other dynasty of comparable stature in north India is the Rajput clan of **Chauhans**, based in Ajmer, Rajasthan.

c.1100 **Govindachandra**, a grandson of the founder of the Gaharwar dynasty, restores much of the past glory of the Kanuj kingdom.

Kirtivarman of the Chandel dynasty dies.

c.1122 Kulottunga I of Chola dies.

c.1150 **Vigraharaja** of the Chauhan dynasty expands his domain into eastern Panjab and Delhi. An inscription added by him to an Ashokan pillar alludes to his battles with 'impure foreigners', probably meaning the Muslim Ghaznavis.

1150–51 In Afghanistan, **Sultan Bahram** of Ghazni executes two princes of **Ghor**, provoking an attack on him by Emir Aladdin Hussein. Aladdin Hussein defeats Bahram, and sacks Ghazni, razing everything except the tomb of Sultan Mahmoud.

c.1160 Govindachandra of the Gaharwar dynasty of Kanuj dies.

1165 Following Vigraharaja's death, the Chauhan dynastic line becomes confusing.

1173 Emir Ghiyasuddin bin Sam of Ghor annexes Ghazni. His younger brother **Shihabuddin Muhammad Ghori** seizes the Ghaznavi territories in Panjab and Sind.

1175 **Prithviraj Chauhan III**, having eloped with the daughter of King Jaichand Gaharwar of Kanuj, ascends the Chauhan throne in Ajmer.

1175–76 Muhammad Ghori enters the subcontinent through the Gomal Pass, south of the more commonly used Khyber Pass, and conducts raids against Multan and Uchh.

1178 Ghori attempts the conquest of Gujarat, ruled by the West Chalukyas, but is repelled.

1178 In the south, the Chola empire falls into decline when Kulottunga III is defeated by the **Pandyas**.

1182 Prithviraj Chauhan III defeats Parmal Chandel of Budelkhand.

1185 Muhammad Ghori wrests **Lahore** in Panjab from the Ghaznavi dynasty.

1186–88 Muhammad Ghori deposes Khursu Malik, the last ruler of the Samani dynasty of Sabuktigin and Mahmoud of Ghazni. By annexing Panjab, Ghori gains complete control over the Indus Valley.

1191 As Muhammad Ghori's army of Turks, Afghans, Persians and Arabs advances beyond Panjab, it confronts a small confederacy of northern Hindu kings led by Prithviraj III. Ghori is seriously injured in personal combat with Govindaraja of Delhi during a battle fought at **Tarain**, 150km north of Delhi, and retreats with his troops. Prithviraj III fails to pursue the vanquished enemy and lives to pay a heavy price.

1192 After recuperating in Afghanistan, Muhammad Ghori, at the head of 120,000 horsemen, returns to Tarain to face 300,000 horses led by Prithviraj III. He sends a message to Prithviraj to surrender or embrace Islam. Spurning this ultimatum, Prithviraj proposes an armistice if Ghori will consider alternative conditions. Ghori's reply is deliberately equivocal. Construing it as an acceptance of his proposal, Prithviraj and his troops celebrate well into the night.

At dawn Ghori's mounted archers attack in waves until the Indians unleash their elephant phalanx with devastating effect. The archers retreat. But as the Indian forces advance, they are attacked by the Turkish cavalry. Towards afternoon, the spirits of Prithviraj's men sag. Ghori, leading an elite force of 12,000 mounted archers, puts the Hindus to flight. Prithviraj is captured and killed.

Thus ends the decisive **Second Battle of Tarain**, breaking the will of the northern rajas to resist the Muslim Afghan onslaught. Ordering his generals to make further conquests, Muhammad Ghori returns in triumph to Afghanistan. His leading general, **Qutbuddin Aibak**, a manumitted Turkic slave, annexes Delhi, an important possession of the Chauhans, and makes it his headquarters. In the course of his eastward march, he seizes Baran (present-day Bulundshahr), Meerut and Kol (later Aligarh).

1193 Qutbuddin starts work on the **Quwwat al Islam** (Victory of Islam) Mosque in Delhi, constructed on the site of the earlier Chauhan citadel using pillars, capitals and lintels taken from the demolished Hindu and Jain temples.

1194–5 Muhammad Ghori leads his forces against **Jaichand Gaharwar**, a powerful king with his capital at Varanasi. The battle near Chandrawar on the Jamuna results in Jaichand's defeat and death. In its wake Ghori gains Bayana, Gwaliar and Patan.

1199 One of Ghori's generals, **Ikhtiyaruddin Khilji**, conquers large areas in south Bihar and adjoining Bengal, thus ending the 450-year-old Pala dynasty.

1203 With the capture of the Chandel kingdom of Bundelkhand by another of Ghori's commanders, Muhammad ibn Bakhtiar, the **Muslim conquest** of the northern subcontinent is an accomplished fact.

1203 Following the death of his elder brother Ghiyasuddin, Muhammad Ghori becomes the Sultan of Ghor.

1205 Muhmmad ibn Bakhtiar, an Afghan lieutenant of Muhammad's chief commander Qutbuddin Aibak, dies after annexing Bihar and Bengal.

1206 Muhammad Ghori, who has left his Indian empire in the care of **Qutbuddin Aibak**, is assassinated. Aibak, a one-time slave, succeeds his heirless master, and founds the **Slave dynasty**.

By proclaiming himself Sultan of the Ghaznavi dynasty's Indian territories, Aibak creates a distinct sultanate which, in his view, ceases to be a mere extension of the Afghan kingdom. To reinforce this interpretation, he moves his capital from Delhi to Lahore, where he is crowned.

7
The Delhi Sultanates

1206–1526

The sultanate set up in the northern subcontinent by Muslim conquerors from Afghanistan was **theocratic**. In theory at least, the **Sultan** (literally 'ruler') derived his legitimacy from the Baghdad-based **Caliph**, the nominal head of all Islam, and he governed according to the *Sharia* – the Islamic canon, as interpreted by leading *ulema* (religious-legal scholars). At the Sultan's court, the order of precedence was as follows: the chief judge of the *Sharia*, the chief preacher, other Islamic judges, senior Muslim lawyers, *Sayyids* (descendants of Prophet Muhammad), holy men with the honorific 'Shaikh'; brothers, brothers-in-law and sons of the Sultan; principal nobles; foreign notables and, finally, military commanders.

As stipulated by the *Sharia*, legitimate revenues included a tax on agricultural produce, varying from one-fifth to one half of the crop; *khums* (literally one-fifth), one-fifth of any booty captured in battles against infidels; *zakat* (literally 'purifier'), an alms tax, ranging from 2.5 to 10 percent of crops and merchandise; customs and import duties, varying from 2.5 to 10 percent; and the *jizya*, a poll tax on non-Muslims exempted from military service. In addition, the Sultan derived income from royal lands administered directly by his own revenue department. In predominantly non-Muslim India, the *jizya* was the most contentious. A commutation tax, it applied only to male adults who, had they been Muslim, would have been recruited into an army. It was a protection levy that a non-Muslim paid his Muslim ruler.

The Sultanate, mostly centred on **Delhi**, was divided into **provinces**. Each provincial governor took a fixed share of land revenues with which – as well as defraying administrative expenses – he maintained a quota of cavalry and infantry to serve the Sultan when required. In addition, the Sultan gave non-hereditary land grants to his nobles in return for supplying him with troops. This arrangement meant that, in times of crisis, the Sultan could potentially call on a gigantic army. In normal times, he maintained a standing force, consisting of bodyguards (often slaves) and other soldiers posted in the capital and at garrison forts along the frontiers. These were either paid cash or given small land grants. Compared to the levies maintained by the governors and noblemen, the Sultan's army was small.

Having established themselves in North India during the 12th century, the Sultans, whether of Afghan or Turkic origin, failed to expand their realm. Throughout the following century they had to contend with **Mongol incursions** in the northwest and **Hindu resistance** in their annexed territories.

Given the incompatibility of Hinduism and Islam – encapsulated by Hindu idol worship and Muslim idol-breaking – Hindu resistance to conversion remained strong. Even the aggressive proselytizing bid by **Timur the Great** (also known as Tamerlaine) – who massacred idol worshippers during his brutal, lightning invasion of the northern subcontinent in 1398 – failed to reduce Hindu resistance. This finally made the Sultans more realistic about converting Hindus to their faith.

On their part, after two centuries of Muslim subjugation, Hindus set aside their superiority complex and started forging a *modus operandi* with their masters. By then, there was a sufficient body of voluntary Hindu converts to introduce inadvertently into Indian Islam, customs, ideas and outlook associated with their Hindu past. This created an environment conducive to genuine Hindu-Muslim dialogue. Against this backdrop emerged the poet **Kabir**, who preached amity between Hindus and Muslims, and later **Nanak** who, in his own creed of Sikhism, tried to synthesize Hinduism and Islam.

A similar synthesis can be detected in the evolving styles of **architecture**. The sultans brought with them architectural concepts based on what had been constructed in Baghdad, Damascus, Mecca and other cities of the Islamic world. But these were gradually modified by local influences and Hindu craftsmen.

Among the sultans, **Alauddin Sikander Sani Khalji** in the late 13th century stands out. His intellectual brilliance was as extraordinary as was his physical ugliness. An illiterate, he intuitively grasped the link between economic power and political authority – a correlation that was to be firmly established by Karl Marx (1818–83) after much study and thought in the second half of the 19th century. Alauddin Khalji's micro-managing of the economy through price controls focused not merely on basic necessities but also on cattle, slaves and prostitutes. Maintaining food granaries through imposition of grain procurement quotas on provincial officials was one of the earliest examples of state-planned economy. But by allowing only small profit margins to the producers of goods, he deterred private enterprise; and the living standards of agriculturists, forming the bulk of the population, already weighed down with excessive taxes, fell.

As with earlier alien rulers in the subcontinent, once the Sultan conquerors and their entourage had been absorbed into the easy-going Indian society, their sultanate steadily atrophied, making it vulnerable to yet another conquest from the northwest – by fellow Muslims albeit of Mongol (Mughal) stock.

In central and southern India a different environment prevailed. During this period several powerful kingdoms emerged, among them **Vijayanagar**. Towards its end, an entirely new development impinged on Indian history. In the aftermath of **Vasco da Gama**'s pioneering voyages in search of the Indies, the source of spices required *inter alia* for meat preservation, Portugal established a trading colony at Goa in the early 16th century, a fact virtually unnoticed by the Delhi sultanate which was then tottering.

1206 **Qutbuddin Aibak** founds the **Slave dynasty**, which lasts 84 years. Although he maintains his capital in Lahore, he leaves his imprint on Delhi by completing the Quwwat al Islam Mosque there.

Around this time **Genghis Khan** (aka Jenghiz, born Temujin) completes his conquest of the **Mongol** tribal confederacy.

1210 Sultan Aibak falls from his horse playing polo and dies. His adopted son Aram Shah rules briefly, but is overthrown by the Delhi-based Turkic nobles who favour **Shamsuddin Iltumish**, a manumitted Turkic slave who is Aibak's son-in-law.

1211 Sultan Iltumish moves the capital back to **Delhi**. To consolidate his position, he secures from the Baghdad-based Abbasid Caliph al-Mustansir Billa a robe of honour conferring on him the title of Sultan-e-Azm, the Great Sultan. While in theory the Caliph is the overlord of all Muslim kings, in practice Iltumush is an absolute ruler, the ultimate judicial authority, subject only to the tenets of the *Sharia* (Islamic Law).

In retrospect, he will be seen as the real architect of Muslim power in the Indian subcontinent. Pious, learned, and reverent toward the *ulema* (religious-legal scholars), he patronizes the arts and continues work on the **Qutb Complex**.

The Qutb Complex

Inaugurated by **Qutbuddin Aibak**, continued by **Iltimush**, and completed by **Feroz Shah Tughluq**, the **Qutb Complex** is the earliest surviving collection of Islamic monuments in **Delhi**. At its centre are the **Quwwat al Islam Mosque** and the **Qutb Minar** (Pivotal Tower). A five-tiered victory tower with balconies, the 78-metre-high Qutb Minar remains unrivalled in the world of Islam for height and mass.

Built of red sandstone, it was surmounted by a cupola which survived until an earthquake in 1803. In the words of Sir John Marshall, the director-general of the Archeological Survey of India, 'Nothing certainly could be more imposing or more fittingly symbolic of Muslim power than the stern and stupendous fabric [of the Qutb Minar], nor could anything be more exquisite than its rich but restrained carvings.' Small wonder that it remains a distinguished landmark of southern Delhi today. Also located within the complex are the later **Alai Darwaza** and **Alai Minar**.

The Qutb Complex is now contained within the larger **Red Citadel** (*Lalkot*), which also includes the **White Palace** (*Safedkot*), the site of the court of Sultan Iltumish and his successors. Although the White Palace is ruined, Iltumish's tomb, combining elements of Indian and Islamic architectures, is extant.

The Qutb Minar, the first monument of Muslim rule in India

1218 Mongols under Genghis Khan control most of China as well as Turkestan, Transoxania, Khorasan and Afghanistan.

Genghis Khan's conquests in Central Asia and Afghanistan result in a massive exodus of local princes, commanders, intellectuals and chieftains, who pour into the northwestern Indian subcontinent.

1220 Armed resistance to the Sultanate by Hindus in Oudh, led by Bartuh, probably an aboriginal chief, results in the deaths of some 120,000 Muslim troops.

1222 Genghis crosses the Indus in pursuit of Emir Jalaluddin Mangabarni of Khiva. By refusing the fugitive prince asylum, Sultan Iltimush averts invasion by Genghis.

1226 Iltimush dispatches his son Nasiruddin to overpower the rebellious Khalji governor of Bihar.

1227 Death of Genghis Khan.

1229 Following Nasiruddin's death, Sultan Iltimush himself subdues the Khalji governor of Bihar.

1234 Iltimush captures Malwa in central India.

1236 Iltimush dies. Ignoring his nomination of his daughter **Raziyya** as his successor, court nobles place her brother Ruknuddin Feroz on the throne. He continues his earlier life of debauchery, and the governors of Multan, Lahore, Jhansi, Oudh and Bihar declare independence. He is overthrown by Raziyya, and killed.

1236 Acquiring the title of **Jalaluddin** (Glory of Faith), Raziyya ascends the throne. Wearing a coat and cap, and riding an elephant, she leads her troops unveiled and subdues rebellious **Bengal**.

> ❝ Sultan Raziyya was a great sovereign, and sagacious, just, beneficient, the patron of the learned, a dispenser of justice, the cherisher of her subjects, and of warlike talent, and was endowed with all the admirable attributes and qualifications necessary for kings. But as she did not attain the destiny in her creation of being computed among men, of what advantage were all these excellent qualifications unto her? ❞
>
> Minjahu as Siraj, *Tabakat-i Nasiri*, trans. G.H. Raverty

During a second expedition to re-capture a fort in Panjab, however, Raziyya is toppled in favour of her younger brother **Muizuddin Bahram** by a cabal of Turkic aristocrats known as **The Forty**, who are pitted against a coalition of Muslim nobles of Afghan origin and Indian converts. Fleeing, Raziyya is killed by a Hindu rebel faction.

1241 A Mongol horde sacks **Lahore**, destroying every relic.

1242 Sultan Muizuddin Bahram, considered a worthless ruler, dies, and is succeeded by his nephew **Alauddin Masoud**, who also proves unequal to the task of governing the sultanate.

1246 Alauddin Masoud is deposed and succeeded by his uncle **Nasiruddin Mahmoud**. He too lacks kingly qualities, but is saved by the highly competent **Ghiyasuddin Balban**, married to his younger sister. A manumitted slave of Turkic origin, Balban quells revolts and acts as *de facto* ruler.

1250 The Islamic **Caliphate** passes from the Baghdad Abbassids to the Turkic **Mamalukes** based in Cairo, Egypt.

Periodic Mongol incursions into the Indian subcontinent, led by Genghis Khan's grandson **Hulagu**, continue. The Mongols reach the Bias River in Panjab, but are repulsed by Balban.

1255 In the south, the enfeebled royal house of **Chola** is overthrown by King Sundra of the **Pandya** dynasty based in Madurai.

1258 Hulagu, serving under his brother the **Great Khan Mongke**, overruns Mesopotamia and sacks Baghdad, the climax of his conquests that include Turkestan, Khorasan and Persia.

1259 The Great Khan Mongke dies. The Mongol empire is divided into four separate khanates, with **Chagatai** and the **Ilkhanate** bordering northwestern India.

1260 Sultan Nasiruddin Mahmoud welcomes an ambassador from Hulagu Khan, now ruler of the Ilkhanate, thus signalling a rapprochement with the Mongol ruler despite having provided asylum and stipends to fifteen sovereigns and princes as well as scores of scholars fleeing Mongol aggression.

His position is strengthened by a string of fortified garrisons built along the northwest frontier by Balban and placed under the command of Sher Khan Sunqar, an Afghan noble.

Closer to Delhi, Balban savagely crushes Mewati brigands operating in the area. About a hundred outlaws are flayed alive. Their skins, stuffed with straw, are exhibited above the city gates.

c.1260 **Hindu temple architecture** reaches its apogee in the monumental temples of **Orissa**, three of which survive: the Shivaite Lingaraja Temple at Bhuvaneshwar; the Vishnuite Jagannatha Temple at Puri; and the Surya (Sun)

Temple at Konarak. The Orissa style is noted for its main tower which starts to curve inwards at about a third of its height ending with a rounded top crowned by a flat stone disc and finial.

1265 Hulagu Khan dies, but sporadic Mongol raids on the subcontinent continue.

The Surya Temple of Konarak

The only shrine of its kind dedicated to Surya, the Sun God, the **Surya Temple** (aka Black Pagoda), completed around 1264, is among India's largest and most splendid. The roof of its *manadapa* (hall) is divided into three sections, instead of the usual two. Although its 65-metre tower has fallen, its spacious assembly halls are extant, as are two smaller outer halls standing apart from the main structure.

The main assembly hall is built on an imposing platform surrounded by a dozen carved wheels three metres in diameter. The steps leading up to the temple entrance are flanked by prancing horses, the whole composition representing a chariot in which the Sun God rides across the heavens. The temple compound is embellished with free-standing sculptures of stunning beauty and force. Images of powerful horses and a great elephant crushing a criminal in his trunk display a facility with animal form rivalled in the East only by the statuary and ceramics of China during the Tang period.

Equally compelling, and rivalling the erotic masterpieces at the Khajuratho temples (see p.115), are seductive images of human males and females engaged in sexual intercourse. Various explanations have been offered for their presence. Some see in them the carnal joys of heaven; others, visual representations of the sexual mysticism that permeated contemporary Hindu thought; still others, portrayals of the sexuality of *devadasis* (literally maids of gods), temple prostitutes. Aesthetically, these sculptures, representing a universe of the flesh, are a dramatic contrast to the temple's austere interior.

1266 Following Nasiruddin Mahmoud's death, **Balban** becomes Sultan. Determined to break the Turkish military oligarchy which has so far monopolized high offices, Balban arrogates unprecedented powers. Declaring himself the 'Shadow of Allah' and His viceroy, he decrees that anybody approaching the royal seat must kiss the ground and then

ROBERT HARDING

The Surya Temple, a masterpiece of Medieval Orissan art

his feet before speaking. Even laughter is all but banished from his court.

Balban is also ruthless in dispensing summary justice. Overhauling the intelligence apparatus, he appoints secret informants at every level of government and orders them to submit daily reports on significant events. He systematizes administrative procedures. Elderly and infirm land-grant holders no longer fit to serve in the army are retired. In their place, Balban recruits able young men and settles soldier-farmers in troublesome regions. He deploys garrisons at strategic sites and improves communications.

1271 In **western Deccan**, Ramchandra of the **Yadava dynasty** accedes to the throne at Devagiri on the Godavari River. The capital is the site of much wealth accumulated from land revenue over generations.

1280 A Hindu inscription in central India alludes to 'the security and bounty enjoyed under the rule of Balban'.

c.1285 **Tughril Khan**, the governor of **Bengal**, revolts against the Delhi sultanate. Balban dispatches three armies against him, but in vain. He then leads a force of 200,000 to the Bengali capital Lakhnauti. Tughril flees to the east but is captured and put to death along with his family.

In Lakhnauti, Balban impales the heads of hundreds of Tughril's followers on stakes set up on both sides of a three-kilometre-long bazaar.

1286 Muhammad Khan, Balban's eldest son and commander of garrisons along the northwest frontier, dies fighting the Mongols.

1287 Grief-stricken by the loss of Muhammad, and in his 80s, Balban dies. His grandson **Muizuddin Kaiqabad** becomes Sultan.

1288 The Venetian traveller **Marco Polo** visits southern India during his seventeen-year expedition to China. He describes Kayal – a port frequented by ships from Arabia and the Far East – as 'a great and noble city' where much business is done. 'The king possesses vast treasures and wears on his person the most costly jewels. He maintains splendid state, shows favour to merchants and foreigners so that they are glad to visit his city, and administers his realm with equity.'

1290 Following the assassination of Sultan Muizuddin Kaiqabad, 70-year-old **Jalaluddin Feroz Shah** of the Khalji clan, and governor of Samana (modern Northwest Frontier province in Pakistan) seizes the throne in Delhi. Instead of fighting the **Mongols**, he allows several thousand of them to settle near Delhi on condition they convert to Islam.

1293 During a second visit to southern India, Marco Polo visits the tomb of St Thomas near modern Madras and notes its popularity as a place of pilgrimage. He takes particular note of horses imported from the Arabian peninsula, a key element in the battles that rage all over the subcontinent.

> **❝** You may take it for a fact that the merchants of Hormuz and Kais, of Dhofar and Shihr and Aden, all of which provinces produce large numbers of battle chargers and other horses, buy up the best horses and load them on to ships and export them to this [Indian] king and his four brother kings. Some of them are sold for as much as 500 saggi of gold, which are worth more than 100 marks of silver.... This king buys 2,000 of them or more every year, and his brothers as many. And, by the end of the year, not a hundred of them survive. They all die through ill-usage, because they have no veterinarians and do not know how to treat them. **❞**
>
> *The Travels of Marco Polo*, ed. Milton Rugoff

1294–4 Jalaluddin Feroz Shah I dispatches his barely literate nephew and son-in-law **Alauddin Sikander Sani Khalji** to capture Bhilsa near Bhopal. He plunders Bhilsa and a nearby Buddhist stupa at Sanchi.

1296 Concealing his movements from his uncle, Alauddin marches to Devagiri in the spring, defeats King Ramachandra, and seizes his wealth.

Returning to his base at Kara near Allahabad, he lures the Sultan to visit him. As Jalaluddin Feroz Shah I disembarks from his boat he is decapitated by Alauddin's bodyguards.

Alauddin marches to Delhi, bribes the Turkic aristocracy with the gold plundered from Devagiri, and assumes the throne, taking the titles *Yamin al Khalifa* (Deputy to the Caliph) and *Nasiri Emir al Muminin* (Victorious Commander of the Faithful). To consolidate his power, he assassinates potential rivals.

1297–1300 With **Mongol incursions** becoming virtually an annual event, the Mongol converts to Islam in the Delhi area attempt an uprising. In reprisal, the Sultan orders the massacre of some 20,000 males. Incensed, their kinsmen from across the northwest frontier besiege Delhi, ravage the Doab – the area between the Jamuna and Ganges rivers – and occupy Sind and Panjab.

1298 Sultan Alauddin Khalji conquers **Gujarat**, a fertile cotton-producing land rich in cattle, with a thriving sea trade, and sacks the rehabilitated Hindu temple at Somnath.

In the bustling port of Cambay, Aluaddin pays 1000 dinars for Kafur, a striking-looking Hindu eunuch-slave. Once Kafur adopts Islam, the Sultan appoints him *malik-naib*, senior commander, and he becomes known as **Malik Kafur**.

1300 Enriched by his plunder, Alauddin strengthens his army and inflicts a humiliating defeat on the Mongols, retaking Sind and Panjab.

The Rajputs

Even though the **Rajputs** originated with the Huna invasions of the 6th century, the term – a derivative of *rajputra* (raja's son), describing more the profession of soldiering and governing than ethnicity – only gained currency during the late Mughal period (see p.163). Accompanying the Hunas were Gujaras, Maitrakas and other groups who supplanted the decimated or scattered older martial tribes of Rajasthan (literally Place of Rajas).

Brahminical endeavours to accord the early Rajputs *kshatriya* status by furnishing them with genealogies linking them to the solar or lunar branches of royalty, as laid out in the *Puranas*, emphasized their foreign ancestry. Of the Rajput clans exercising power in the 9th and 10th centuries, **Pariharas**, **Chauhans** (or Chahamans), **Solankis** and **Pawars** (or Paramaras) enjoyed special status. Collectively known as *Agnikula* – Fire Family – they claimed descent from a mythical figure emerging from an enormous fire-pit near Mount Abu in Rajasthan. (Since the fire rite was purificatory, it implied that Rajputs were aliens who had to be purified.)

Following the demise of the Gurjara-Pratihara dynasty in late 9th century, the Pariharas governed southern Rajasthan, the Solankis north Gujarat, the Pawars Malwa, and the Chauhans eastern Rajasthan. The Chauhans, however, were an Aryanized indigenous tribe from the Lake Sambar area near Jaipur, and had become part of the Gurjara-Pratihara kingdom through intermarriage. After its break-up, Ajayraja Chauhan established a new capital, Ajay-Meru (Ajay Mountain), or Ajmer, in the early 12th century. Among the non-*Agnikula* clans were the **Chandels**, related to the Gond tribe, in the Khajuraho region; the **Guhilas** in Mewar; the **Tomaras** in and around Delhi; and the **Rahstrakutas** of western Deccan. The Rajput clans were notable for their endless feuds. The temporary alliance of a few of them to battle Muhammad of Ghori in 1192 failed to stop the Muslim forces.

1301 Alauddin prepares for a conquest of the south by capturing the strategic natural fortress of Ranthambhor in Rajasthan along an important route to the Deccan.

1302 Led by Malik Kafur, the nine-year **southern campaigns** begin.

1303 Alauddin captures and plunders the **Rajput**-held fortress at Chitor in **Rajasthan**. To save their honour, the wives, sisters and daughters of the defeated Rajputs immolate themselves.

Having escaped the siege, **Hamir Guhila** conducts guerrilla actions against the Sultan's troops in the nearby Aravalli Hills. After founding the state of **Mewar** (modern

Alauddin Sikander Sani Khalji r. 1296–1316

The consolidator of the Turkic Muslim rule in the subcontinent, **Alauddin** possessed the most analytical intellect among the Delhi Sultans, which he used to eradicate rebellions and institute a state-planned economy. Attributing rebellious activity to excessive wealth among certain groups, immoderate consumption of alcohol at aristocratic gatherings, and poor espionage, he attacked the causes. He confiscated the Islamic religious trusts, often richly endowed. He undermined the economic base of Muslim nobles by stopping fresh land grants and later cancelling earlier ones. He ended the privileges enjoyed by Hindus serving as hereditary revenue assessors and collectors as well as revenue farmers, called *zamindars* (literally owners of land) – intermediaries whom the Sultan paid a certain percentage of land taxes they collected. He posted informers in public offices and the households of dignitaries; prohibited the consumption of alcohol and banned intermarriage among Turkic, Persian and Afghan nobles.

  The first Muslim monarch to raise a standing army, he recruited able, young men, paying them cash salaries and providing them

Udaipur) he recaptures the Chitor fort. Mongol forces besiege Delhi for two months, retiring only when they extract a sizeable ransom.

1304 Alauddin Sikander Khalji inscribes the legend 'Second Sikandar' (ie Alexander) on his coinage, and decrees that Muslim preachers should refer to him by the same title in their sermons.

1305 Mongol raiders attack Multan.

1306 As a succession crisis flares in Transoxania, centre of the Ilkhanate kingdom, the Mongols temporarily abandon their attacks on the subcontinent.

with horses and weapons. At its peak his cavalry numbered 475,000. To maintain this huge force, and to squeeze Hindus, who were major landholders, he raised land revenue from one sixth of the produce to one half. He also introduced a property tax, and plundered during his military campaigns in the Deccan, where he successfully combined highly mobile Turkish horsemen with the behemoth of an Indian elephant phalanx.

When these measures failed to enable his soldiers to maintain a decent living standard, he imposed price controls not only on foodgrains and other necessities, but also on cattle, slaves and prostitutes. He ordered commodity dealers to register with the Inspector-General of Bazaars, who ruthlessly supervised grain stocks and prices. To counter supply fluctuations, the Sultan decreed stockpiling of yield from crown lands into urban granaries, and imposed procurement quotas on provincial officials. Food prices fell and stayed low even during drought. But the downside of his reforms was that – by stifling incentive due to reduced profit – they deterred economic activity, especially in the crucial agricultural sector.

1307 When **King Ramachandra** fails to pay annual tribute, the Sultan dispatches Malik Kafur to Devagiri. Kafur brings Ramachandra to Delhi where he and Alauddin Sikander are reconciled.

1309 Aided by Ramachandra, Malik Kafur attacks Pratap Rudra of the Kakatiya dynasty, the sovereign of Warangal, a region of modern Andhra Pradesh. Pratap Rudra surrenders, hands over a large part of his treasure, and agrees to pay annual tribute to the Delhi Sultanate.

1310-11 Malik Kafur attacks Ballall III, the Hoysala king of Karnataka, then secures his support for an assault on the **Pandays** to the south. The Panday ruler proves elusive. Kafur loots the temple cities of Madurai, Srirangam and Chidambaram. He returns to Delhi with 612 elephants, 20,000 horses, 240 tonnes of gold, and numerous boxes of jewellery.

Alauddin Khalji builds the citadel of Siri near Delhi and adds the **Ala-i-Darwaza** (Alauddin's Gateway) to the Qutb Complex.

I am an unlettered man, but I have seen a great deal. Be assured then that the Hindus will never become submissive and obedient till they are reduced to poverty. I have therefore given orders that just sufficient shall be left [for them] from year to year of corn, milk and curds, but that they shall not be allowed to accumulate hoards and property.

Sultan Alauddin Khalji, addressing an Islamic religious-legal scholar

c.1315 The Sultan's forces raid Kabul, Kandahar and Ghazni, all ruled by the Mongols.

1316 Following Alauddin Khalji's death, his 6-year-old son Shihabuddin Omar is enthroned by Malik Kafur, who acts as his regent. A month later, Malik is assassinated by a slave guard at the behest of Alauddin's elder son, **Qutbuddin Mubarak**, who then proclaims himself Sultan. His brief reign is notable for his debauched extravagance.

1318 Qutbuddin Mubarak overpowers Harpal Dev Yadava in Devagiri and annexes his kingdom. After his triumphal return to Delhi, the young Sultan appears in court in female clothing and jewellery. He orders a bevvy of prostitutes to parade naked along the terraces of the royal palaces and urinate on courtiers below as they walk to the royal court. In Devagiri his Muslim governor rebels.

1320 Qutbuddin Mubarak promotes **Khusru Khan** to prime minister, a low-caste Hindu convert to Islam. Khusru has the Sultan murdered and usurps the throne.

The Turkic nobles, led by **Ghazi Malik**, the warden of the marches in the north, defeat and kill Khusru in September.

Ghazi Malik, a son of a Turkish slave of Sultan Balban and his Hindu wife, is proclaimed Sultan. He takes the title **Ghiyasuddin Muhammad Tughluq**, and founds the **Tughluq dynasty**. He starts building a new city, called **Tughluqabad**, 6km sq in area, with a massive fort as its nucleus, east of the Qutb Complex in Delhi.

1321–23 Sultan Ghiyasuddin Tughluq sends his son **Muhammad Adil** to the Deccan to capture Warangal, ruled by Raja Pratapa Rudra, and nearby Bidar. Prince Muhammad uses the Devagiri fort as his base and triumphs.

1324 The Sultan campaigns against rebellious Bengal while Muhammad Adil acts as his viceroy in Delhi. Truimphant,

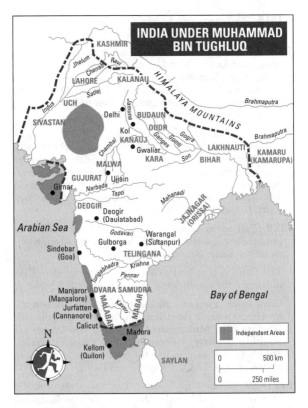

INDIA UNDER MUHAMMAD BIN TUGHLUQ

Ghiyasuddin Tughluq orders Prince Muhammad to erect a timbered pavilion at Afghanpur near the banks of Jamuna.

1325 Father and son stage a reunion in July. But as evening prayers approach, and the Sultan, his favourite son Mahmoud, and a few aides are left inside the pavilion to pray,

Prince Muhammad sets off a stampede of his elephants to demolish the pavilion.

To ensure the deaths of the occupants, Muhammad obstructs the arrival of pickaxes and shovels. Feigning grief while securing the throne for himself, Muhammad accords his father an impressive mausoleum below the walls of the Tughluqabad citadel. According to the official version, promulgated by **Sultan Muhammad Adil bin Tughluq**, a thunderbolt struck the pavilion which fell, crushing its occupants. His territories nominally include Uttar Pradesh, Bihar, Bengal, Panjab, Sind, Gujarat, Malwa, and parts of the Deccan, including Malabar.

Muhammad Adil Bin Tughluq r.1325–1351

Few rulers have combined such contrary characteristics as **Muhammad Adil Bin Tughluq**. Endowed with a prodigious memory and intellect, he was proficient in logic, Greek philosophy, mathematics and medicine. He was also a poet, an elegant calligrapher and a patron of the arts. He built hospitals and almshouses and his generosity to Muslim scholars was legendary. While he was regular in his prayers, abstained from alcohol, and shunned luxury, he was neither a religious nor an ethnic bigot. On the battlefield he was a distinguished commander. Yet he was also myopically self-righteous, deeply introverted, contemptuous of advice, however well-meaning, and incredibly cruel. Early on in his reign, he followed up his generous bribes to Turkic, Persian and Afghan nobles with gruesome punishment of a political dissident. After having him flayed alive, the Sultan ordered his victim's skin to be stuffed and displayed in public. He then offered the bereaved family the rebel's minced innards cooked with rice. This turned out to be a rehearsal for similar retribution meted out on a large scale later on after he had quashed a rebellion.

1327 A Mongol army led by Tarmashirin Khan of the Chagatai Khanate reaches the gates of Delhi, but withdraws after receiving a hefty tribute.

1328 Wishing to re-trace the campaigns of Alexander the Great in reverse, and seize Afghanistan, Uzbekistan, Khorasan, Iran and Iraq, Muhammad bin Tughluq enlarges his cavalry to 357,000, then abandons the enterprise when costs spiral.

1328–29 To combat a shortage of silver, the Sultan mints grossly adulterated coinage, then issues additional token coins of copper and brass. These measures exacerbate **monetary chaos** when the new currency is widely counterfeited. Within two years, and at great cost to the treasury, Muhammad bin Tughluq is forced to buy back the real as well as forged coins.

Dismissing the old royal aides of non-Indian origin, he favours Indian converts to Islam, a policy that prompts a series of poisoned-pen letters addressed to him.

1330–31 To get even with his anonymous but influential enemies, Muhammad bin Tughluq moves his capital to Devagiri, renamed **Daulatabad**, 1400km south of Delhi. Less exposed to Mongol attacks, Daulatabad is also better situated to deal effectively with the problematic territories of Malwa and Gujarat, and to consolidate the Sultan's shaky control over the defeated Deccan kingdoms.

Ordering the **evacuation of Delhi**, Muhammad offers to compensate its citizens for the loss of homes and shops. When they refuse to leave, he gives them three days' notice. A city spread over 70 sq kms is so thoroughly emptied that, according to the chronicler Ziauddin Barani, 'not a cat or a dog was left among its buildings'. But, having reached Daulatabad, he changes his mind when he realizes that an abandoned Delhi is more vulnerable to attacks by the Mongol than a populated one. Thus begins a forced migration back to Delhi.

1334 The Moroccan traveller **Ibn Battuta**, visiting Delhi, describes it as 'one of the greatest cities of the universe', and 'the most magnificent city in the Muslim world', but finds it rather sparsely populated for a settlement of its size.

1336 The south-central Hindu kingdom of **Vijayanagar** is founded by Harihara I of the Shivaite Sangama dynasty, with Vijayanagar (now Hampi, Karnataka) on the southern bank of the Tungabhadra River as its capital.

1337 The Sultan dispatches 100,000 cavalry under his nephew **Khusru Malik** to capture the mountains between India and China. Khusru marches to Kullu (present-day Himachal Pradesh) in the foothills of the western Himalayas. Forced by freeezing weather to abandon the campaign, Khusru's retreat is blocked by local Hindu forces. All but ten horsemen perish in the snows.

1338 The Muslim governor of **Bengal** stages a successful rebellion against the Delhi sultanate, and the province retains its independence for the next two centuries.

Muhammad bin Tughluq builds a new administrative quarter in Delhi, called the **Jahanpanah**, between Siri and the Qutb Complex.

1340 Rebellion in Malabar marks an irreversible decline of the Delhi Sultanate. The Sultan's intensified tyranny is becoming increasingly intolerable while his capacity to quell revolts is diminishing due to reduced land revenue caused by the neglect of heavily taxed agriculture by peasants and landlords. In desperation, he sends an envoy to the Mamaluke Caliph in Cairo to secure his investiture. On receiving it, he issues special coins calling himself *Yamin al Khalifa* (Deputy to the Caliph)

1341 The Sultan appoints Ibn Battuta chief justice of Delhi, then marches south to quash a rebellion in Warangal. But his army is struck by cholera, and he himself falls ill.

Ibn Battuta c.1304–1378

Born in Tangiers (present-day Morocco), **Muhammad ibn Abdullah ibn Battuta** was the most widely travelled man of pre-modern times, who spent 12 of his 29 peripatetic years in the Indian subcontinent, beginning in 1333, where he was a courtier of Sultan Muhammad bin Tughluq. At 21, he left home on pilgrimage to Mecca via Algeria, Tunisia, Libya and Egypt. He returned when he was 50, by which time he had visited forty countries according to the modern atlas. He went as far north as the Volga basin, as far south as Zanzibar, and as far east as China – chalking up a total of 120,000km, three times the distance covered by Marco Polo. In the Arab world, he is known simply as 'The Traveller of Islam'. He made it a point to adopt the country he visited by marrying several times, partly to satisfy his immense libido, and settling down, if only briefly.

Impressed by his learning, Muslim rulers often appointed him as a judge or ambassador, and lavished him with expensive gifts and gold. He recorded his journeys in a four-volume work, *The Mirabilia of Metropolises and the Wonders of Wandering*, usually called *The Travels (Al Rihala)*. In this he provides an invaluable account of the customs, thinking, religions and events of the peoples he came across in Africa, Asia and Europe. 'Ibn Batutta it was who hung the world, that turning wheel/Of diverse parts, upon the axis of a book,' wrote a 17th-century admirer.

1342 A severe famine, caused by drought, burdensome taxes and neglect of agriculture, sets in. The Sultan releases stocks from state granaries, and imports food from afar.

1346 Muhammad bin Tughluq dispatches Ibn Battuta to China as his ambassador. Shipwrecked near Calicut, Ibn Battuta will explore South India, Sri Lanka and the Maldives.

1347 Seceding from the Delhi Sultanate, Alauddin Hassan, a Persian noble, now calling himself **Alauddin Bahman**

Shah, founds the **Bahmani dynasty** – named after the Persian hero Bahman – in western **Deccan**, with its capital at Daulatabad/Devagiri.

1350 The Sultan invades Gujarat to put down the 22nd rebellion during his quarter-century rule.

1351 While pursuing the Gujarat rebel leader into Sind, Muhammad bin Tughluq falls ill and dies in a military camp, leaving no direct male heir. His commanders choose **Feroz Shah II Tughluq**, a 42-year-old cousin of the dead Sultan as his successor.

Feroz Shah leads the army back to Delhi. He later seeks and receives investiture from the Mamaluke Caliph as his *Yamin al Khalifa* (Deputy to the Caliph). Unusually, the new Sultan maintains a journal in which he lists such virtuous acts as his ban on torture. A learned man, he encourages translation of Sanskrit works into Persian.

To relieve pressure on the state exchequer, he discontinues cash salaries to his army and reverts to awarding **land grants** to Muslim nobles to maintain soldiers, and makes such grants hereditary.

He turns slave contingents, often Hindu, into workers for state-owned workshops producing weapons and such luxuries as robes, perfumes and gems, and for constructing and repairing public works.

1353–54 Sultan Feroz Shah II fails to regain Bengal.

1358 In Daulatabad, **Muhammad Shah I** of the Bahmani dynasty succeeds his father Alauddin. He battles with the neighbouring Hindu kingdom of Vijayanagar.

1360 Feroz Shah II's first attempt to recapture rebellious Sind and Gujarat fails.

1361 The Sultan attacks the Ganga king of **Orissa**, sacks the Lord Jagannatha Temple in Puri and massacres local Hindus.

> Among the many varieties of torture carried out during the earlier Sultans' reign were amputation of hands and feet, ears and noses; tearing out of eyes, pouring molten lead into the throat, crushing the bones of the hands and feet with mallets, burning the body with fire, driving iron nails into the hands, feet and bosom; cutting the sinews, sawing men asunder; these and many tortures were practiced. The great and merciful God made me, His servant, hope and seek for His mercy by devoting myself to prevent the unlawful killing of Muslims and the infliction of any kind of torture upon them or upon any men.

Sultan Feroz Shah Tughluq, journal entry

But he does not annex the province and hands it back to the Raja for an annual tribute, which the Raja will later neglect to pay.

1362 Firoz Shah II regains **Sind**.

1364 The Sultan begins building an administrative complex, **Ferozabad**, centred around a citadel with gardens and a seminary, north of Tughluqabad. He brings to Delhi two massive Ashokan pillars from Topra (Panjab) and Meerut (Uttar Pradesh), one of which is re-erected in Ferozabad.

1369 The Mongol conquerer, **Timur the Great**, (aka Timurlane, Timur the Lame, Tamerlane), a reputed descendant of Genghis Khan, becomes ruler of his native Samarkand (in modern Uzbekistan). A staunch Muslim, he will forge an empire containing Persia, Afghanistan and Mesopotamia, and reaching the shores of the eastern Mediterranean.

1377 Muhammad Shah I of the Bahmani dynasty is succeeded in Daulatabad by Mujahid Shah.

1378 Mujahid Shah is succeeded by Muhammad Shah II.

1379 Harihara II ascends the throne in Vijayanagar. Enjoying peace with the neighbouring Muslim Bahmani

In this Mughal miniature, Timur's descendants kneel in front of him

dynasty, he consolidates his dominion covering most of southern India.

1388 Sultan Feroz Shah Tughluq II is succeeded by his grandson Ghiyasuddin II in Ferozabad.

1389 Ghiyasuddin II is succeeded by Abu Bakr, another grandson of Feroz Shah II.

1390 Abu Bakr is followed by his uncle Muhammad bin Feroz.

1394 Muhammad bin Feroz is succeeded by his son Alauddin Sikander.

1395 Sultan Alauddin Sikander is followed by his cousin **Nusrat Shah Tughluq**.

1397 In Daulatabad, Muhammad Shah II is succeeded by Feroz Shah of the Bahmani dynasty.

1398 Sultan Nusrat Shah Tughluq is expelled from Delhi by **Nasiruddin Mahmoud Shah** who proclaims himself Sultan – just as an army led by Timur's grandson Pir Muhammad captures Multan after a long siege.

Encouraged by the weakness of the Delhi Sultanate and the famed riches of India, and determined to end Hindu idol-worship, Timur crosses the Indus in the autumn with 90,000 cavalry.

At **Panipat**, 80km north of Delhi, he defeats Nasiruddin Mahmoud Shah, who flees to Gujarat. Timur's forces then cross the Jamuna just below Ferozabad, the capital of Nusrat Shah. He escapes and dies soon after in exile.

To forestall a rebellion by 100,000 Hindu prisoners, Timur orders their massacre before entering Delhi on 18 December. He declares himself Sultan. His jubilant soldiers are cruel to local Hindus. When the latter resist, Timur decrees their wholesale slaughter and the sacking of the city. Over five days and nights his troops plunder the wealth accumulated over decades.

1399 On 2 January Timur departs for Samarkand. Marching via Hardwar and Jammu in the Himalayan foothills, he leaves behind a trail of carnage and famine. He appoints Sayyid Khizr Khan his governor of Multan to rule Panjab.

1405 Timur dies in Samarkand and is succeeded by his son **Shah Rukh**.

1406 **King Deva Raya I** accedes to the throne of **Vijayanagar**. His capital is besieged by the neighbouring Bahmani ruler Feroz Shah. He gives his daughter in marriage to Feroz Shah, who lifts the siege. Reconciliation is short-lived, however.

1412 Deva Raya I is succeeded by King Viyajaya I.

1413 With the death of Nasiruddin Mahmoud Shah, the Tughluq dynasty effectively ends.

1414 **Khizr Khan**, the governor of Panjab, invades Delhi and overthrows Nasiruddin's feeble successor. Regarding himself as merely a viceroy of Shah Rukh, he does not assume the title of Shah, meaning Sultan. His jurisdiction extends only to Delhi, Panjab and the Doab.

1419 King Vijaya of Vijayanagar dies.

1421 Khizr Khan's son **Mubarak** assumes the title Shah and founds the **Sayyid dynasty**. He tries to quell rebellion in the Doab, but in vain.

In (independent) Bengal, the ruler Iliyas Shahi receives the Chinese admiral-diplomat Zheng-Ho, representing the Ming dynasty.

1422 In Daulatabad, Feroz Shah of the Bahmani dynasty is succeeded by Ahmad.

1434 In Delhi, Mubarak Shah is assassinated at the behest of his prime minister, Sarwar al Malik. He is succeeded by his nephew Muhammad Shah who is unable to reverse the disintegration of the Delhi sultanate.

1435 In Daulatabad, Ahmad Shah is followed by Alauddin Ahmad.

1440 Birth of **Kabir**, a poet and a preacher of Muslim-Hindu amity.

Kabir 1440–1518

A poet and religious reformer, **Kabir** sought to promote Hindu-Muslim amity by drawing equally upon the tradition of *bhakti* (devotion) among Hindus (see p.99) and of mystical Sufism (see p.175) among Muslims. Born out of wedlock to a brahmin widow living near Varanasi, he was adopted by a Muslim weaver. As a young man he became one of the twelve disciples of **Ramanand**, a southern-born Vishnuite reformer who preached in Hindi his simple creed of the unity of God to which he admitted all, irrespective of caste or creed. But Kabir broke away from Ramanand and developed his own doctrine, which he expressed in memorable couplets.

He argued that, as organized religions, Hinduism and Islam were keeping humans apart. He either denied altogether the Hindu and Muslim concepts of the Supreme Being – Brahman and Allah – or put them on a par by declaring them identical, and found himself denounced by both brahmins and *ulema*. Furthermore, by advocating the reform of society on an egalitarian basis, Kabir went beyond the idea of co-existence between differing faiths. His denunciation of the caste system appealed particularly to artisans – disliked equally by high caste Hindus and upper-class Muslims – who formed the bulk of his followers, called *Kabirpanthis* (Travellers on the Way of Kabir).

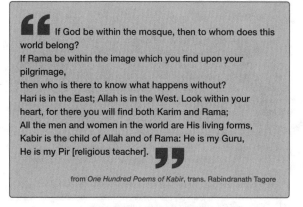

1445 Muhammad Shah is succeeded by his son Alauddin Alam Shah. The disintegration of the Delhi Sultanate continues.

1446 King Deva Raya II of Vijayanagar is the last effective ruler of the Sangama dynasty.

1447 Shah Rukh, son of Timur, dies.

1451 Alauddin Alam Shah is forced by court nobles to abdicate in favour of **Bahlul Lodi**, a former governor of Panjab, whose earlier attempt to topple Muhammad Shah had failed. He now establishes the **Lodi dynasty**. An ethnic Afghan, he goes out of his way to befriend the Turkic aristocracy while allocating large land grants to Afghan nobles, thus moderating the absolutism of earlier sultans.

Foiling an attack on Delhi by the rebellious governor of Jaunpur in the Gangetic plain, he leads his army into Jaunpur, then conquers the adjoining area to the south between Kalpi, Dholpur and Gwaliar. By the end of his rule, his dominion extends from the foothills of the Himalayas in the

Guru Nanak (1469–1539) and Sikhism

Guru Nanak was the founder of **Sikhism**, which attempts to synthesize Hinduism and Islam, and which today has 20 million followers in India. Born into the household of Kalu, a Hindu of the *khatri* (trading) sub-caste in Raypura di Talwandi village (later renamed Nanakwada) in West Panjab (present-day Pakistan), he was educated through the generosity of a Muslim family friend. Later, dissatisfied with his humdrum life as a government storekeeper, he abandoned his wife and three children to join the *sufis* (see p.175), followers of mystical Islam. He parted company with them as well, and travelled through the subcontinent, exploring the possibility of an accommodation between Hindu and Muslim religions.

He came to regard brahmins and *ulema* as co-conspirators bent on fragmenting and appropriating the Infinite, Indivisible, Unknowable God and dividing His followers into Hindus and Muslims, Vishnuites and Shivaites, Sunnis and Shias. He taught that by focusing on the transcendental deity – his Name and his Word as revealed to him, Nanak – and by living virtuously, humans could place themselves on a path to transcend the birth-death cycle and achieve salvation. He denounced idol-worship, and his reiteration of the essential unity of God and the equality of all believers underlined his opposition to the caste system. He abandoned his sub-caste/family name, and became known simply as Nanak.

north to the frontiers of Bundelkhand in the south, and from Panjab in the west to Varanasi in the east.

1457 In Daulatabad, Alauddin Ahmad Shah of the Bahmani dynasty is succeeded by Humayun.

1461 Humayun Shah is followed by Nizam.

1463 Nizam Shah is succeeded by Muhammad III.

1469 Nanak, the founder of **Sikhism**, is born in Panjab.

Eventually returning to his family and village, he refined his doctrine and gathered disciples, who were called *Sikhs* (Learners), he being their Guru (Teacher). Among Hindus he attracted members of the trading and agricultural sub-castes. His insistence that Sikhs discard all outward signs of Hinduism or Islam engendered a strong sense of community. His sayings are contained in the *Adi Granth* ('Original Book'), a compendium of hymns and teachings contributed by him and the nine succeeding Sikh Gurus, the last being Guru Gobind Singh (1666–1708).

Guru Nanak and his companion Mardana meeting King Shivanabh, in a Mughal miniature c.1500

1482 In Daulatabad, Muhammad Shah III is succeeded by Mahmoud Shah.

1489 Sikandar Lodi succeeds his father Bahlul in Delhi. Overcoming several challenges to his authority, he annexes Jaunpur, Bihar and the area south of Gwaliar as far as Nagpur.

He introduces an audit system for government income and expenditure and a code of conduct for Muslim aristocracy.

He reinvigorates the espionage apparatus, withdraws duties on corn and reduces trade tolls.

A religious bigot, he dispenses justice in accordance with the *Sharia*, desecrates many Hindu temples, particularly in Mathura, bans Hindus bathing in the Jamuna, and seeks conversions to Islam through both force and inducements. **Agra**, rather than Delhi, is his preferred capital.

1494 Following his father Shaikh Omar Mirza's death, 11-old Zahiruddin Muhammad, better known as **Babur**, becomes the ruler of the Central Asian kingdom of **Fergana**, a region of modern Uzbekistan. His father is a descendant of Timur while his mother, Qutluq Nigar Khanim, is a descendant of Jenghiz Khan.

1498 **Vasco da Gama**, a Portuguese navigator seeking maritime access to the Eastern pepper and spice trade, rounds the Cape of Good Hope, the southernmost tip of Africa, and anchors at **Calicut** in Kerala. He pioneers annual voyages by a fleet of armed Portuguese merchant vessels.

1500 Babur, embarking on a programme of conquest, captures Samarkand.

1503 The Portuguese build a fort in **Cochin**, and suborn the local raja.

1504 Babur captures Kabul and sets up his headquarters there. In Kabul, people of the Mongol stock are called Moghul or Mughal.

1505 Portugal appoints Dom Francisco de Almeida as its viceroy for its 'State of India'. Babur crosses the Khyber Pass, the first of five incursions into the subcontinent.

1509 Rana Sangha becomes King of Mewar and begins defying the Delhi Sultanate.

1509 Under **Krishna Deva Raya** of the **Tuluva dynasty**, Vijayanagar's forces establish control over all of the peninsula south of the Krishna River and successfully resist the Bahmani sultans of north Deccan.

The key to Krishna Deva's triumphs lies in his pragmatic yet professional military planning: recruiting soldiers from among forest dwellers and non-agriculturists, hiring skilled Muslim and Portuguese gunners, engaging Muslim cavalry, and putting brahmin commanders in charge of a string of fortresses. Emulating the southern sultans, he requires his commanders, called Nayaks, to collect and remit land revenue as well as maintain troop contingents.

Domingo Paes, a Portuguese visitor, estimates the raja's army at one million. To maintain such a huge force, Krishna Deva exacts heavy taxes from his vassals, and levies import-export duties on the burgeoning overseas maritime trade.

1510 **Viceroy Alfonso Albuquerque** captures **Goa** (area 3370 sq km) on the west coast from the Bijapur sultanate, and turns it into the fortified nucleus of Portugal's farflung maritime empire in the Indian Ocean. Portugal also establishes a monopoly in the lucrative horse trade.

1517 Ibrahim Lodi succeeds his father Sikander. Inept and tactless, he alienates the nobility, but its attempts to oust him fail.

In the **Islamic empire**, the Caliphate passes from the Cairo-based Mamalukes to the **Ottomans** in Constantinople (present-day Istanbul).

1518 Following the death of Sultan Mahmoud Shah, the Bahmani dynastic kingdom disintegrates.

1519 Ibrahim Lodi's annexation of Gwaliar adds to his overconfidence and that alienates even his close relatives. Babur advances as far as Bhira in Panjab, then returns to Kabul. Throughout his campaigns, he very effectively combines his mastery of the use of **firearms**, acquired through his long association with Persians, with the Uzbek tactic of *tulgh ma* – a cavalry manoeuvre that involves turning the enemy's flank, then charging it simultaneously in the front and the rear at break-neck gallop.

1522 Domingo Paes, a Portuguese traveller, provides a glowing account of **Vijayanagar**, describing it as being as large as Rome – with more than 100,000 houses and a population of some 500,000 – and admiring its numerous lakes, water courses and orchards. After checking out markets covering 30 sq km, he calls Vijayanagar 'the best provided city in the world'.

He deals at length with the variety of animal and bird meat, with every street having sellers of mutton 'so clean and fat that it looked like pork'. Noting that prostitution is a recognized occupation and a source of government revenue, he writes: 'The women attached to the temples are of loose character, and live in the best streets that are in the city … They are very much esteemed and are classed among the honoured ones who are mistresses of the captains.'

1523 Rebelling against his own kinsman, Panjab's governor Daulat Khan Lodi invites Babur to overthrow Sultan Ibrahim Lodi.

1524 In his fourth Indian expedition, Babur captures large swathes of land east of the Indus. He entrusts these to his lieutenants before returning to Kabul.

1525 Babur is invited by Alam Khan, the Sultan's uncle, and Rana Sangha of Mewar to attack the Delhi Sultanate. In November he leaves Kabul with 12,000 troops.

The Koh-i-Noor Diamond

Originally weighing 186 carats, **Koh-i-noor** (literally Mountain of Light), the globe's most famous diamond, once valued at the equivalent of 'two-and-a-half days' food for the whole world', most probably came from a mine in the **Golkanda/Hyderabad** region of the Deccan. While its early history is obscure, by 1526 it was owned by **Raja Virkramaditya** of Gwaliar, having earlier been the property of **Sultan Alauddin Khalji**, acquired during his Deccan campaigns. Vikramaditya's relatives traded it for their lives with Babur's son Humayun after the climactic Battle of Panipat. Famously, Babur recorded in his journal *Baburnama* how 'Humayun offered it to me when I arrived at Agra. I just gave it back to him.'

During his forced exile in Persia and Afghanistan, Humayun held on to the diamond. In 1739 Nadir Shah of Persia took away the Koh-i-noor and the Peacock Throne to Persia. Following his assassination in 1747 by the Abdali Aghans, the Koh-i-noor passed to their leader **Ahmad Shah**, who established the Durrani dynasty. In 1814, during his forced exile from Afghanistan, **Shah Shuja Durrani** exchanged it for refuge in the domain of **Sikh King Ranjit Singh** (see p.234). In 1849, Ranjit Singh's youngest son **Dalip Singh** was obliged to hand it over to Lord Dalhousie, who then presented it to Queen Victoria, to become part of the British Crown Jewels. It was re-cut in 1852 by Garrards of London. In 1937, weighing 109 carats, it was incorporated as the centrepiece of a crown designed for the coronation of George VI, to be worn later by his consort Elizabeth, better known since 1952 as the Queen Mother until her death in 2002.

1526 On 21 April at the **Battlefield of Panipat**, Babur, leading 12,000 soldiers, faces Ibrahim Lodi's force of 100,000 troops and 1000 elephants. To safeguard his front-line, he lashes together 700 carts, among which are positioned his matchlock-shooters, leaving sufficient gaps for his cavalry to break through. Babur holds in reserve additional flying columns. When battle commences, these columns swing around their foes' flanks and press from the rear, thus depriving them of any room for manoeuvre. Ibrahim Lodi charges repeatedly but fails to break through the cordon of the carts. His army is squeezed so hard that its wings are forced in upon its centre, and it cannot move forward or backward. The Sultan and 15,000 of his followers are killed.

As Babur marches on Delhi to found the **Mughal dynasty**, his eldest son Humayun advances on Agra. There, he encircles the family of Raja Vikramaditya of Gwaliar, a Lodi feudatory killed at Panipat. Among the treasures they offer him in return for their lives is the **Koh-i-noor**.

8
The Mughals
1526–1806

In establishing his Indian empire, **Babur** supplanted fellow-Muslims, Islam providing a continuity of sorts between the Delhi Sultanates and the Mughal dynasty, the two eras together covering six centuries. Since Hindu subjects had become accustomed to Muslim rule by the time Babur arrived, his dynasty presided over a period that saw the flowering of a synthesis between the indigenous and foreign cultures. Out of this emerged a distinctive school of miniature painting, the Kathak dance, the Urdu language, the Mughlai cuisine, and the Red Fort of Delhi and the Taj Mahal.

As often happens with a new dynasty, the **early Mughal rulers** were extraordinarily dynamic, **Akbar** being the most outstanding. Reigning from 1556 for almost half a century, he proved adept at co-opting Hindu nobles into his government and army. This enabled him to put his enlarged dominion on a firm footing. Akbar's policy of tolerance and inclusiveness remains the touchstone of Indian politics at their best. It served his successors well until the accession – amidst debilitating filial bloodletting – of **Aurangzeb**, the last of the Great Mughals, in 1658.

Ironically, Aurangzeb's rule marks both the Mughal empire's territorial zenith as well as the beginning of its end. Re-imposing the much-detested *jizya* poll tax on Hindus, debilitating his army and exchequer by prolonged and unecessary wars, and wary of delegating authority, he proved incapable of controlling the sons he had failed to train for the responsibility of government during his overly long reign. Those who succeeded Aurangzeb are rightly called the **Lesser Mughals**. Without exception, they were ineffectual rulers, powerless to resist the aspirations of the long-suppressed Hindus in the north, now

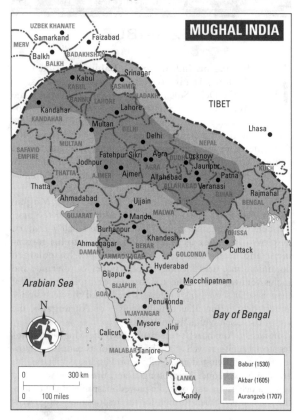

MUGHAL INDIA

UZBEK KHANATE
Samarkand • Faizabad
MERV
Balkh • BADAKHSHAN
BALKH
Kabul • Srinagar
KABUL KASHMIR LADAKH
Kandahar Lahore
KANDAHAR LAHORE
Multan DELHI
MULTAN Delhi
SAFAVID Fatehpur Sikri Agra Lucknow
EMPIRE Jodhpur OUDH Jaunpur
THATTA Ajmer Allahabad Patna
AJMER Varanasi
Thatta ALLAHABAD BIHAR
Ahmadabad Ujjain BENGAL
GUJARAT Mandu MALWA
Burhanpur Rajmahal
Ahmadnagar Khandesh ORISSA
BERAR
DAMAN AHMADNAGAR GOLCONDA Cuttack
Bijapur Hyderabad
BIJAPUR Macchlipatnam
Arabian Sea GOA
Penukonda
N VIJAYANGAR Bay of Bengal
Calicut Mysore Jinji
MALABAR Tanjore
LANKA
0   300 km
Kandy
0   100 miles

TIBET

Lhasa •

NEPAL

KUCH

Babur (1530)
Akbar (1605)
Aurangzeb (1707)

supplemented by the newly emergent Sikhs. Nor could they counter the separatist tendencies of Bengal in the east, or meet the challenge posed by the Marathas in the Deccan.

Once again, the northwest frontier became a liability, with the Persian army making periodic incursions into the northern plains. Yet the next foreign conquest of the subcontinent would come from an unexpected quarter – **Europe**. The presence of Europeans in South Asia, heralded by **Alexander the Great**, was not new. What was novel was the way they came – by sea.

Once the dominance of Islam in the Middle East and the Crusades had blocked existing land routes, including the Silk roads, European merchants did their utmost to find a maritime alternative to break the Muslim monopoly over the trade in spices, essential for the preservation of food as well as enhancing its taste. By the early 16th century, Portuguese merchants were perched on the western coast of India at Goa, surrounded by a spice-growing hinterland. Yet it was not the Portuguese, nor the Dutch and French following in their footsteps, who set about suborning India. It was the **English**. Their instrument was the **East India Company**, established in 1600, to trade with the East.

The Great Mughals 1526–1707

Though Babur reigned for only five years, he remained a source of inspiration for his successors. His eldest son, **Humayun**, survived long enough to reclaim the throne he had earlier lost to his Afghan rival, Sher Khan Sur. However, there would certainly not have been a long-lasting Mughal empire but for the many-faceted genius of **Akbar**.

The first Mughal ruler to be born in the Indian subconti-

An informal portrait sketch of Akbar the Great c.1605

nent, Akbar resolved to win the loyalty of all his subjects irrespective of their faith. During the first half of his reign, he expanded the nobility from 55 members – almost all non-Indian Muslim – to 222, with nearly half of them Indian, including 43 Rajputs. With their help, he expanded and consolidated his domain, which included two-thirds of the subcontinent and almost all of Afghanistan.

Akbar's successor **Jahangir** was equally tolerant of Hindus, and **Shah Jahan**'s intolerance was tempered by the liberal disposition of his favourite daughter, Jahanara, and by his eldest, favourite son, Dara Shikoh, a free-thinker. Politically, by controlling their Afghan subjects, the successors of Akbar freed the Persian empire to challenge its rival to the west, the Ottomans, at the same time encouraging it to deter an invasion of the Mughal domain by Central Asian nomads. This in turn enabled the Mughals to focus on the south.

Yet they faced a dilemma. On the one hand, any attempt at outright annexation of territories below the Mughal Deccan carried the risk of upsetting the delicate balance between several diverse forces within the empire at large; on the other it was essential for the emperor to periodically exercise his restive soliders. Shah Jahan solved the problem by conducting occasional skirmishes with the Persian emperor over Kandahar, taking care not to escalate hostilities into full-scale war.

By contrast, **Aurangzeb** needlessly provoked revolt in Rajputana even before he had fully pacified rebellious tribes in the Afghan region. He thus alienated two powerful Rajput clans that had hitherto fought for the Mughals enthusiastically since Akbar's reign. His action stemmed from his propensity for Muslim exclusivity, a counterpoint to Akbar's inclusiveness. By alienating the Hindu literate castes, who largely manned the Mughal administration, he undermined the nerve system of his empire. His re-introduction of the **jizya tax** provided common grievance for such disparate non-Muslim groups as the Rajputs and Sikhs in the north and the Marathas in the south.

Overall, the synthesis that the successful Great Mughals achieved went beyond statecraft. It permeated all walks of life – language, art, music, painting, architecture and cuisine. **Urdu** – a hybrid language written in Persian script, with its syntax rooted in north Indian tongues, and its vocabulary borrowed from the local vernacular, Arabic and Persian – evolved in military camps but soon spread among civilians.

Impressive monuments like the **Red Forts** in **Delhi** and **Agra**, the **Fatehpur Sikri** complex and the **Taj Mahal** were made possible only as a result of the Mughals' efficient administrative and revenue-collecting system that was, ironically, introduced by **Sher Shah Sur**, the Afghan interloper. It collected surplus from agriculture, commerce and industry more effectively than before. **Todar Mal**, the energetic finance minister of Akbar, conducted extensive surveys of agricultural yields and prices, and devised new revenue districts with similar soil and climate which he assigned to freshly recruited revenue collectors or *zamindars* (revenue farmers) in order to eliminate corruption and fraud. Having calculated assessments for each crop and area, he ordered village headmen or *zamindars* to maintain written records. He could do so only after suspending all existing imperial land grants and placing all land – irrespective of its ownership – under central authority for a period of about five years.

When he restored the old ownership, land revenue, the primary source of imperial income, almost doubled.

Akbar divided his empire into fifteen provinces, each under a governor who was rotated. He maintained his court along military lines. Administrative officials, exercising civilian and military responsibilities, were called *mansabdars* (office-holders). Akbar graded them into 33 ranks, according to the number of soldiers, ranging from 10 to 5000, a *mansabdar* was required to provide for the imperial army. The rank of 7000–10,000 soldiers was reserved for royal princes.

Mansabdars maintained their troops through land revenue derived from the fiefs, or *jagirs*, that came with their office, and which reverted to the emperor upon their retirement, dismissal or death. Some 2000 *mansabdars* commanded a total of 150,000–200,000 cavalrymen, while Akbar's standing army had 25,000–45,000 cavalry. By integrating administrative officials into a single system, Akbar ensured loyalty to the crown by assorted groups – Afghan, Persian, Turkic, Turkoman, Uzbek, Indian Muslim, and Rajput and other Hindus.

But, in the absence of a hereditary peerage – a norm in Europe – there was no countervailing centre of power to the sovereign whose arbitrariness remained unchecked. There was an absence, therefore, of any seed of political democracy. Also, conscious of the return of their property to the crown on their demise, *mansabdars* squandered whatever cash they possessed, thereby preventing accumulation of private capital. Subsequently, it was the private capital available to the English and French trading companies from local sources that would bring about the Mughals' downfall.

The absence of a universally accepted protocol regarding royal succession proved disastrous to the interests of the Mughal empire, as did the impatience of the eldest son when his father's rule lasted too long. Although the preferential claim of an emperor's eldest son to the throne was generally acknowledged, his prerogative was not absolute. Bloody conflicts often erupted, justifying the adage *takht ya takhta*, 'throne or coffin'.

Jahangir, the eldest prince, was the first to rebel against his father, Akbar. He in turn was challenged by his eldest son, **Khusru**, albeit in vain. Khusru's defeat paved the way for **Shah Jahan**, who was the third in line. In his old age, Shah Jahan was imprisoned by **Aurangzeb**, who again was the third in seniority. In turn, the ageing Aurangzeb was challenged, unsuccessfully, by his fourth son, **Prince Muhammad Akbar**, after his senior brothers had either defected, fled or faced arrest. When Aurangzeb protested, Muhamamd Akbar retorted that the emperor was merely reaping what he had sown.

1527 **Babur**, the founder of the **Mughal empire** in northern India, confronts Rana Sangha of Mewar who, refusing to accept Mughal overlordship, defeats the Mughal garrison at Bayana, 70km from Agra, causing many desertions and low morale.

On the eve of a battle at Khanua, 30km from Agra, Babur reminds his commanders that the Rajputs (see p.139) are infidels, and that fighting them means participating in *jihad* (holy war). To underscore his renewed commitment to Islam, he vows never to drink again and orders all goblets and decanters to be smashed and wine skins emptied. Taking an oath on the *Quran* he promises to fight until death. His commanders follow suit. As a result Babur triumphs, despite the numerical advantage Rana Sangha has, commanding 100,000 men.

1529 In **Vijayanagar**, King Krishna Deva Raya is succeeded by his brother Achyuta Deva Raya. Babur defeats an army of Afghans on the banks of the Ghaghra near its junction with the Ganges, west of Patna.

1530 Babur is succeeded by his eldest son **Muhammad Humayun**, an urbane and witty ruler more inclined to

Zahiruddin Muhammad Babur 1483–1530

Babur, the founder of the Mughal dynasty – who combined the daring restlessness of nomadic Mongols and the sophisticated urbanity of settled Persians – is a link between his rapacious antecedent, steppe warrior Timur, and his own suave grandson, Emperor Akbar. He was both a soldier of fortune and a man of refined taste – as much at ease with his sword, commanding the unquestioned loyalty of his troops, as with his pen, an accomplished poet and writer whose wide range of subject matter was matched by critical perception and refined sensibility.

Babur began keeping a journal at the age of 11, when he became the ruler of **Fergana**, and continued the practice until his death 36 years later. Known as the *Baburnama* (Babur's Journal), and described by the 19th-century British historian Mountstuart Elphinstone as 'almost the only specimen of real history in [South] Asia', it is written in his mother tongue, Turki, in a style that is at once sinewy and candid. Except for the missing years 1508 to 1519, the journal details the emperor's experiences in Fergana, Samarkand, Kabul, and the Indian subcontinent, describing their geography, scenery, climate, people, agriculture, industry and works of art, as well as political, military and personal events. Always lively and acute, the *Baburnama* can be refreshingly poignant, as when its author confesses to weeping for days on end at the death of a boyhood friend.

savour stimulating conversation than to consolidate his father's victories.

1534 Portugal annexes **Bassein**, a port just north of present-day Bombay.

1534–36 Emperor Humayun conquers Rajputana, Malwa and Gujarat.

1536 Death of Guru Nanak, the founder of Sikhism (see p.156).

1537 Portugal annexes the district of Diu in north Gujarat to control access to the thriving ports of Cambay, Surat and Broach.

1538–39 Humayun, defeated by Sher Khan Sur, an Afghan noble, at Chausa between Varanasi and Patna, narrowly avoids capture. Sher Khan, well into his 50s, assumes the royal title **Sher Shah**.

1540 Humayun suffers a second defeat at the hands of Sher Shah, whose 15,000 mainly Afghan cavalry overpowers his well-equipped army of 40,000 at Kanuj. The empress is taken prisoner, but Humayan escapes. Sher Shah installs himself on the throne in Delhi.

Sher Shah adds Panjab, Sind and Malwa to his dominion. Drawing on his experience of running a large estate in Bengal, he rationalizes assessment and collection of land revenue, grants security of tenure to cultivators, and holds village headmen accountable for unsolved crimes. Separating authority between civil, military and religious offcials, he rotates them. He constructs military posts as well as roads and caravansarais, and builds a new administrative centre in Delhi at **Shergarh**, 10km north of the Qutb Complex. He is the first to mint the **Indian silver rupee**, which survives four centuries.

1542 In Vijayanagar, **Rama Raja**, son-in-law of Krishna Deva Raya, accedes to the throne with the assistance of the Deccani sultans. The ousted emperor Humayun, still on the run after being refused sanctuary by his younger brother Kamran, the governor of Kabul, fathers **Jalaluddin Muhammad** (later Akbar) by his newly wedded wife, Hamida Bano Begum, at Umarkot in Sind.

1544 Humayun meets Persia's Shah Tahmasp, a Shia Muslim, at Sultaniye in north-west Persia. After he has adopted Shia Islam, the two exchange gifts. Shah Tahmasp provides Humayun with 12,000 troops, as well as courtiers and artists.

1545 Sher Shah is fatally burned in an accident involving artillery rockets as he lays siege to Kalinjar Fort between Allahabad and Khajuraho. His five-storey, fifty-metre high mausoleum at Sasaram, between Varanasi and Gaya, resting on an octagonal platform in the midst of a lake, will be acclaimed as an outstanding example of synthesized Indian and Muslim architectures. He is succeeded by his son **Islam Shah**.

1545 Humayun seizes Kandahar in southern Afghanistan.

1553 Humayun captures Kabul from his brother Kamran and recovers his young son, Jalaluddin Muhammad. For his earlier transgression Kamran is blinded.

1554 Islam Shah is succeeded by his 12-year-old son Firoz Shah Sur. The boy is soon murdered, and his uncle **Muhammad Adil Shah Sur** assumes the throne. His territory fragments into quasi-independent provinces, and this encourages Humayun to recover his empire.

1555 Humayun defeats the Sur governor of Panjab at Sirhind, occupies Delhi, and reclaims the imperial throne.

1556 Emperor Humayun falls to his death from the roof of his palace where he has installed a temporary observatory. He is succeeded by his eldest son, Jalaluddin, aged 13, who is in Panjab with his guardian **Bairam Khan**, a Turkoman of Shia persuasion.

Jalaluddin is crowned at Kalanaur, assumes the title **Akbar** (Great), and appoints Bairam Khan as his regent.

The Mughal garrison at Delhi is put to flight by an army of Muhammad Adil Shah Sur led by his chief minister Hemu, a Hindu general with 22 military victories to his credit.

At the **Second Battle of Panipat** in November, however, Hemu is hit in the eye by an arrow and collapses in his elephant howdah. His soldiers lose heart and run. Hemu is captured and decapitated.

1557 Akbar transfers his capital from Delhi to **Agra** on the banks of the Jamuna and orders the construction of the **Red Fort**. Bairam Khan regains Panjab, Gwaliar, Ajmer and Jaunpur (present-day eastern Uttar Pradesh).

1560 Sharp differences in age and temperament between Akbar and Bairam Khan lead to the dismissal of the regent, who is advised to go on pilgrimage to Mecca. The power vacuum is filled by Akbar's mother Hamida Bano Begum, his former chief nurse Maham Anaga and her son Adham Khan.

1561 Emperor Akbar appoints Shamsuddin as his chief minister.

Emperor Jalaluddin Muhammad Akbar, r.1542–1605

Of the Great Mughal emperors **Akbar** was the greatest, and stands beside Ashoka as one of India's most widely admired rulers. What is remarkable is that he grew up an illiterate, having resisted learning at the palace of his uncle, Kamran. Most probably he was dyslexic, but he had an unbounded curiosity, a sharp intellect and a prodigious memory, as well as a strong athletic physique and a courageous personality. Soon after assuming full imperial power at 20, he took to appearing early each morning at a balcony window of his palace, to show himself to his subjects, a presentation ritual – called *darshan*, viewing (an idol or god) – which his two successors followed. But Akbar's majesty was more than a matter of parade or presentation. He was an outstanding general who lived by his martial doctrine: 'A monarch should ever be intent on conquest, otherwise his neighbours rise in arms against him. The army troops should be exercised in warfare lest from want of training they become self-indulgent.' As his court record shows, Akbar seldom if ever wavered from his principles, military or civil, during his long reign.

1562 When Shamsuddin is fatally stabbed by Adham Khan, Akbar orders Adham Khan to be hurled from the palace walls. From this point onwards, Akbar exercises supreme civil and military authority without a chief minister.

The Red Fort at Agra is finished.

1563 Akbar marries **Jodh Bai**, a daughter of Raja Bihar Mal of Amber (later Jaipur), a Kachhwaha Rajput who, having been loyal to Humayun, accepts Akbar's suzerainty.

The emperor inducts Bihar Mal, his son Bhagwan Das and grandson Man Singh into the imperial order as *mansabdars* (office-holders), allowing them to keep their fiefdoms, Hindu religion and caste in return for providing specific numbers of cavalry during imperial campaigns.

Akbar, attracted to **Sufism**, claims to have visions that bring him into direct communion with Allah. Adopting the principle *Sulh-i-kul* (tolerance of all), he abolishes pilgrimage tax on Hindus, the *jizya* poll tax on non-Muslims and forbids the enslavement of prisoners-of-war.

1565 In the south, an alliance of four Deccani sultans defeats and beheads Rama Raja of **Vijayanagar** at Talikota. As Vijayanagar is abandoned, the raja's officials cart away 550 elephant-loads of treasure from the city. Its destruction damages the trade of Portuguese Goa.

1565–67 Akbar quells a rebellion of Uzbek officers in Afghanistan seeking to elevate Kamran's son to the imperial throne.

1567–68 Akbar besieges the **Chitor fort** of Rajput Raja Udai Singh of Mewar (later Udaipur). The Raja and his son escape to the hills, but Akbar continues the siege. As Rajput womenfolk undertake self-immolation, the defenders fight to the death. Furious, Akbar orders the massacre of some 25,000 non-combatants. His troops loot the fort and then abandon it.

Sufism

While subscribing to the general theory of mysticism – that direct knowledge of God is attainable through intuition or insight – **Sufism** is rooted in doctrines and methods derived from the *Quran*. Some early Muslims – inspired by Prophet Muhammad's withdrawal into a cave and nightly vigils – resorted to ascetic exercises as a means to getting close to Allah. They stressed meditation and contemplation of the Creator, and regarded involvement in worldly affairs as a distraction from the path of seeking Allah within.

These men were called Sufis, from the word *suf* (wool) because of the simple woollen garments they wore. Over time two types of Sufi emerged: the ecstatic and the sober. Among the latter, **Abu Hamid Muhammad al Ghazali** was the most prominent. He tried to furnish the Islamic legal system with a spiritual infrastructure originating in Prophet Muhammad's mystic consciousness. His work became the basis for the orders that sprouted after his death in 1111. It was common for a Sufi order to establish its own convents. An example of a mainstream order was the **Naqshbandi**, named after **Bahauddin Naqshband** (1318–89), in Tajikistan. Believing that piety was best expressed through social activity, Naqshbandis opposed withdrawal from the world. Whereas ordinary Islamic rituals were austere, Sufi orders provided a framework within which rich and colourful liturgical practices grew.

Sufism spread rapidly between 1250 and 1500 when the caliphate was based in Cairo under the Mamluke sultans, and when Islam penetrated South and Southeast Asia as well as Central and West Africa. It was through Sufism that Islam was often able to absorb pre-Islamic beliefs and practices of the new converts. Today many Sufi orders exist among Muslims of the Indian subcontinent.

1569 Akbar captures a Rajput fort at **Ranthambhor**. For his thanksgiving he visits the shrine of the Sufi saint Muhy-iuddin Chishti in nearby Ajmer. Then he calls on the saint's descendant Salim Chishti at Sikri, 50km west of Agra. Here Akbar's Rajput wife Jodh Bai gives birth to a son whom he names Salim. The prince will grow up learning Persian, Turkish, Arabic and Urdu, and takes an interest in botany, zoology, music and painting.

Akbar begins building a mosque and other facilities near Sikri, all in striking red sandstone and called **Fatehpur** (Town of Victory) **Sikri**.

1570 Fatehpur Sikri becomes Akbar's capital.

1572 Akbar conquers Gujarat with its cotton and indigo crops, and its port city of Surat which trades with Arabia, the Persian Gulf, Egypt and East Africa. To commemorate this victory, he builds a 57-metre-high, 42-metre-wide entrance gate at Fatehpur Sikri. Called the **Buland Darwaza** ('Lofty Gate'), it becomes the symbol of his empire.

1574 Akbar appoints **Abul Fazl**, the son of his liberal-minded courtier Shaikh Mubarak, official chronicler. A loyal, industrious, learned man of commanding intellect, Abul Fazl will write the 2500-page *Akbarnama* ('Akbar's Journal'), a year-by-year account of Akbar's reign, and the 1500-page *Ain-i-Akbari* ('Institutions of Akbar').

1576 Akbar conquers **Bengal**, with its abundance of rice, silk and saltpetre. During this campaign he gains some knowledge of Christianity from Father Julian Pereira, Jesuit Vicar-General of Bengal.

1577 The Emperor grants a land site and water tank to the Fourth Sikh Guru Ram Das at **Amritsar** in Panjab. Sikhs will later build the **Golden Temple** there and make Amritsar their centre.

1579 The **Portuguese** obtain imperial permission to establish a trading post at **Satgaon** in Bengal from where they later migrate to a site on the **Hooghli River**, which becomes an important commercial centre.

Emperor Akbar upsets orthodox Muslims by declaring from the pulpit of the main Fatehpur Sikri mosque that he is the final authority on interpreting the *Sharia* (Islamic law), until then the prerogative of the Chief Mufti.

1580 At Akbar's invitation, two **Jesuit missionaries** arrive in Fatehpur Sikri from Goa. They join debates, chaired by Akbar, between scholars of different faiths – Islam, Hinduism, Jainism, Zoroastrianism – that are held at the court. Akbar's secret aim is to devise a faith that will transcend religious differences and unite his subjects.

1581 Disgusted by Akbar's idiosyncratic religious initiatives, and encouraged by a *fatwa* (religious decree) issued against him by the Mufti of Jaunpur, his younger brother **Muhammad Hakim**, governor of Kabul, tries to seize Panjab, but fails. Akbar leads an expedition to Kabul and overthrows his brother.

1582 Akbar proclaims *Tauhad Illahi* (Divine Monotheism), popularly called *Din Illahi* (Divine Faith). It is an eclectic creed based on the concept of one God with the emperor serving as his viceregent on earth and authorized exponent of His will. He issues coins with the Islamic invocation 'Allah-u Akbar' (God [is] Great), a play on his own regnal name. He decrees that his subjects must prostrate themselves before him, and that his portraits carry a halo. Yet Akbar does little else to institutionalize *Din Illahi*, which will die with him. All eighteen of its professed adherents are courtiers, and all but one Muslim.

1583 The Jesuit mission returns to Goa, having failed to convert Akbar to Christianity.

1585 Prince Salim marries a sister of Raja Man Singh, a Rajput courtier. Ambitious to conquer the northwest, Akbar moves his capital from Fatehpur Sikri to **Lahore**.

1586 Akbar annexes **Kashmir** when the local ruler resists total submission and an annual tribute.

1587 **Shah Abbas** accedes to Persia's imperial throne.

1588 England's defeat of the Spanish Armada presages greater English involvement in the lucrative Eastern spice trade.

1591 Akbar annexes southern **Sind**.

1592 Raja Man Singh conquers **Orissa** on Akbar's behalf.

1594 The Emperor annexes **Baluchistan** with its Makran coast.

1595 Akbar seizes **Kandahar** from Shah Abbas of Persia. The strategic Kandahar fort, guarding the passage to both the Indian subcontinent from the west, and to Kabul from the south, gives the Mughal Emperor control of all the subcontinent north of the Narmada, as well as Ghazni and Kabul, with an estimated combined **population** of 100 million.

1595–98 As monsoon rains fail in consecutive years, Akbar's measures to relieve famine prove inadequate.

1597 Having secured the northwestern sector of his empire, Akbar turns his attention to Deccan, moving his capital from Lahore to **Agra**.

1599 Prince Murad, the second of Akbar's three sons, dies of excessive drinking.

1600 Elizabeth I of England grants a charter with exclusive trading rights to the 'Governor and Company of Merchants of London trading into the East Indies', subsequently known as the **East India Company**.

1600–1 In his **Deccan campaign**, Akbar captures Khan-desh and part of Ahmadnagar.

1602 Prince Salim, viceroy of the eastern sector of the empire, declares himself emperor at the Allahabad Fort, and issues imperial decrees. Convinced that Abul Fazl is poisoning the ears of Akbar against him, Salim persuades Raja Bir Singh of Bundel to murder the royal chronicler then *en route* to Agra from the Deccan.

1603 Salim and Akbar are reconciled in Agra. But when the Emperor orders his son to lead a campaign against the rebellious Rajput Rana of Mewar, Salim prevaricates. Akbar sends him back to Allahabad where he again sets up an independent court.

1604 Daniyal, the youngest of Akbar's sons, dies of alcoholism. Akbar summons Prince Salim, an opium addict, to court under threat of naming Salim's 17-year-old son Khusru his heir. When Salim prostrates himself before the emperor, Akbar appears satisfied. But afterwards he takes the prince to his private quarters, slaps him and confines him to a bathroom, depriving him of opium for ten days. After releasing him, the emperor names him the crown prince. Under the guidance of the Fifth Guru, Arjun Das, the Sikh holy book, ***Adi Granth*** ('Original Scripture'), is compiled.

1605 Salim re-erects the **Ashoka pillar** (see p.84) at Allahabad having inscribed it with his own genealogy. When his father falls ill with dysentery, Salim is summoned to Agra. Unable to speak, Akbar gestures that his imperial turban be placed on Salim's head and the imperial sword be hung on his side.

Akbar is buried at Sikandara, near Agra. Salim assumes the throne, taking the name **Nuruddin** (Light of Faith) **Muhammad Jahangir** (World Conqueror). His official chronicler will be Abdul Hamid Lahori, author of *Badshah-*

nama ('emperor's journal'). Incongruously combining decadence, cynicism, childish naivete and candour, Jahangir takes as much delight in witnessing men flayed alive, impaled or torn to pieces by elephants as in sighting wild flowers in Kashmir. 'Sovereignty does not regard the relations of father and son,' he notes in his memoirs *Tuzuk-i Jahangiri*. 'The king, it is said, should deem no man his relation.'

1606–7 Prince Khusru escapes semi-confinement in the Agra Fort and rebels unsuccessfully against his father. On Jahangir's orders, Khusru's eyes are sealed with stitches. Years later, when his father relents, his eyes are unstitched, with one eye regaining vision.

1608 Captain **William Hawkins** of England arrives at Jahangir's court, presents gifts worth 25,000 gold pieces, and delivers a letter from King James I. The emperor appoints him a *mansabdar*, commanding 400 soldiers, with

> 66 In the course of nine years I got up to 20 cups of double distilled spirit [arak], 14 of which I drank in the afternoon and the remaining six at night. My food in those days was one fowl and some bread. No one dared to expostulate with me, and matters reached such an extreme that when in liquor I could not hold my cup for shaking and trembling. I drank but others held the cup for me. One of my father's doctors told me that six more months of drinking would put me in my coffin. So I tapered off to six cups of mixed wine and spirits daily. Then I took to opium. 99
>
> Jahangir, cited in Waldemar Hansen, *The Peacock Throne: The Drama of Mogul India* (1968)

an annual salary of 30,000 rupees, and arranges his marriage to a daughter of the Armenian Christian Mubarikesha. He joins Jahangir in his drinking bouts. In his memoirs, the emperor will boast of being more alcoholic than his great-grandfather, Babur, having started on wine at the age of 14, before graduating to *arak*. Despite the Islamic injunction against alcohol, Jahangir appears on his coins with a drinking cup to hand.

c.1609 Tobacco is first introduced into India. Like James I of England and Shah Abbas of Persia, Jahangir considers it obnoxious and forbids its consumption.

1611 Jahangir marries 33-year-old Mihr un Nisa ('Light among Women') and renames her first Nur Mahal ('Light of the Palace'), to match his own name Nuruddin, and then **Nur Jahan** ('Light of the World'). Her brother Asaf Khan becomes master of the imperial household. Captain Hawkins returns to England.

1612 Jahangir consolidates Mughal control of **Bengal** following the death of the last Afghan rebel, Usman Khan, in battle.

The East India Company sets up a factory at Surat, and defeats the Portuguese navy in the nearby Swally estuary.

Twenty-year old **Prince Khurram** (lit. Joyous), the third son of the Emperor after Khusru and Parwez, marries Asaf Khan's 19-year-old daughter **Arjumand Banu**, who acquires the name **Aliya Begum**. She is Khurram's second wife, bears him fourteen children (of whom four sons and three daughters survive), and becomes his confidante.

1615 Khurram defeats Rana Amar Singh of Mewar and his son, Karan. Jahangir is so delighted to succeed where his illustrious father Akbar had failed that he gives Karan Singh a high rank of 5000 soldiers.

Nur Jahan 1578–1645

Nur Jahan, the Mughal empress with the highest public profile, was born Mihr un Nisa in Kandahar, the daughter of Ghiyasuddin Muhammad, a Persian noble. In 1591 Ghiyasuddin travelled to India and entered Emperor Akbar's service.

Mihr grew up as a woman of stunning beauty, raven-haired and blue eyed. She was married to Ali Quli Sherafkun ('Lion Thrower'), a noble with a fiefdom in Bengal by whom she had a daughter, Ladila. In 1607, after her husband had stabbed Bengal's governor and was killed by the latter's attendants, Mihr and her daughter were brought back to the royal court at Agra. There, Emperor Jahangir became infatuated with her. After four years' wooing, she agreed to marry him. Following their wedding, her father was given the title Itimad al Dawla ('Trust of the Realm'), and became virtual prime minister. Mihr's brother too, Itiqad Abul Hassan, renamed Asaf Khan, was promoted head of the imperial household.

As Nur Jahan, she became co-ruler in all but name. When Jahangir fell ill, she signed imperial decrees. She held her own court, and was renowned for her horsemanship, her tiger hunts and her Persian poetry. Domineering, highly intelligent and astute, she set trends in fashion. Unprecedently in Islam, her imperial husband struck coins in her name, with the inscription: 'By order of Emperor Jahangir, gold has a hundred splendours added to it by receiving the name of Nur Jahan, the Empress Begum'. Her daughter Ladila married Shahriyar, the youngest of Jahangir's sons.

Having been part of a trio – Asaf Khan, Shah Jahan and herself – that effectively ran the empire for several years, Nur Jahan broke with Shah Jahan when she realized she could no longer manipulate him. She then backed Shahriyar as the successor to the throne, but in vain. She died a natural death.

18th century Mughal miniature of Nur Jahan (seated) with attendants on a terrace

> Greatly bejewelled, the Emperor entered the royal scales, sitting like a woman on his legs while being balanced against silver, gold and gems ... endless weighings followed – against gold and silk, spices, then meat, butter and wheat. The weighing over, the emperor ascended his throne and threw basins of silver nuts and fruits to scrambling nobles.
>
> Sir Thomas Roe, in Waldemar Hansen, *The Peacock Throne: The Drama of Mogul India* (1968)

Sir Thomas Roe, English King James I's exceptionally able envoy, arrives at Jahangir's court in Ajmer to negotiate a treaty with the Mughal Emperor. Immediately taking note of the court's ambiance of velvet and silk canopies, carpets and an elevated throne set above a railed precinct, Roe later describes other facets of court life, including ceremonial weighings of the emperor on his birthday in a large garden, attended by nobles sitting on rugs.

1616 At a ceremony in Agra, Prince Khurram reviews his army – including 600 richly trapped elephants and 10,000 cavalrymen – before Emperor Jahangir, who bestows upon him the title **Shah Jahan** (Ruler of the World).

When bubonic plague strikes the Agra area, Jahangir decides to move his court to follow Prince Khurram/Shah Jahan's southern campaign. On joining the royal camp, the English diplomat Roe is overwhelmed by the sight of the emperor in his ceremonial attire, with his belt of gold, his sword and scabbard 'encrusted all over with great diamonds and rubyes'.

1618 Sir Thomas Roe leaves for England without the treaty sought by James I, but with a written confirmation of the rights Jahangir has bestowed on English traders.

1620 Jahangir conquers **Kangra** in the foothills of the Himalayas. He hands over the custody of Prince Khusru to Prince Khurram/Shah Jahan, now based at Burhanpur, the Mughal administrative capital of north Deccan.

1622 In January, Khurram (Shah Jahan) informs his father that Khusru has died of dysentery. Khusru is in fact murdered at Khurrram's instigation.

Shah Abbas of Persia retakes **Kandahar**. Jahangir orders Khurram to march against Shah Abbas, but he refuses and stages a rebellion.

1623–25 Prince Parwez defeats Khurram (Shah Jahan), who withdraws to Bengal. Defeated again, he retreats to Deccan where he befriends an old enemy, **Malik Ambar**,

> ❝ On his head he [Emperor Jahangir] wore a rich turbant with a plume of herne tops, not many but long; on one syde hung a ruby unsett, as big as a walnut; on the other syde a diamond as greate; in the middle an emarlld like a hart, [but] much bigger. His shash was wreathed about with a chaine of great pearles, rubyes and diamonds, drilld. About his neck he carried a chaine of most excellent pearle, three-strand double (so great I never saw); at his elbows, armletts sett with diamonds; and on his wrists three rowes of several sorts; and every finger boasted a ring. A chain of pearls, rubies and diamonds covered his midriff. ❞

from *The Embassy of Sir Thomas Roe to India, 1615–19*

in Ahmadnagar, and gains respite. He is reconciled with Jahangir after sending his sons, Dara Shikoh and Muhyiuddin Muhammad Aurangzeb, to Agra as hostages, but does not himself appear at court.

1625 The East India Company sets up factories on the eastern coast of India. Prince Parwez dies, ostensibly of drink, but is more likely to have been poisoned by Khurram (Shah Jahan).

1626 In the south, Malik Ambar, the Nizam Shahi sultan of Ahmadnagar, dies, and is succeeded by his son **Fateh Khan**. Muhammad Adil Shah becomes the ruler of **Bijapur** and slowly expands his kingdom until it extends from coast to coast.

1627 Emperor Jahangir dies in October at Rajaur, in the foothills of Kashmir, while Khurram (Shah Jahan) is in Junnar (near present-day Bombay). His younger brother **Shahriyar**, the only other surviving prince, being at the court in Lahore, declares himself emperor.

> ❝ Let your heart be as fresh as a sweet garden. The letter of love and friendship which you sent and the presents, token of your good affection toward me, I have received by the hands of your ambassador Sir Thomas Roe (who well deserveth to be your trusted servant) .... I have given my general command to all the kingdom and ports of my dominion to receive all the merchants of the English nation as the subjects of my friend, that in what place soever they choose to live they may have reception and residence to their own content and safety, and what goods soever they desire to sell or buy, they may have free liberty without any restraint. ❞
>
> Jahangir's 1618 Letter to James I of England

In Agra, Asaf Khan names **Dawar Baksh**, the minor son of Khusru, as acting emperor. In a battle near Lahore, Asaf Khan defeats Shahriyar, who is blinded.

1628 In January Khurram (Shah Jahan) marches on Agra. He decrees the execution of Prince Shahriyar, Dawar Baksh and the sons of the deceased Prince Daniyal. He then assumes the imperial title **Shihabuddin** (Flame of Faith) **Muhammad Shah Jahan**, and Aliya Begum, his favourite wife, becomes **Empress Mumtaz Mahal** (Favourite of the Palace). He appoints Asaf Khan his chief minister, and Mahabat Khan his commander-in-chief. Behind the scenes, Mumtaz Mahal acts as Shah Jahan's confidante.

The tomb of **Itimad al Dawla** in Agra is finished according to the design of Nur Jahan, his daughter. A delicately constructed monument in white marble, with snub-minarets, a square-cut dome, latticed windows, and inlay decoration of semi-precious stone, its feminine refinement becomes a bridge between the muscular sandstone structures of Akbar and Jahangir and the Taj Mahal (see p.188).

1629 Death of the poet **Tulsi Das**, born nearly a century earlier in Varanasi. His many books include a free translation of Valmiki's *Ramayana* (see p.28) from Sanskrit into Hindi, entitled ***Rama Charita Manasa*** ('Rama's Life Story'). Enjoyed as much by the literate elite as the illiterate masses, it lays the foundation for modern Hindi. An outstanding poet with an extraordinarily sensitive ear for the melody and harmony of Hindi words, Tulsi Das laces his predominantly spiritual verse with sensuous imagery.

1630–32 Monsoon failures cause famine in Gujarat and the Deccan. Shah Jahan, by now widely recognized as a just ruler, acts effectively to alleviate suffering. His intolerance toward non-Muslims is tempered by Dara Shikoh, his eldest and favourite son, and Jahanara, his favourite daughter.

The Taj Mahal

Regarded as one of the wonders of the world, the **Taj Mahal** transcends history as, in the final analysis, it is a truly spiritual achievement. Working closely with his chief architect, **Ustad Ahmad**, **Shah Jahan** decided that his homage to the departed empress **Mumtaz Mahal** should combine the bulbous dome of Emperor Humayun's mausoleum with the white marble and delicate semi-precious stone inlay of Itimad al Dawla's. It should also integrate the dramatic safeguarding by minarets at the four corners of the platform as in Emperor Akbar's tomb, with the feminine grace provided by the expert landscaping of Emperor Jahangir's gardens.

It took 20,000 workmen twenty years to complete the complex. Their ranks included master masons, calligraphers, dome specialists, pinnacle builders and stone-cutters recruited not only from all over India but also from Kandahar, Samarkand, Baghdad and Istanbul. The procurement of the building materials too was eclectic. While its white marble came from quarries in Jodhpur, and red sandstone for its gateway, garden walls, mosque and guesthouse from Fatehpur Sikri, its precious and semi-precious stone inlays were purchased from further afield: turquoise from Tibet, lapis lazuli from Sri Lanka, jasper from Gujarat, malachite from Russia, carnelian from Baghdad, and chrysolite from Egypt. Agate, amethyst, black marble, chalcedony, jade, quartz and sardonyx were procured from equally sundry sources. Lifting heavy marble slabs to the height of 80 metres required a four-kilometre ramp – a device similar to that used to build the Egyptian Pyramids.

Shah Jahan's aim was to evoke paradise on earth. His almost floating edifice erected between the flowing waters of the Jamuna at the back and a clear pool of water in front comes close to building the divine throne. A remarkable combination of fine art, scientific calculation, outstanding technical skill, flawless construction, perfect layout, sensuous charm, and its essentially spiritual ambiance makes the Taj Mahal unique.

The classic view of the Taj Mahal, which Tagore described as 'a solitary tear suspended on the face of eternity'

1631 Shah Jahan mounts a campaign to annex Ahmadnagar, Bijapur and Golkonda in the south. He is at Burhanpur when his empress Mumtaz Mahal dies in childbirth, aged 39. Her body is interred there for six months and then transferred to a provisional sepulchre in Agra on a plot beside the Jamuna. As a sign of bereavement, the emperor refuses to wear coloured or embroidered clothes, appearing only in white, the Islamic colour of grief. He forswears music as well as perfume.

1632 At **Hooghli port** the Portuguese tax local merchants heavily and kidnap children for conversion to Christianity. In retaliation, the Mughal governor Qasim Ali Khan captures Hooghli, kills many Portuguese and dispatches many more to Agra.

Mahabat Khan, leading a Mughal army, takes over the Ahmadnagar Fort by bribing the Nizam Shahi boy sultan Hussein Shah and his regent Fateh Khan. Following his appointment as governor of the Deccan, Mahbat Khan attacks Daulatabad, the new capital of Hussein Shah, and deposes the young sultan, thus ending the **Ahmadnagar dynasty** of the Nizam Shahis.

As work begins on a mausoleum for Mumtaz Mahal, to be called the **Taj Mahal** (Crown of the Palace), the emperor ends his long, self-imposed bereavement.

1634 Supervised by its designer, Berbadal Khan, the **Peacock Throne**, one of seven constructed for the Mughal emperors, is completed after six years' labour. Built as a cot bedstead standing on golden legs, it is covered by a pearl-fringed enamelled canopy supported by twelve golden pillars, each resting on two peacocks encrusted with gems and separated by a tree of diamonds, emeralds, pearls, rubies and sapphires. Other Moghul thrones include an oval-shaped bath-tub. Shah Jahan's personal treasure consists of gold and silver stored in two underground strong rooms each measuring 23 x 23 x 10 metres, and jewellery kept in the imperial jewel house.

1635 Pressured by Shah Jahan, Abdullah Qutb Shah of **Golkanda** accepts Mughal suzerainty, and issues coins in the emperor's name.

1636 Following his refusal to accept Shah Jahan's overlordship, Sultan Adil Shah of Bijapur is attacked and defeated. He accepts Mughal suzerainty. Between them, the two rulers divide up the remaining Ahmadnagar kingdom. Shah Jahan appoints his third son **Prince Aurangzeb**, aged 18, viceroy of Deccan, now consisting of four renamed provinces – Khandesh, Berar, Telangana and Daulatabad – with 64 forts.

1638 The governor of **Kandahar** defects from the Persians to the Mughals. Finding the Red Fort in Agra too small, the emperor orders the construction of a new city, called **Shahjahanabad** (later known as **Old Delhi**) on the banks of the Jamuna, to the north of the earlier Khalji–Tughluq settlements (see p.143 and p.130)

1640 The East India Company sets up a factory in **Madras** and builds Fort St George.

1643 The central dome of the Taj Mahal is completed.

1645 Nur Jahan dies. Shah Jahan transfers Prince Aurangzeb from Deccan to Gujarat.

1647 John Albert de Mandelslo, a French aristocrat, visiting employees of the (London) East India Company stationed at Surat, notes their white linen coats and turbans, and finds them playing darts and enjoying 'wheat bread, beef, and mutton prepared by English cooks, and Indian delights of kedgeree and pickled mangoes'.

1648 In April Shah Jahan and his court move to the newly completed Shahjahanabad. In October the Persians recapture Kandahar.

Shahjahanabad

Shahjahanabad (literally Shah Jahan's Town) is the original name of today's **Old Delhi.** A planned city of 26 sq km with wide roads, shaded canals, bazaars and inns – enclosed by massive walls, adorned by 27 towers and open at 11 gates – it ultimately became home to some 400,000 people. Hidden behind the towering red sandstone walls of the **Red Fort**, rose an impressive ensemble of royal palaces, representing an austere culmination in white marble. The court consisted of the **Diwan-i Khas** (Hall of Special Audience) and **Diwan-i Aam** (Hall of Public Audience). The inscription in Persian letters of gold in the Diwan-i Khas -'If there be paradise on earth, it is this, it is this, it is this' – summed up the aspiration of **Shah Jahan.**

Outside the Red Fort stood the **Jama Masjid**, Friday Mosque, then the largest mosque in the Indian subcontinent, and the imposing thoroughfare of **Chadni Chowk**, Silver Square. The imperial complex of the Red Fort remains mostly intact, its parapet providing a dramatic setting for such state occasions as Independence Day, when a speech is delivered by the incumbent prime minister.

The Moti Masjid, or Pearl Mosque, was built by Aurangzeb in 1662 for his own use

1649 Shah Jahan transfers Prince Aurangzeb to Multan.

1652 Aurangzeb fails to retake Kandahar, and Shah Jahan loses confidence in his military abilities. The emperor returns Aurangzeb to the Deccan as Viceroy.

1653 An attempt by Shah Jahan's eldest son, **Dara Shikoh** – viceroy of Allahabad, Panjab and Multan – to regain Kandahar also fails. The Taj Mahal is completed.

1655 On February 3, his 65th birthday by the Islamic (lunar) calendar, Shah Jahan confers on Prince Dara Shikoh the title Shah Buland Iqbal (Lucky Lofty Ruler), and seats him on a golden chair next to the Peacock Throne. Dara Shikoh thus becomes co-ruler. Although a Sunni Muslim of the Hanafi school, he is steeped in Sufism (see p.175). A scholar and a believer in the principle of *Sulh-i Kul* (tolerance of all), he studies the Talmud and the Bible, Hindu scriptures and the writings of Sufi saints.

He translates the *Upanishads* from Sanskrit to Persian under the title, *Sir al Asrar* ('The Secret of Secrets'), and argues that the essential nature of Hinduism is identical with Islam's. He is critical of those *ulema* who apply the *Sharia* literally. 'Paradise is where no mullah abides,' he quips. His behaviour angers orthodox Muslims, including his austere brother Aurangzeb.

1656 A strict Sunni, Aurangzeb resolves to destroy the Shia ruling dynasties of Bijapur and Golkonda, especially as they have rich treasuries, with the Golkondan capital of Hyderabad being the world centre of the diamond trade. Since Golkonda's Sultan Qutb Shah is in arrears with his annual tribute, Aurangzeb besieges his fort and the Sultan surrenders.

In Bijapur, Muhammad Adil Shah is succeeded by his 18-year-old son **Adil Shah II**.

1657 Aurangzeb invades Bijapur and cedes its Bidar region. A total conquest of the kingdom is within sight when Emperor Shah Jahan intercedes and ratifies a treaty with the Bijapur sultan, allowing him to cede only three districts to the Mughal empire and pay a large indemnity.

In September Shah Jahan falls ill. Officially, he suffers acute constipation; in reality he has overdosed on aphrodisiacs taken to satisfy his lust for a young Moorish woman. He rallies after a week and appears at the *jharoka* window of the palace. But this is not enough to stave off the War of Succession. **Prince Muhammad Shuja**, the second in royal seniority and governor of Bengal, declares himself emperor and strikes coins in his name. The youngest prince, **Muhammad Murad Baksh**, based in Gujarat, does the same. Shah Jahan moves from Delhi to Agra to be near the Taj Mahal.

1658 Aurangzeb joins in the succession struggle by making imperial land grants. He strikes a deal with Prince Murad Baksh whereby, once in power, they will divide the empire, Murad claiming the northwest, and Aurangzeb the rest.

Their combined forces defeat an imperial army sent by Shah Jahan and led by Prince Dara's eldest son, Suleiman Shikoh. They march toward Agra, but are intercepted by Prince Dara. During the battle Murad Baksh is injured, but when Dara abandons his elephant after it is targeted by enemy guns, his troops, disheartened by the sight of the empty howda, disperse. Dara flees.

The royal Red Fort at Agra surrenders to Aurangzeb and Murad Baksh. Aurangzeb imprisons his father Shah Jahan. Murad Baksh attempts to defect, but is seized and jailed. Aurangzeb ascends the throne.

1659 Aurangzeb defeats Prince Shuja's forces at Khajwa in Fatehpur district. His general, Mir Jumla, chases Shuja and his family into the Arakan region of Burma, where they are reportedly slaughtered by the Magh tribe a year later.

Emperor Shihabuddin Muhammad Shah Jahan 1592–1666

As the builder of **Shah Jahanabad** and the **Taj Mahal**, **Shah Jahan** is the most renowned of the Great Mughals at home and abroad. For three decades his stern hand maintained the empire built by his grandfather Akbar. Although the first signs of military weakness appeared when he failed to recapture Kandahar from the Persians, the inherited military-administrative machine had enough momentum to continue functioning effectively. Having led an extraordinarily eventful life, and having acceded to power only by eliminating his two elder brothers, in his later years he helplessly witnessed the internecine warfare for the throne between his sons – **Dara Shikoh**, the Mystic; **Shuja**, the Playboy; **Aurangzeb**, the Schemer; and **Murad Baksh**, the Reckless. In this bloody contest, his favourite, Dara Shikoh, lost, and success went to Aurangzeb, who was unmoved by the pleas of his father from a prison cell. In response to Shah Jahan's advice against intrigue, Aurangzeb merely retorted: 'How do you still regard the memory of [your brothers] Khusru and Parwez, whom you did to death before your accession and who had threatened no injury to you?'

Prince Muhammad Sultan, Emperor Aurangzeb's eldest son, who has joined Shuja's camp out of his hatred for Mir Jumla, becomes his father's prisoner. Aurangzeb then defeats Prince Dara near Ajmer, but again Dara escapes.

Aurangzeb enters Delhi, claims the Peacock Throne, acquires the title Alamgir (Conqueror of the Universe) and issues coins in his name. As he does not want a Quranic epithet customarily inscribed on Mughal coinage to be defiled by the touch of infidels, he prescribes a Persian couplet: 'This coin has been stamped on earth like the shining full moon by Emperor Aurangzeb Alamgir.'

In line with the Islamic injunction of 'enjoining virtue and suppressing vice', he appoints *muhtasib*, guardians of public morals, to supervise bazaars and suppress such unIslamic pusuits as gambling and the consumption of alcohol. He dismisses court dancers, musicians and artists, discontinues his predecessors' practice of appearing on a palace balcony at dawn as unnecessarily immodest, and commissions a contingent of *ulema* to compile a comprehensive document on Hanafi jurisprudence within the Sunni sect.

Overall, Aurangzeb's zealotry is tempered only by the presence at his court of such senior Hindu aristocrats as **Raja Raghu Nandan** (the finance minister), and **rajas Jaswant Singh** of Marwar and **Jai Singh** of Jaipur (senior commanders).

When Prince Dara is finally captured near the Bolan Pass, connecting the subcontinent with Afghanistan, Aurangzeb consults the court *ulema*. They rule that Dara is guilty of apostasy, punishable by death. Dressed as a beggar, he is placed on a small, unwashed elephant and paraded through Delhi before being decapitated. On receiving Dara's severed head, Aurangzeb dispatches it to their imprisoned father.

1659 Having captured forty forts in the mountainous Western Ghats region of Ahmadnagar and Bijapur, **Shivaji Bhonsle**, son of a Maratha Hindu landowner in Bijapur murders Afzal Khan, a senior commander of Aurangzeb.

1661 Aurangzeb encourages a son of Ali Naqi – the finance minister of Gujarat murdered by Prince Murad Baksh in 1657 – to demand blood money according to the *Sharia*. Murad Baksh is tried by an Islamic judge, found guilty and beheaded.

Forming an alliance with England against Holland, Portugal cedes its settlement of Bom Bahia (lit., Good Bay; later **Bombay**) Island as part of Catherine of Braganza's dowry on her marriage to King Charles II.

> **"** When Aurangzeb learned that the head of Dara had arrived, he ordered it to be brought to him in the garden on a dish, with the face cleaned of surface blood and a turban on [his crown]. He called for the lights to be brought so that he might see the mark borne by the Prince on his forehead, and might make sure that it was Dara's head, and not that of another person. After he had satisfied himself he told them to put it on the ground, and gave it three thrusts in the face with the sword he carried by way of his staff, saying, 'Behold the face of a would-be king and emperor of all the Moghul realms. Take him out of my sight.' He gave secret orders to place the head in a box, to be sent by runners to the eunuch Itibar Khan, who had charge of Shah Jahan's prison, with orders to deliver it to him when seated at the table. **"**

Niccolao Manucci, *Storia do mogorl, Story of the Moghul*, trans. W. Irvine

1663 Death of Aurangzeb's Hindu finance minister Raja Raghu Nandan.

1664 Shivaji Bhonsle sacks Surat, but fails to dislodge the East India Company. The French meanwhile establish **La Compagnie des Indes Orientales**.

1665 Aurangzeb introduces differential customs duties, 5 percent for Hindu traders and half as much for Muslims, only to make Muslims exempt two years later.

Under the protection of Raja Jai Singh of Jaipur, Shivaji Bhonsle visits the Mughal court, expecting to be recognized as a sovereign prince. Instead, he is given the rank of a commander of 5000 men. Feeling insulted, he escapes.

Mughal Art and Architecture

The originality and appeal of Mughal art and architecture lie in their synthesis of Indian and Persian elements. **Mughal architecture** reached its apogee during the reign of **Shah Jahan**, manifest in the **Taj Mahal** and the **Moti Masjid (Pearl Mosque)** at Agra, as well as Shahjahanabad. Shah Jahan's monuments are characterized more by feminine elegance (derived from white marble) than masculine strength from red sandstone used by his father, Jahangir, and grandfather, Akbar, and by the lavish use of costly decoration, seen strikingly in the delicate *pietra dura* inlay of Florence, but executed in precious and semi-precious stones, which supplanted the simpler marble mosaic of the sandstone carvings of the earlier Mughal period. At the same time, the indigenous Indian features that figured prominently in his predecessors' edifices faded.

In **painting**, Shah Jahan's court artists permitted themselves to be influenced by European pictures that arrived with the Portuguese and the English, and began introducing certain amounts of shading and more subdued colours. This, coupled with their sharpness of vision and steadiness of hand, resulted in portraiture that was refreshingly free from the stiffness characteristic of earlier and succeeding periods.

Jahangir was himself a painter and draughtsman. Besides designing some of the wall decorations for the Agra palace, he made drawings of beasts and birds local to Kashmir. He also had an eye for miniatures, which, under his patronage, developed into a high point of Indian art. Earlier, Akbar had gathered numerous artists to decorate his palaces at **Fatehpur Sikri**. Eminent among these were **Khwaja Abdul Samad**, a Persian, and **Daswa Nath** and **Baswan** of North India. What emerged as a result of their collaboration was a series of animated and crowded scenes in dramatic motifs embellishing the palaces.

Jahangir's great love of nature is reflected in this painting by Abdul Hasan and Mansur entitled 'Squirrels in a Plane Tree'

1666 Shaista Khan, the Mughal viceroy in Bengal, captures Chittagong from the King of Arakan. The imperial court's announcement that the emperor has secured the submission of 'Tibet' applies, in reality, to Ladakh at the western extremity of the Tibetan plateau, whose ruler has agreed to mint coins bearing the name 'Alamgir'.

Shah Jahan dies in captivity in Agra Fort and is buried next to his wife at the Taj Mahal.

1667 The Afghani Yusufzai tribe rebels in the northwest.

Raja Jai Singh dies while campaigning in the Deccan, and is succeeded by his son Raj Singh.

Aurangzeb dispatches battle-hardened Raja Jaswant Singh to the Deccan to assist Prince Muazzam, the emperor's second son. Bribed by Shivaji Bhonsle, the two men successfully advise Aurangzeb to grant Shivaji the title Raja.

1668 Charles II of England leases Bombay to the East India Company.

Aurangzeb orders his official chroniclers to stop recording events as he considers such activity immodest and therefore un-Islamic.

1669 Aurangzeb is angered by reports that in Varanasi, Multan and Sind brahmins are giving public lectures on Hindu scriptures which are attracting Muslims. He orders provincial governors to destroy Hindu schools and temples and prevent the teaching and practice of idolatrous forms of worship.

As the centre of phallic worship, repugnant to most Muslims, **Varanasi** is Aurangzeb's prime target: its Vaishvanath Temple is razed and replaced later by the Great Mosque of Aurangzab. A similar fate befalls the imposing Keshava Deva Temple in Mathura.

1670 Shivaji Bhonsle again sacks Surat, and once more the East India Company defends itself.

1671 Aurangzeb transfers Raja Jaswant Singh from the Deccan to the Jamrud garrison near the Khyber Pass. He decrees that all imperial clerks and accountants must be Muslim, but as there are insufficient qualified Muslims he reduces their quota to 50 percent.

1672 The Afridi and Khatak Afghan tribes rebel.

1674 Aurangzeb moves his capital to the Afghan region and conducts a series of successful campaigns against the rebels. These campaigns empty his treasury, however. Also, by alienating Afghans, their recruitment into the imperial army to quash other rebels is precluded. Further, by deploying his best Mughal soldiers to fight in the northwest, Aurangzeb relieves pressure on **Raja Shivaji**, who is crowned as an independent sovereign in the Deccan.

The **French** establish a trading settlement at Pondicherry in the south.

1675 On learning that some Muslims have embraced Sikhism, Aurangzeb orders the execution of the ninth Sikh Guru, Tegh Bahadur. Under the leadership of his son **Gobind Singh**, Sikhs withdraw to the Himalayan foothills in Panjab where the young Guru moulds them into the militant **Khalsa Panth** (Pure Brotherhood). They take up arms first against local hill rulers, then the Mughals.

1676 Prince Muhammad Sultan is executed by Aurangzeb.

1678 The death of Raja Jaswant Singh of Marwar (later Jodhpur) – the highest ranking Hindu commander – removes the last restraint on Aurangzeb's intolerance toward non-Muslims. He annexes Marwar.

1679 Aurangzeb reimposes the *jizya* poll tax, assessed at 0.65 percent of the value of property, on non-Muslims,

The Khalsa Sikhs

The **Khalsa Sikhs** came into being in the late 17th century. The tenth and last Sikh Guru, **Gobind Singh** (1666–1708), prescribed a baptismal rite, called *pahul*, that required initiates to drink consecrated water stirred with a dagger. This done, a male added Singh (Lion) to his name, and a female Kaur (Princess). Gobind Singh further decreed that males must adopt the 'Five Ks': *kess* (uncut hair); *kanga* (comb); *kachha* (underpants); *kara* (steel bangle); and *kirpan* (dagger). These prescriptions made male Khalsa Sikhs distinctive from Hindus and Muslims, giving them a lasting identity. His ban on smoking – included in his saying 'Wine is bad, *bhang* (hemp) destroys one generation, but tobacco destroys all generations' – is yet another notable characteristic of Khalsa. He revised and enlarged the Sikh scripture, *Adi Granth*, and declared that it was on a par with a (human) Guru, thereby precluding the need for further human Gurus to guide Khalsa Sikhs. The scripture was henceforth called *Guru Granth Sahib*.

Concentrated in the Panjab and its northern foothills, the Khalsa Sikhs would emerge as a combative political-military force, taking advantage of and contributing to the waning of the Mughal empire. Their holy warriors, called *Akalis* (eternals), matched the Muslim *Ghazis* (warriors).

abolished by Akbar over a century earlier. He calls on Rajput Maharaja Raj Singh of Mewar (later Udaipur) to enforce the tax. The maharaja refuses.

Two imperial armies under **Prince Muhammad Akbar**, the emperor's fourth son, attack Mewar as well as the Rajput-ruled Marwar. They destroy 200 Hindu temples. Raj Singh escapes to the peaks of the Aravali Hills, which stand between the two Mughal armies, and harassses them alternately. In desperation, Aurangzeb orders his third son, **Prince Muhammad Azam**, to take charge of the Rajputana campaign. Politically, the reintroduction of the *jizya* tax provides a common platform to disparate, non-Muslim opposition, consisting of Rajputs, Sikhs and Marathas.

1680 Raja Raj Singh of Jaipur and Shivaji Bhonsle are succeeded respectively by their sons Jai Singh and Shambhaji Bhonsle.

1681 Muhammad Akbar defects to the rebel Rajputs, then declares himself emperor. Aurangzeb endeavours to win him back with threats and promises, but the Prince retorts 'All sons have equal claim to the property of their father.'

Muhammad Akbar marches toward Aurangzeb's camp at Ajmer, but his slow progress allows the emperor to gain reinforcements from Delhi. Aurangzeb also plants a forged letter, supposedly written by Muhammad Akbar, into the Rajputs' hands, detailing the prince's intention to betray his newfound allies.

Abandoned by the Rajputs and most of his own soldiers, Muhammad Akbar flees to the Deccan where he allies with the rebellious **Marathas**.

> ❝ What good did you do to your father
> That you expect so much from your son?
> O thou who art teaching wisdom to mankind,
> Administer to thine own self what thou art teaching to others!
> Thou art not curing thyself,
> Then, for once, give up counselling others. ❞
>
> Prince Muhammad Akbar, admonishing his father, Emperor Aurangzeb
> in 1681

Raja Jai Singh concludes peace with the emperor and cedes three sub-districts in lieu of paying the *jizya*. But the Rajput Marwar kingdom remains unbowed during Aurangzeb's lifetime.

1682 Anticipating a direct challenge from Maratha-backed Prince Muhammad Akbar, and wishing to enlarge his domain, Aurangzeb marches southward to the Deccan, but fails to capture his son.

The Marathas

The **Marathas** are the inhabitants of **Maharashtra**, bounded by the Tapti River to the north, Goa to the south, the Arabian Sea to the west, with the line of its eastern border running through Bidar to Chand on the Wardha River. Maharashtra's most prominent geographic feature is a chain of mountains running parallel with its coastline, called the **Western Ghats**. Their flat summits – well supplied by monsoon rain water and protected by walls of smooth rock – form natural fortresses. Down the centuries these were fortified into virtually impregnable strongholds from which guerilla warfare could be waged.

Aside from a brahmin minority – among whom the Chitpawans are best known as the providers of the Peshwas rulers – the Marathas belong to the *shudra* caste. Small and sturdy, they are renowned for their perseverance. As agriculturists they are sober and frugal, with a touch of guile. As village chiefs they supplied the administrative backbone of the kingdoms of Ahmadnagar and Bijapur. As soldiers they were as courageous and enterprising as Rajputs, but did not share Rajput concepts of honour, valour and self-sacrifice. For a Maratha, victory was to be achieved by any means, fair or foul. His adversaries therefore regarded him as a formidable foe.

1685 Aurangzeb entrusts a campaign against Golkonda to his eldest surviving son, **Prince Muazzam**, who promptly makes a pact with Golkonda's sultan. His father reluctantly endorses it.

1685–87 The East India Company chairman Sir Josiah Child persuades English King James II to send twelve ships to seize the Bengali port of Chittagong, but the Mughal navy defeats them.

1686 Much to the disapproval of Prince Muazzam, who thinks it unwise to destroy Muslim sultanates in the south, Aurangzeb annexes **Bijapur**, ending the Adil Shahi dynasty.

1687 The East India Company transfers its west Indian headquarters from Surat to strategically safer Bombay.

1687–88 Aurangzeb arrests Prince Muazzam for corresponding with the Deccani sultans. He annexes Golkonda and ends the Qutb Shahi dynasty. In so doing, however, he frees Maratha chiefs from local rivalry. They begin channeling their joint resources into an armed struggle against the Mughal empire.

1688 The East India Company, whose ships have begun attacking Mughal naval vessels off Bombay, is expelled by Aurangzeb from Bengal, where La Compagnie des Indies Orientales is allowed to establish a settlement at Chandernagore on the Hooghli River.

1689 Aurangzeb's troops capture and execute **Shambhaji Bhonsle**. His young son Shahu is taken hostage and handed over to the royal household. Shambhaji's brother, Raja Ram, succeeds him.

On the west coast, Aurangzeb's forces capture Bombay, thus ending the **First Anglo-Indian War** with a victory for the Mughals.

WERNER FORMAN ARCHIVE

An official of the East India Company smoking a water-pipe

1690 The East India Company's envoys seek Aurangzeb's pardon. In return for a sizeable indemnity and a promise of future good conduct, the emperor restores the Company's commercial privileges, hands back Bombay, and allows it to resume its operations in Bengal. Job Charnock, the former head of the Company's base in Hooghli, returns there and founds the future city of **Calcutta**, with a fortified factory at Fort Williams.

1691 By exacting tribute from Tanjur and Trichinopoly in the deep south, Aurangzeb establishes the maximum extent of the Mughal empire, which now consists of 21 provinces, six of them in the south.

1694 To Muhammad Azam's displeasure, the emperor releases Prince Muazzam and appoints him Governor of Kabul. There, Muazzam defeats his renegade brother Prince Muhammad Akbar who, with Persian assistance, commands 12,000 cavalry.

1695 Aurangzeb forbids Hindus, except Rajputs, to ride elephants or horses, use palanquins, or carry weapons.

1698 Despite his old age and use of a walking stick, Aurangzeb continues his fort-capturing campaign in the Deccan, believing it to be a *jihad* against the idol-worshipping Marathas. Most of his spare time is spent transcribing the *Quran* and stitching skull caps for the pious. Disappointed in three of his four surviving sons, he now bestows his favours on the youngest, **Kam Baksh**.

1700 Raja Ram Bhonsle is succeeded by his wife, Tara Bai.

1705 Aurangzeb occupies the Maratha fort at Wakinkera after it has been evacuated by the enemy, his last military exploit.

1706 Emperor Aurangzeb moves his capital to Ahmadnagar.

1707 Aurangzeb dies. His corpse is laid to rest beside the tombs of local saints at Khuldabad near Daulatabad. In accordance with his wishes, his own tomb is a plain block of plastered masonry on an open platform with no canopy.

In the inevitable contest for the succession that follows, Muhammad Azam is killed fighting Prince Muazzam south of Agra. At 63, Muazzam, becomes emperor with the title **Bahadur Shah I** (Brave King). In this contest, the tenth Sikh Guru Gobind Singh sides with the eventual winner.

The Lesser Mughals 1708–1806

Aurangzeb's long campaign in the Deccan prevented him from properly attending to the administration of the empire in the north, the bastion of the Mughals. Long and recurring wars of succession ruined the imperial fabric, debilitated the military machine and created an environment conducive to anarchy.

To administer an expanded empire required a larger number of *mansabdars* (office-holders), who had to be provided with crown land. But in the post-Aurangzeb era, as the empire contracted, there was not enough royal land for distribution. There was also a decline in the size and quality of the nobility due to the recurring wars of succession, fighting between competing peers for governorship, alienation of Rajputs, gross favouritism by weak and incompetent emperors, and the luxurious and extravagant lifestyle of nobles, aware of the loss of their land grant on death.

This was the beginning of the end. What finally brought about the fall of the Mughal empire a century after Aurangzeb's demise was the rot that set in the army, starting at the top. The increasingly degenerate imperial leadership led to the loss of loyalty to the crown and the strengthening of ethnic solidarity – Afghans, Turks and Indians.

The result was an undisciplined and incohesive military, served by shoddy commisariats. The infantry, armed with outmoded, cumbersome matchlocks, came to resemble watchmen rather than trained troops. In the cavalry, the system of strict roll call broke down. As for gunners, their equipment was so outdated that they could fire cannons only once every 25 minutes.

The watershed came in 1739 with the invasion of the northern subcontinent by **Nadir Shah** of Persia. The Mughal empire failed to recover from this body blow. It slid into anarchy, a state highlighted by repeated Maratha incursions into Gujarat, Malwa, Budelkhand and the Doab region between the Ganges and Jamuna.

Equally seriously, the failure of the Mughals to develop their navy left them virtually powerless to resist **European coastal incursions**. As early as 1510, the Portuguese had captured Goa and turned it into the nucleus of a maritime empire in the Indian Ocean. They were followed by the Dutch, the English and the French who, in turn, set up small colonies along the Indian shoreline. It was in this context that **Nawab Siraj al Dawla** (literally Mirror of the Realm), the ruler of Bengal, suffered an ignominious defeat by a small force led by **Robert Clive** of the **East India Company** in 1757 at Plassey.

Even though Clive triumphed more through chicanery than superior generalship or military might, the **Battle of Plassey** is regarded as the event that laid the foundation for the **British empire** in the subcontinent. Without Clive's derring-do and duplicity, this empire would not have been born. Without the calculating cold-mindedness of **Warren Hastings**, it would not have survived its infancy; and without the Subsidiary Treaties of **Marquess Wellesley**, it would not have reached adulthood.

1708 Emperor Bahadur Shah I releases **Prince Shahuji Bhonsle** from captivity. On his return to the **Maratha** domain, civil war breaks out between him and his aunt Tara Bai. Having accepted service at the Mughal court, **Sikh Guru Gobind Singh** accompanies the emperor on a campaign against Prince Kam Baksh in the Deccan. When the Guru is murdered in Nander by an Afghan commander, the Sikh military leadership passes to **Banda Bahadur**, who vows to avenge the execution of Gobind Singh's sons by the Mughal commander of Sirhind, Panjab.

1709 Kam Baksh dies of his wounds having been defeated by his brother Bahadur Shah I in a battle near Hyderabad in the Deccan.

1710 The Sikh leader Banda Bahadur assumes a royal title and mints his own coins. He and his Khalsa Sikh forces sack Sirhind and massacre Muslims. Following their defeat by Bahadur Shah I, however, they retreat to the hills.

1712 Bahadur Shah I is succeeded by his eldest, but worthless, son **Jahandar Shah.**

1713 Jahandar Shah is murdered and the Mughal throne is occupied by his debauched nephew **Farrukh Siyar**. In the Maratha kingdom, on the demise of chief minister (*Peshwa*) Balaji Vishvanath Peshwa, his office passes to his son **Baji Rao**.

1715 Farrukh Siyar defeats and slaughters Banda Bahadur along with 1000 Khalsa Sikh warriors.

1717 The East India Company presents £30,000 worth of gifts to the Mughal Emperor. In return, all duties payable by the Company in Bengal and Surat are commuted to nominal annual payments of £300 and £1000 respectively.

1719 Farrukh Siyar is murdered and the Mughal throne passes to **Muhammad Shah**. An indecisive, pleasure-seeking ruler, he will preside over the slow dissolution of the

Mughal empire, with provincial governorships turning into the hereditary office of **nawab** (aka *nabob*, from *na'ib*, meaning deputy), particularly in Oudh, Bengal and the Deccan. He abolishes the contentious *jizya* poll tax.

1720 On the death of Baji Rao Peshwa, his office of chief minister passes to his son **Balaji Baji Rao**.

1723 **Chin Kilich Khan**, the grandson of a Bukhara noble, and a former viceroy of the Deccan, bearing the title Nizam al Mulk, leaves his post as chief minister at the imperial court and retires to Hyderabad with a view to turning the Deccan into an autonomous kingdom. Unable to stop him, the emperor confirms him as Nizam al Mulk, and gives him the personal title of Asaf Jah.

1727 In the Maratha territory, Raja Shahuji formally hands over all his authority to his chief minister Balaji Baji Rao Peshwa, known henceforth as **Baji Rao II**. In Bengal, Murshid Quli Khan, the long-serving governor who has moved the provincial capital from Dacca to Mushidabad, dies, and is succeeded by his son, Shujauddin Muhammad Khan.

1735 The Marathas under Baji Rao II reach Rajputana.

1736 Nadir Quli Khan, an Afghan nobleman, overthrows the Safavids in **Persia** and takes the royal title **Nadir Shah**.

1737 The Marathas reach the suburbs of Delhi but fail to take the Mughal capital.

1739 Nadir Shah invades the Mughal empire and captures Delhi. After two months in the capital, he carts off 80–90 million silver rupees, an equivalent amount in gold and unminted silver, a store of jewellery including the Koh-i-noor diamond and the Peacock Throne. The Mughal empire, unable to recover from this blow, slides into anarchy.

1740 Alivardi Khan, the deputy governor of Bihar, over-throws **Bengal**'s governor Shujauddin Muhammad Khan, and is recognized as the Viceroy/Nawab of Bengal, Bihar and Orissa by the Mughal emperor. When he stops sending annual tribute to Delhi, however, the region becomes virtually autonomous.

At the Maratha court, Baji Rao II is succeeded by his son **Madhava Rao Peshwa**. Due to a tenfold increase over two decades, the value of La Compagnie des Indies Orientales' trade is now almost half that of the East India Company's annual income of £880,000 a year – equivalent to over 10 percent of the British government's revenue. The East India Company deals in Indian cotton yarn and fabrics, silks, indigo, rock salt, spices, molasses and saltpetre. Both companies also trade with China.

1740–48 During the European War of the Austrian Succession, **Anglo-French enmity** spills over into the Indian subcontinent.

1746 The French take Madras from the East India Company. Among their English captives is **Robert Clive**, a junior clerk.

1747 Ahmad Shah Abdali is elected ruler of Afghanistan by the Abdali Afghans after they have assassinated Nadir Shah of Persia, which includes Afghanistan. He assumes the title Durr-e Durran, Pearl of the Age, which becomes Durrani.

1748 The Mughal emperor Muhammad Shah is succeeded by his son **Ahmad Shah**.

1749 Raja Shahuji Bhonsle of the Maratha court dies heirless. Following an Anglo-French peace accord, Madras is returned to the (London) East India Company.

1750 Balaji Rao Peshwa makes Pune capital of the Maratha confederacy.

1751 Robert Clive, leading 210 armed men, seizes the southern city of Arcot and retains it despite a fifty-day siege.

1752 Following Ahmad Shah Durrani's third and most successful raid on India, the Mughal Emperor Ahmad Shah cedes him the region west of the Indus.

1754 Ahmad Shah is deposed by **Alamgir II**, a son of the deceased Emperor Jahandar Shah. The Marathas make territorial gains in the north.

1756 At Murshidabad in Bengal, Alivardi Khan is succeeded by his grandson Mirza Mahmoud, who assumes the title **Siraj al Dawla** (aka Suraja Dowlah).

In June, reacting to the East India Company's unauthorized fortification of its factory in Calcutta, Siraj al Dawla seizes its factory at Qasimbazar (near Murshidabad) and then, after five days' fighting, captures Calcutta itself, now a city of 300,000 with the Company's Fort Williams at its centre.

While most of Calcutta's 2500 Britons, having taken refuge in Fort Williams, escape by ship, an unknown number are detained in the Fort's prison cell – the so-called 'Black Hole' of Calcutta – measuring six by five metres, with two barred windows. The next morning all but 23 are found dead, their corpses thrown into a ditch and covered with earth. The survivors are set free, except John Zephaniah Holwell, a member of Fort Williams's Council, and three others.

1756–57 Invading northern India, Ahmad Shah Durrani of Afghanistan sacks Delhi.

1757 In January, arriving from Madras by sea, Robert Clive and Admiral Charles Watson retake Calcutta. With Britain and France again at loggerheads during the Seven Years War (1756–63), Clive and Watson sail upstream and over-run the French trading colony at Chandernagore.

The 'Black Hole' of Calcutta

The unfortunate deaths of between 41 and 50 Britons in a detention cell of **Fort Williams** in Calcutta in 1756, were presented as a glaring example of the barbarity of Indians – with a long, compulsory description (much embroidered and exaggerated) appearing in British history text books. First published in 1945, and reprinted as recently as 1967, one such narrative tells us how 'Suraja Dowlah, the Nabob ... a violent youth of nineteen ... marched against Calcutta at the head of 30,000 men. The European residents with fruitless heroism tried to defend Calcutta; but after three days they were forced to surrender ... A mixed company of ... 146 in number, were driven into a narrow prison-cell of the Fort, about 18 feet x 15 feet, with only two small barred windows to admit the air ... Scarcely able to breathe, they had to endure the intense heat of a June night, from seven until six in the morning ... The Nabob allowed the survivors to come forth. But there were only 23 of them.' (Sir Henry Marten and E. H. Carter, *Histories, Book IV: The Modern Age*).

In reality, although Siraj al Dawla's soldiers relieved the British of their valuables, they spared their lives, an act of 'unexpected forbearance', as a more recent British historian puts it. How many lives were actually claimed overnight by dehydration and suffocation remains unresolved to this day. Allowing two sq ft per (standing) person, a 270 sq ft cell would have accommodated 135 persons, all of them standing upright, making John Holwell's figure of 146 an apparent fabrication. Accepting his actual list of less than 50 dead gives a total of about 70 being thrown into the cell. Others have offered a figure of 64, with 41 dying. Whatever the total, the tragic event was unintended. In the late 1970s, the obelisk unveiled by Lord Curzon next to the General Post Office in Calcutta was moved to the compound of St John's Church, next to Job Chamock's grave.

The 'Black Hole' quickly developed into a grisly myth. This French
engraving from the 18th century plays up its most gruesome aspects

On 23 June, at **Plassey**, a village near Qasimbazar on the banks of the Bhagirathi River, Clive joins battle with the forces of Nawab Siraj al Dawla. Despite an overwhelming numerical superiority, Siraj is defeated, losing 500 of his men to the enemy's 18. He flees, but his cousin Miran, son of Mir Jaafar, captures and executes him. Clive's victory paves the way for British domination of India.

The Battle of Plassey

The day after Plassey, the victor **Robert Clive** wrote in a letter, 'It is scarcely hyperbole to say that tomorrow the whole Moghul empire is in our power.' In retrospect, it is hard to dispute the truth of his declaration: subjugation of Bengal paved the way for the British conquest of the subcontinent. The outcome of the battle itself, however, was determined more by politics and duplicity than military skills.

The young, headstrong **Nawab Siraj al Dawla** had already alienated his older, experienced nobles, who preferred his uncle Mir Jaafar, the commander-in-chief. Exploiting intrigue at Siraj's court, Clive bought the loyalty of Mir Jaafar through bribes funded by Aminchud, a Calcutta-based banker to the East India Company. When Aminchund threatened to divulge the plot to Siraj, Clive silenced him by promising (in writing) £200,000 once Siraj had been replaced by Mir Jaafar – a promise he never kept.

Clive led 2200 Indian and 800 European soldiers equipped *inter alia* with 8 six-pounder cannons and 2 howitzers against an enemy armed with 12 cannons and 50,000 troops, three-quarters of them under Mir Jaafar's direct command. After an initial cannonade exchange, Clive retreated behind a hill. Then came a monsoon downpour. It drenched Nawab Siraj's ammunition while Clive's soldiers kept their powder dry under cover. When the rain stopped, Clive's superior artillery fired round after round of cannon balls. Siraj was unable to retaliate. At this point, Mir Jaafar told the Nawab he had no intention of deploying his cavalry against the British. As Siraj's men fled, Clive's advanced.

Nawab Siraj al Dawla in an engraving by Cogneret after Bourdier

1758 The Marathas conquer Panjab, much to the chagrin of Ahmad Shah Durrani. John Holwell, now appointed deputy-governor of Fort Williams, erects an obelisk at the burial place of his fellow prisoners.

1759 Alamgir II is murdered. The Mughal throne passes to his son, Prince Guahar Ali, who takes the title of **Shah Alam II**. He is recognized by Ahmad Shah Durrani.

1760 Following Clive's departure for England, the East India Company replaces the ageing Mir Jaafar as the titular ruler of Bengal with his young nephew **Mir Muhammad Qasim** following the death by lightning of Jaafar's son Miran. Mir Qasim will prove an efficient administrator and tax collector.

1761 In January Ahmad Shah Durrani, heading a coalition of ten armies led by Muslim generals – 42,000 cavalry and 38,000 infantry – joins battle at Panipat with Sadashiv Rao Bhao, a cousin of (Maratha) Madhava Rao Peshwa, leading a coalition of eight armies commanded by six Hindu and two Muslim generals – 55,000 cavalry, 15,000 infantry and 15,000 freebooters. The Marathas lose. With defeat dies their dream of a Maratha empire in the subcontinent. The **Third Battle of Panipat** is as important as the First in 1526, which ended the Delhi Sultanates; or the Second in 1556, which firmly established Mughal rule. At the Maratha court, Madhava Rao Peshwa dies and is succeeded by his brother Naryana Rao Peshwa.

1763 In Bengal, Mir Qasim quarrels with the East India Company over commercial liberties taken by private British merchants. He moves his capital northwards, from Murhsid-abad to Monghyr, and raises an army along European lines. The Company defeats him, and he escapes to Patna where he kills all the British prisoners he has taken. As the Company's troops march to Patna he flees to Oudh. The Company restores his ageing uncle, Mir Jaafar, as the Nawab of Bengal.

1764 Mir Qasim – now allied with Nawab Shuja al Dawla of Oudh, and backed by Shah Alam II, the nominal Mughal Emperor – sets out to regain Patna. But, in the battle at Baksar (aka Buxar) situated between Varanasi and Patna, the 30,000-strong Indian allied army is defeated by the East India Company's 7500 mainly Indian soldiers, led by Major Hector Munro. As a straight armed confrontation without any underhand deception – the determining feature of the Battle of Plassey – the later battle is more important in establishing Britain's military superiority in India.

1765 The East India Company appoints Robert Clive as its Governor of the Bengal 'Presidency'. He restores Shah Alam II to the throne, but only after the Mughal ruler agrees to grant the Company the right to collect land revenue in Bengal-Bihar-Orissa in perpetuity, and enjoy a monopoly over trade in salt, tobacco and betel-leaf as well as permanent exemption from any taxes. In return, the Company agrees to pay Shah Alam II £260,000 annually at his new capital of Allahabad.

1766 John Holwell publishes an account of 'The Black Hole of Calcutta' (see p.214) in which he claims that 123 Britons died in Fort Williams.

1767 Ahmad Shah Durrani mounts his last invasion of India. Clive returns home.

1769 James Watt patents a steam engine, and Sir Richard Arkwright a spinning-frame – crucial developments in Britain's **Industrial Revolution** that – leading to a rapid spread of textile mills in northwest England – will destroy exports of India's handloomed textiles, one of the staples of the East India Company's early trade.

1770 As Bengal is struck by **famine**, the revenue of the East India Company, heavily pillaged by its own merchants, plummets. To reverse the trend, the Company starts auctioning the *zamindari* (ie revenue collection) rights in each village to the highest bidder every five years. This will lead to rack-renting of cultivators and minor rebellions by them.

1772 East India Company directors appoint **Warren Hastings**, with eighteen years' service in India, Governor of the Bengal Presidency. For a substantial fee, he deploys a brigade of Company soldiers to assist the Nawab of Oudh in expelling invaders from his territory, and so sets a precedent for the Company's mercenary activities. Facing bankruptcy, the Company applies for a loan of £1.5 million from the British government, equal to one-tenth of its total revenue.

At the Maratha court, Narayana Rao Peshwa is succeeded by Madhava Rao Narayana Peshwa.

1773 The **Regulating Act** is piloted through British Parliament by Prime Minister Lord North. It approves a loan to the East India Company subject to the Company's agreeing to parliamentary supervision, making its Bombay and Madras Presidencies subordinate to the Bengal Presidency, which henceforth is to be ruled by a Governor-General, assisted by four councillors, with a five-year tenure.

1774 Warren Hastings becomes the first Governor-General of the Bengal Presidency. Lord Clive of Plassey dies.

1775 The East India Company's first war with the **Marathas**, over Bassein and Salsette on the west coast, ends in victory for the Company.

1776 The American War of Independence (1776–81) diverts Britain's attention away from the affairs of India.

1777 Following the loss of its American colonies and their cotton plantations, British governmental and commercial interests encourage cotton-growing in India's Deccan region and in Egypt.

1778 The first Bengali grammar is published.

1779 Warren Hastings is appointed Governor-General of the Bengal Presidency for a second five-year term.

1781 Warren Hastings founds a Muslim theological college (*madressa*) in Calcutta.

The Calcutta Gazette, the first Indian newspaper, appears.

1784 The **India Act**, piloted through Parliament by Prime Minister William Pitt the Younger, invests the British government with ultimate power over the East India Company through a **Board of Control** in London, consisting of the Chancellor of the Exchequer, a Secretary of State for India and four privy councillors appointed by the Crown. The Board is given the authority to recall the Governor-General or any other Company official. Parliament also passes the Commutation Act, which leads to increased tea trade with China.

The Royal Asiatic Society is founded in London to further research into Oriental literature, history and philosophy.

The first sample of machine-made British muslin arrives in Bengal.

1785 Unhappy with the India Act, Warren Hastings resigns and is followed briefly by Sir John McPherson.

1786 **Earl Cornwallis**, an English aristocrat with no East India Company experience, is appointed Governor-General of the Bengal Presidency. He creates a separate class of officials (called **civil servants)**, and distinct from the Company's commercial and military divisions, to administer its Indian territories. He bars Indians from the Company's civil service as well as its military officer corps. He separates judicial from executive functions, and ensures that all judges are British.

Lord Clive of Plassey 1725–1774

Robert Clive, the founder of the British empire in India, was described by a colleague as 'short, corpulent, awkward, unmannerly, gloomy, morose and untractable'. A problem child, his lawyer father found him a clerical post with the East India Company when he was 17. His boredom at the Company's counting house in Madras twice drove him to attempt suicide. Both times his pistol misfired. In 1751 he carried out a daring military manoeuvre that saved the Company's puppet Nawab from being overthrown by the French. Allowed to conduct private trade, Clive enriched himself by suppling provisions to Company soldiers. With £40,000 to his credit, he returned to England and purchased a parliamentary seat.

By 1756 he was back in Madras, and was immediately ordered to retrieve Calcutta from Siraj al Dawla. After his victory at Plassey, the Company received huge compensation from Mir Jaafar and the right to collect revenues worth £500,000 annually. Clive's personal share of the indemnity was £234,000, plus a land grant worth £30,000 a year. On his second return to England, his fortune of £401,000 enabled him to purchase a controlling interest in the Company.

Created Lord Clive of Plassey, he undertook his third and final trip to the subcontinent in 1765. As the Company's Governor of Bengal he struck a deal with Shah Alam II, whereby the latter was restored to the Mughal throne and given a stipend. In return, the Company appropriated land revenues in Bengal-Bihar-Orissa and secured the right to tax-free trading. In 1767 Clive returned home for good. In 1773 the British Parliament censured him for the manner in which he had amassed his Indian fortune. A year later, in poor health, he finally succeeded in killing himself by cutting his throat.

1789 When **Tipu Sultan** of Mysore attacks the British-protected Travancore kingdom in the south, Cornwallis intervenes. He defeats Tipu, who cedes most of the Malabar coast to the Company, giving it a foothold in the far south.

Clive in casual pose, from an engraving by Stoddart

1792 Cornwallis stops periodic auctioning of *zamindari* (ie revenue collection) rights and introduces a system of **permanently settled** estates with annual land revenue, fixed in perpetuity, to be paid to the government by *zamindars*.

This will win the British administration loyalty of *zamindars,* now assured of their landownership rights in perpetuity. Cornwallis also founds a Sanskrit college in Varanasi.

1793 Parliament renews the East India Company's charter for twenty years. **Sir John Shore**, a civil servant, succeeds Cornwallis as Governor-General. Aware that the Company's coffers are depleted, and its army understrength, he pursues a non-interventionist policy in the affairs of local rulers.

Silting of the harbour at Surat leads to the migration of its mainly Parsi merchants to Bombay, where the Company develops its cotton and **opium** exports to China.

1795 At the Maratha court, Madhava Rao Narayana Peshwa commits suicide, and is succeeded by his uncle **Baji Rao II**. In London, Warren Hastings is acquitted of charges of corruption by Parliament after impeachment proceedings lasting nine years.

1798 Marquess Wellesley, a former East India Company Control Board member, is appointed Governor-General of the Bengal Presidency. An interventionist, his declared aim is to elevate the British government to a position of paramount power in India. During his tenure the British Empire *in* India becomes the British Empire *of* India. He introduces the **Subsidiary Treaty**, an instrument for securing formal allegiance of local rulers in India, who are to be called 'subsidiary allies'. He thus creates a two-tiered British rule: direct and indirect.

1799 Wellesley annexes Tanjore in the far south.

Ranjit Singh, a 19-year-old illiterate Sikh warlord, acquires Lahore by siding with Zaman Shah Durrani, a grandson of Ahmad Shah Durrani of Afghanistan, when Zaman Shah attacks Panjab.

1800 Following his treaty with the East India Company, the Nizam of Hyderabad cedes territory to the Company.

1801 Wellesley annexes Carnatic in the south and parts of Oudh in the north.

1802 With the capture of **Amritsar**, Ranjit Singh becomes a formidable Sikh chief.

1803–4 In the **Second Maratha War**, the British destroy Maratha power in central India and the Maratha-administered Mughal government in northern India.

In the Deccan, Wellesley's younger brother Arthur (later Duke of Wellington) defeats a Maratha army. A British force under General Gerard Lake triumphs over the Marathas in Aligarh, and then at Pratabgarh. Lake enters Delhi in September 1803, commandeers Shah Alam II (the blind octogenarian Mughal emperor) and reduces his status to nominal king of Delhi.

1805 An order issued by the East India Company effectively turns Shah Alam II into a pensioner. He ceases to be the overlord of the Company in India and his authority is limited to the Red Fort in Delhi. Lord Cornwallis becomes Governor-General for a second time, but rules only for a few months. He makes peace with the Marathas and withdraws from central India and Rajputana.

1806 Former Mughal emperor Shah Alam II dies, and is succeeded by Akbar Shah II, a ruler without subjects or soldiers.

Invited by one of the quarrelling chieftains in Cis-Satlaj, a region south of the Satlaj River, Raja Ranjit Singh crosses the river and occupies Ludhiana.

Hindu soldiers under British command at Vellore mutiny when new army regulations require them to remove caste marks on their foreheads.

The East India Company

Established by royal charter in 1600, the privately owned 'Honourable Company of Merchants of London Trading Into the East Indies' evolved into a mighty commercial-political-military entity, with its own army and navy and civil administrators, and its activities spreading to China and beyond. It was in India, however, that it acquired its character as 'a delegation of the whole power and sovereignty of the United Kingdom sent into the East', to quote Edmund Burke, an eminent British politician (1783).

Its attempts to secure a Mughal decree, formalizing its trading status and privileges in the empire, succeeded only after its navy had defeated the Portuguese near Surat in 1612. In return, it protected Mughal sea traffic from the Portuguese. By 1700, it had fortified trading stations in Calcutta, Madras and Bombay. With its victory at Plassey in 1757, it became the dominant political power in eastern India.

Financially weakened by its newly acquired administrative task, in 1773 it applied for and secured a loan from the British government, subject to its accepting parliamentary supervision. By now it had commercial, land revenue and judicial branches. In 1784, while the India Act invested the British government with ultimate power over the Company, the Commutation Act set the scene for its increased trade with China. Integral to this was the practice of using **opium**, grown in India, as a barter for tea and other Chinese goods. Indeed, the opium trade proved so lucrative that it became a potent argument for maintaining British hegemony over India.

9
The British Raj

1807–1947

nitially, **East India Company** traders and representatives in South Asia evinced much interest in, and fascination for, the indigenous people and their religions, philosophy and languages. But, as the Company's trading interests became allied to territorial ambition, and as the British – by virtue of successive military victories over the subcontinent's feuding rulers – acquired self-confidence, their curiosity declined.

Unlike previous rulers, **the British**, arriving by sea as fixed-term contracted employees of the East India Company, had an island homeland with a distinct identity to which they returned after their tour of duty. This was not the case with their Afghan, Turkic and Mughal predecessors. Little wonder then, that the British in India kept their identity intact. With the loss of Britain's American colonies in 1783, the centre of its empire shifted to India. Consequently, the distance of the ruling British from the subjugated Indians widened. The new rulers found less and less to admire in anything Indian.

By the late 18th century it had become commonplace among the British, irrespective of class, to despise Indians. 'A race of lamentably degenerate and base [people] with a feeble sense of moral obligation and governed by a malevolent and licentious passion,' was how Charles Grant, a historian, not untypically described Indians in 1792. Forty years on, Edward Trelawny, a contemporary of Percy Shelley and Lord

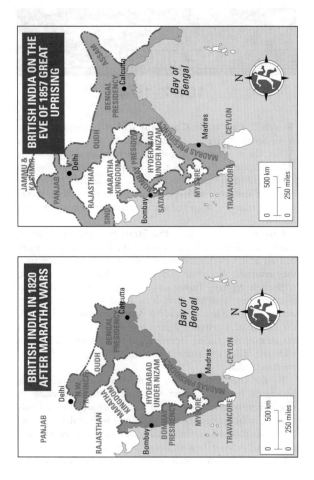

BRITISH INDIA ON THE
EVE OF 1857 GREAT UPRISING

ASSAM

BENGAL
PRESIDENCY

Calcutta

Bay of
Bengal

N

JAMMU &
KASHMIR

OUDH

Delhi

PANJAB

RAJASTHAN

MARATHA
KINGDOM

SIND

BOMBAY PRESIDENCY

HYDERABAD
UNDER NIZAM

MADRAS PRESIDENCY

Madras

CEYLON

MYSORE

TRAVANCORE

Bombay

SATARA

500 km

250 miles

0

BRITISH INDIA IN 1820
AFTER MARATHA WARS

Calcutta

BENGAL
PRESIDENCY

Bay of
Bengal

N

OUDH

N.W.
PROVINCES

Delhi

PANJAB

RAJASTHAN

MARATHA
KINGDOM

HYDERABAD
UNDER NIZAM

MADRAS PRESIDENCY

Madras

CEYLON

BOMBAY
PRESIDENCY

MYSORE

Bombay

TRAVANCORE

500 km

250 miles

0

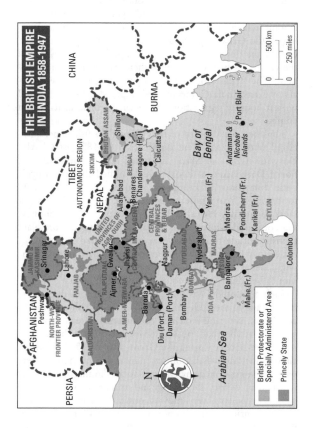

THE BRITISH EMPIRE IN INDIA 1858-1947

CHINA

BURMA

TIBET
AUTONOMOUS REGION

SIKKIM

BHUTAN ASSAM

Shillong

NEPAL

AFGHANISTAN

Peshwar

NORTH-WEST
FRONTIER PROVINCE

JAMMU &
KASHMIR

Srinagar

Lahore

PANJAB

BALUCHISTAN

PERSIA

UNITED
PROVINCES OF
AGRA OUDH

Allahabad

Benares BENGAL
Chandernagore (Fr.)

Calcutta

RAJPUTANA

AJMER-MERWARA

CENTRAL INDIA AGENCY

Gwalior

Ajmer

Jhansi

CENTRAL
PROVINCES
& BERAR

Nagpur

HYDERABAD

Hyderabad

Yanam (Fr.)

Bay of
Bengal

Andaman &
Nicobar
Islands

Port Blair

Baroda

Diu (Port.)
Daman (Port.)

Bombay

BOMBAY

GOA (Port.)

MYSORE

Bangalore

Mahe (Fr.)

MADRAS

Madras

Pondicherry (Fr.)

Karikal (Fr.)

CEYLON

Colombo

Arabian Sea

N

British Protectorate or
Specially Administered Area

Princely State

0   500 km
0   250 miles

Byron, observed: 'Europeans lord it over the conquered natives with a high hand. Every outrage may be committed with impunity.' Such an attitude generated resentment among Indians, which built up over decades, eventually leading to the **Great Uprising** of 1857, when Indians tried to cast off the imperial yoke. The attempt failed, however, and the victorious Britons tightened their grip over the subcontinent. The British government dispensed with its intermediary, the East India Company, and imposed direct rule – and with it housing segregation and racial apartheid in its Indian empire.

Thus began a century of fully fledged British imperialism allied with racism. The publication in 1859 of Charles Darwin's *Origin of Species* spawned, almost immediately, Social Darwinism, a theory which argued that the worldwide dominance of Europeans stemmed from their innate superiority, being inherently better equipped than other races to survive. **Horatio Hubert** (later Lord) **Kitchener**, the comamnder-in-chief of India, summed up the prevalant British attitude thus: 'However well-educated and clever a native may be, and however brave he may have proved himself, I believe no rank we can bestow on him would cause him to be considered an equal of the British officer.'

Such an attitude was prevalent among Britons during the first decade of the 20th century when the British empire was at its peak, covering a quarter of humanity, spread so widely over the globe that the sun never set on it. The empire reached its apogee during the **Great War of 1914–18** when almost one-and-a-half million Indians volunteered for service in the imperial army. Yet no sooner did that armed conflict end in victory for Britain and its allies than nearly 400 unarmed civilians were mowed down by army bullets in a park in Amritsar. The abomination of the **Jallianwala Bagh massacre** in 1919 lodged deep in the Indian psyche. Slowly but surely an independence movement gathered pace. What finally precipitated the end of the British Raj was **World War II** of 1939–45. It left Britain so enfeebled that it lost the will to keep on governing a subcontinent with a population of 360 million.

British rule between 1807 and the Great Uprising of 1857-58

By the beginning of the 19th century, civil administration had supplanted trade as the principal activity of the **East India Company**, which controlled the Bengal, Bombay and Madras presidencies – so called because each of the territories was initially ruled by a president appointed by the Company directors. Given the size of the area under its jurisdiction, the Company needed more manpower for administrative purposes. In 1828 **Lord Bentinck** decided to employ Indians in subordinate positions.

This decision coincided with the aspirations of a rising urban **Hindu middle class**, who were as keen to learn the language of their new masters as they had done of the old ones, in order to serve the British as administrators, moneylenders, revenue collectors and soldiers. By contrast, upper-class **Muslims**, sulking at the loss of their power, shunned the British, and stuck to their social traditions in general, and to Persian and Arabic in particular. Lord Bentinck's order in 1835 to replace Persian with English as the language of government destroyed the last remnant of their influence.

Bentinck's order also foreclosed the debate between **Orientalists**, who wanted education in Sanskrit and Persian to continue, and **Anglicists**, who recommended English as the medium of instruction, in favour of the latter. Their chief spokesman, **Thomas Babington** (later Lord) **Macaulay**, argued that since the Company needed Indian clerks and assistants, it was cheaper to teach them English than teach Indian languages to Britons. 'Our aim should be to create a class of persons Indian in colour and blood, but English in tastes, in opinions, in morals, and in intellect ... who may be interpreters between us and the millions we govern,' he concluded.

Macaulay's sweeping aims were in line with the sentiment prevalent among the Company's directors in London. In the first flush of their success in expelling all other European rivals from the subcontinent, they harboured a wish to lead the heathen natives out of their spiritual darkness into the light of **Christianity**. Indeed, Macaulay confidently assured his evangelical father that in little over a generation there would not be a single idolater left among the respectable classes of Bengal as they all would have embraced Christianity by then.

Faced with Christian proselytization, **Hindu intellectuals** sought to reform Hinduism, attacking its excessive ritual and oppressive caste system, and focusing instead on only one of its three primary gods: Brahma. The result was the **Brahmo Samaj** (Society of Brahma). It was a defensive act, which did not dispel the view then prevalent even among villagers in the north, whether Hindu or Muslim, that the new rulers were determined to impose Christianity. This dreaded perception fuelled the **Great Uprising**, providing the popular underpinning to a mutiny by the British army's Indian soldiers.

The swaggering superciliousness with which the British, from the highest to the lowest, conducted themselves, offended self-respecting Indians of all classes and creeds. In addition, there were other negative developments – social, economic, political – which cumulatively created a feeling of dislocation in different strata of society and accentuated discontent.

India's thriving **cottage cotton industry** was ruined by imports of British mill-made textiles that began flooding the subcontinent from 1824 onwards, leaving many spinners and weavers destitute. The changes to the land revenue system instituted by the East India Company had dispossessed an entire class of Muslim nobles and alienated their long-serving peasants whose loyalty to their masters was as palpable as was their devotion to Islam or Hinduism. The Company's strict application of the **'Doctrine of Lapse'**, whereby adopted or illegitimate sons were disqualified from succeeding their fathers as rulers of the 'Protected States' (aka 'Subsidiary States'), resulted in the annexation of seven such states, creating a host of disgruntled royal families in the years just before the revolt.

From top to bottom, Indian society was rife with resentment. What happened in 1857 was a spontaneous amalgam of an army mutiny, a rural rebellion, and a desperate attempt by various princes to regain their lost patrimony. It was played out in a year-long series of uncoordinated local uprisings, sieges, massacres, attacks and counterattacks, and retributions in northern India – with its epicentre in the province of **Oudh**, where very few estate-holders remained loyal to the British. In the absence of a leader capable of uniting and coordinating the disparate rebellions, the British reasserted control. This heralded the dissolution of the East India Company, the formal end of the **Mughal dynasty**, and the overthrow of the **Marathas** in central India.

1807 **Lord Minto** becomes the **East India Company**'s Governor-General of the Bengal Presidency.

1809 Minto signs the Treaty of Amritsar with **Ranjit Singh**, recognizing the Satlaj as the boundary between the dominions of Ranjit Singh and the East India Company, with Ranjit Singh governing territories north of the river. Minto also signs a friendship treaty with the ruling **Ameers** of Sind.

1813 The British Parliament renews the East India Company charter for twenty years but ends the Company's trading monopoly in everything except opium and China tea.

To protect the burgeoning British textile industry a 78 percent import duty is imposed on Indian fabrics. Parliament also establishes the **Church of England** in India and allows Christian missionaries unrestricted access to the subcontinent. It requires the Company to spend £10,000 annually on education in India.

1813 **Lord Hastings** replaces Lord Minto as Governor-General.

1814 Following his expulsion from Afghanistan, Shah Shuja, a grandson of Ahmad Shah Durrani, seeks refuge in Ranjit Singh's domain. The Sikh ruler agrees to help him in exchange for the **Koh-i-noor diamond** (see p.160).

1816 The Hindu College, the first modern higher education institution in India, is established in Calcutta by **Ram Mohun Roy**, a Hindu thinker and reformer, and his friends.

1818 John Marsham founds the first Bengali weekly newspaper, *Samachar Darpan* (News Mirror) in Calcutta. His example is emulated by Ram Mohun Roy who establishes periodicals in Bengali, Persian and English.

Calcutta's old Fort Williams is demolished and a foundation stone for a customs office is laid.

Following his defeat in two battles, the Pune-based Maratha Peshwa **Baji Rao II** surrenders to the East India

The pleasures of colonial life – an Englishman enjoys his toilet, attended by no less than five servants

Company. Lord Hastings abolishes the office of the *Peshwa*, and retires Baji Rao II on a pension to the Bithur Fort near Kanpur along with his adopted son Dhondu Pant, known as Nana Sahib.

1819 Lord Amherst is appointed Governor-General. During his period of office he alienates Muslim landed aristocracy by abolishing the *taluqdari* land-ownership system prevalent in Oudh that had enabled it to act as tax collectors, policemen and judges.

1820 Amherst renews the 1809 treaty with the ruling Ameers of Sind.

Ranjit Singh consolidates his rule over territory that stretches from the Satlaj to the Indus, and includes Panjab, Multan and Kashmir (wrested by him from the Afghans). Known as *Sher-e Panjab*, Lion of Panjab, he is equally popular among his Hindu, Muslim and Sikh subjects. The professionalism of his army causes concern among the British.

1821 John Holwell's obelisk in Calcutta (see p.214), having fallen into disrepair, is dismantled.

1823 Lord Amherst issues a repressive **Press ordinance**, providing for the confiscation of any printing press found to have printed 'objectionable material'.

Ranjit Singh extends his authority to Peshawar on the Indian-Afghan border.

> **❝** Raja Ranjit Singh's conversation is like a nightmare ... He is almost the first inquisitive Indian I have seen; and his curiosity balances the apathy of the whole of his nation. He has asked me a hundred thousand questions about India, the British, Europe, [Napoleon] Bonaparte, this world in general and the next, hell, paradise, the soul, God, the devil, and a myriad of others of the same kind. **❞**
>
> A. Jaquemont, a French visitor to Raja Ranjit Singh's court

> **"** The present system of religion adhered to by the Hindus is not well calculated to promote their political interest. The distinctions of caste, introducing innumerable castes and sub-castes among them, has entirely deprived them of patriotic feelings, and the multitude of religious rites and ceremonies and the laws of purification have totally disqualified them from undertaking any difficult enterprises. **"**
>
> Ram Mohun Roy, cited in Bipan Chandra et al, *India's Struggle for Independence*

1824 Britain exports one million metres of **cotton textiles** to India. A **mutiny** by the 47th Bengal Native Infantry breaks out at Barrackpore, the Governor-General's country seat 24km north of Calcutta, in protest at being posted abroad (to Burma), where Hindu caste differences cannot be maintained. It is suppressed by British regiments.

In Calcutta, an **Ayurvedic College** of medicine is founded (see p.75).

1828 William Cavendish-Bentinck, known as **Lord Bentinck**, the new Governor-General of the Bengal Presidency, focuses on establishing an efficient administration manned largely by Indians.

Ram Mohun Roy transforms his recently established Atimiya Sabha (Spritual Assembly) into the **Brahmo Samaj** (Society of Brahma), a Hindu reform organization.

1829 Lord Bentinck abolishes *suttee* (see p.242). His administrative economies turn the East India Company's annual deficit of £1 million into a surplus of £1.5 million.

Ram Mohun Roy (1772–1833) and the Brahmo Samaj

Ram Mohun Roy was the first Hindu reformist of modern times. Born into a Brahmin landlord family in Bengal, he spent thirty years mastering Sanskrit, Persian, Arabic, Hebrew, Greek and English, and studied scriptures of major religions in the original. He then served the **East India Company** for twelve years, rising to the position of assistant revenue collector. After retirement, he took up religious, social and political work, and published a Bengali translation of the *Upanishads*. In *Precepts of Jesus* (1820) he rejected Christian theology but accepted its humanitarian and ethical teachings.

In 1823 he appealed to **Lord Amherst** to introduce the teaching of English and sciences into Indian schools while opposing his press censorship. Five years later, he transformed the earlier Atimaya Sabha, aimed at reforming Hinduism, into the **Brahmo Samaj**. Influenced by Christianity and Islam, Samaj members rejected polytheism and expressed belief in only one Hindu deity: **Brahma**, the Creator. They opposed such post-*Upanishads* practices as idol worship and polygamy, and the caste system. They stressed rationalism rather than faith.

The Brahmo Samaj, with its doctrine of universalist theism, won many converts among upper-caste professionals in Bengal and paved the way for the emergence, a century later, of a rich crop of radical nationalists and Marxists. Roy also campaigned against *suttee* (see p.242), influencing Lord Bentinck's 1829 decision to ban the practice. In 1830 Akbar Shah II, conferred the title Raja upon him, and sent Roy to London as his ambassador to plead the Mughal Emperor's case before the British government. In this he was only marginally successful. He did not return home and died in Bristol, England.

MARY EVANS PL

Ram Mohun Roy, depicted in an unattributed engraving from 1824

Dwarkanath Tagore, grandfather of Rabindranath Tagore, founds the Calcutta Union Bank, India's first.

1830 A newly opened sea-and-land passenger route – consisting of a voyage from England to Alexandria, overland travel to Suez and a voyage to Bombay – reduces the journey time between Britain and India from six months to one.

1831 Lord Bentinck signs a friendship treaty with Raja Ranjit Singh.

1833 A new twenty-year East India Company Charter Act abolishes the Company's trading functions. It creates the office of **Governor-General of India in Council**, with four Council members, including a lawyer. It permits Europeans to purchase land in India, a provision which results in the establishment of plantations of indigo vetch – a source of blue dye used for many European uniforms.

Lord Bentinck becomes India's first Governor-General of India, with jurisdiction over the Bengal, Madras and Bombay Presidencies. He inaugurates work on the **Grand Trunk Road** linking Calcutta to Delhi (and later Peshawar).

1834 Britain exports 54 million metres of cotton textiles to India, accounting for more than half of its total exports to the subcontinent. India's cottage textile industry collapses. 'The [ensuing] misery hardly finds a parallel in commerce,' writes Lord Bentinck in his annual report. 'The bones of the cotton weaver are bleaching the plains of India.'

British entrepreneurs begin planting **tea**, introduced from China, in **Assam**.

1835 Thomas Babington **Macaulay**, former secretary to the East India Company Board of Control in London, is appointed Legal Member of the Governor-General's Council. Lord Bentinck further appoints him President of the General Committee of Education. Macaulay favours **English** as the medium of instruction rather than Persian or Sanskrit, partly because he is dismissive of the knowledge available in those languages. Accepting his recommendation, Bentinck replaces Persian with English as the language of governmental and legal business.

1835 The first medical college to train Indian doctors in Western medicine is established in Calcutta.

Sir Charles Metcalfe is appointed acting Governor-General of India.

1836 Lord Auckland, an indecisive ruler, is appointed full Governor-General.

> All the historical information which has been collected from all the books written in the Sanskrit language, is less valuable than what may be found in the most paltry abridgments used at preparatory schools in England ... The question now before us is simply whether, when it is in our power to teach the [English] language, we shall teach languages in which ... there are no books on any subject which deserve to be compared to our own ... whether, when we can patronize sound philosophy and true history, we shall countenance at the public expense medical doctrines which would disgrace an English farrier, astronomy which would move laughter in girls at an English boarding school, history abounding with kings 30 feet tall and reigns 30,000 years long, and geography made up seas of treacle and rivers of butter.

T.B. Macaulay, *Minute on Indian Education*, 2 February 1835

1837 Mughal Emperor Akbar Shah II is succeeded by **Bahadur Shah Zafar**. He is told by Auckland that his titles will expire with his death, and that the Mughal royal family will be moved out of the Red Fort in Delhi.

Landlords in the Bengal Presidency form the **Landholders' Society** in Calcutta.

The British **postal service**, until now used only for official purposes, is opened to the public.

Suttee

The term *suttee* is derived from *sati*, meaning 'truthful female'. In ancient Scythia, widows and slave-girls were routinely sacrificed at their master's sepulchre, and this is believed to be the origin of the Indian practice of female **voluntary self-immolation**. By offering herself to the purifying flames of her god-husband's pyre, a widow wished to rejoin him in the afterworld.

Invading Greeks in the 320s BC were the first Europeans to notice this custom in northwestern India, where it was most common among royalty and the upper classes. Later, in the 1520s, European visitors to Vijayanagar recorded that when a captain died all his wives burned themselves, and the same was true of the king. During 1813–28, between 500 and 850 cases of *suttee* were reported in the Bengal Presidency.

At the local level, many Hindu rulers and British officers had banned the practice. What **Lord Bentinck**'s Regulation XVII of 1829 did was to enforce a ban throughout Bengal. His legislation, subsequently extended to the Bombay and Madras presidencies, made the forced burning or burying alive of widows punishable by criminal courts as 'culpable homicide' – equivalent to 'manslaughter' in English law. In 1832 a group of Bengali Hindus appealed unsuccessfully to the Privy Council in Britain against Lord Bentinck's Regulation. However, since the *suttee* practice was very limited, its outlawing had little popular impact.

1838 Lord Auckland meets Ranjit Singh, now seriously ill. During his reign, the Sikh ruler has transformed his inherited Sikh Khalsa militia into a multi-faith 89,000-strong force, with 54,000 infantry and the rest cavalry and gunners. Equipped with nearly 500 assorted artillery and 300 camel swivels, this army is commanded *inter alia* by French and Italian officers. By comparison, the East India Company's Bengal Army is just over 110,000 strong. Many British colonels allow missionaries to preach and convert Indian soldiers to Christianity.

1839 Raja Ranjit Singh dies in Lahore and is succeeded by his son, Kharak Singh.

1840 Due to the collapse of the handloom cotton industry, the population of Dacca, Bengal, has shrunk from 150,000 to 30,000. Raja Kharak Singh dies in Lahore and the following day his son, Nihal Singh, is killed. The throne in Lahore passes to **Sher Singh**, a younger brother of Kharak.

1842 Lord Ellenborough becomes Governor-General.

British forces suffer defeat in the **Anglo–Afghan War**.

1843 Partly to counter the Afghanistan debacle, partly to control the Indus and Lower Sind for commercial profit, and partly to secure the northwestern subcontinent, **General Charles Napier**, backed by Ellenborough, annexes Sind despite Britain's friendship treaty with the Ameer dynasty. Subsequently, Napier will be remembered for his one-word Latin victory message to the Governor-General: 'Peccavi' ('I have sinned').

The first regular Britain to India sea-land-sea route – via Alexandria, then overland to Suez – is inaugurated. It is run by the Peninsular and Oriental Company, originally set up to service ports in the peninsula of Spain and Portugal.

Following the assassination of Raja Sher Singh, the throne in Lahore passes to 6-year-old Dalip Singh, the youngest son of Ranjit Singh, with the army commander Tej Singh acting as regent.

The **Bengal British India Society** is formed in Calcutta to 'promote general interest in public affairs'.

1844 The 1st Viscount Hardinge begins his term as the Governor-General. Following mutinies by Madras and Bengal regiments in Sind, their leaders are court-marshalled and one regiment disbanded.

1845–46 In the **First Anglo-Sikh War**, the British occupy Lahore. The subsequent treaty requires the Sikhs to pay an indemnity of £1.5 million. To raise this sum the Sikh Council sells **Kashmir** for £1 million to Raja Gulab Singh, the Hindu ruler of adjoining **Jammu**. The administration of the Kingdom of Lahore, much reduced in size, is entrusted to a British Resident, and Dalip Singh placed under British tutelage.

The state of Jammu and Kashmir comes into being when Raja Gulab Singh amalgamates his territories of 95 percent Muslim Kashmir and 60 percent Hindu Jammu.

1848 Lord Dalhousie, an energetic westernizer of 35, is appointed Governor-General. He rules that provisons contained in the **Subsidiary Treaties** between the East India Company and local rulers, whereby the Company acknowledges their heirs, applies only to legitimate sons, and that in the absence of such a successor he will annex the Indian territory. Using this **'Doctrine of Lapse'**, he disinherits (Maratha) Nana Sahib, based at the Bithur Fort near Kanpur. Over the next seven years he will annex seven other Indian states.

1849 Following the **Second Anglo-Sikh War**, Lord Dalhousie coerces 11-year-old Dalip Singh into signing a document that relinquishes his territories, as well as the Koh-i-Noor diamond, to the British. The annexation of Panjab turns the unceasing tribal disorderliness in the adjoining northwestern mountains into a pressing problem for the Governor-General.

1850 Visiting England, Lord Dalhousie presents the Koh-i-Noor to Queen Victoria.

1851 The Landholders' Society and the Bengal British India Society merge to form the **British Indian Association**.

The first electric **telegraph** line is opened between Calcutta and Diamond Harbour, a distance of 40km.

1852 To prevent their caste status being demeaned by travel, soldiers of the 38th Bengal Native Infantry refuse to go to Burma to fight alongside the British.

The **Bombay Association** and the **Madras Native Association** are formed as voluntary bodies to promote the interests of the educated middle class.

The British issue the first Indian **postage stamp** in Karachi, for use only in Sind.

1853 The first Indian **railway**, originally commissioned by Lord Dalhousie, opens between Bombay and Thana, a distance of 37km.

The East India Company charter is renewed, but only for the duration of the current British Parliament. The Company introduces open competition in its **Indian Civil Service** by entrance examination.

1854 The first **steam-powered cotton mill**, owned by C. N. Davar, a Parsi, opens in Bombay. He has to pay an excise duty while British cotton imports are admitted without duty.

'Agony point' loop on the Darjeeling Himalayan railway, one of the steepest ascents in the world

In Calcutta, the first **jute mill** is unveiled by British planters. The fibre, found beneath the bark of *Corchoruss capsularis*, is used to produce burlap, webbing, twines and backing yarns for carpets.

1856 Dalhousie annexes the kingdom of **Oudh**, the heart of North India, on the pretext that its ruler Wajid Ali is incompetent and corrupt.

Lord Canning, replacing Dalhousie as Governor-General, issues the **General Service Enlistment Act**, which requires Indian soldiers to go anywhere they are sent, a point of bitter contention.

After failing to obtain redress in London, Wajid Ali returns to Oudh where some 21,000 *taluqdars* have been deprived of their fiefdoms, and where 40,000 of his former soldiers and retainers are now unemployed in a province that provides more than a third of the 128,000 Indian soldiers in the 151,000-strong Bengal Army of the East India Company.

1857 Following its adoption by the British home army, the **Enfield rifle** arrives in India. The cartridges for this gun, rammed down the barrel, are greased with a tallow that contains pig and cow fat. A military ordinance directs soldiers to bite open the end of the cartridge before loading. This offends Hindu soldiers, mostly high caste – required to

> **"** However infamous the conduct of the sepoys, it is only the reflex, in a concentrated form, of England's own conduct in India, not only during the epoch of the foundation of her Eastern Empire, but even during the last ten years of a long-settled rule ... An officer in the civil service from Allahabad writes, 'We have power of life and death in our hands, and we assure you we spare not.' Another from the same place: 'Not a day passes but we string up 10 to 15 of them (non-combatants).' One exulting officer writes: 'Holmes is hanging them by the score, like a 'brick.'... From Benares we are informed that 30 *zamindars* [landlords] were hanged on the mere suspicion of sympathizing with their own countrymen, and whole villages were burned down on the same plea. **"**

Karl Marx, writing in the *New York Daily Tribune*, 16 September 1857

The Great Uprising of 1857–58

The epidemic of mutinies, uprisings, massacres, sieges, assaults and reprisals that broke out in Calcutta in January 1857 has been called the Great Sepoy/Indian Mutiny by the British, and the War of Independence/Great National Uprising by Indians, with neutral commentators preferring the Great Revolt/Uprising. Of the Bengal, Bombay and Madras armies, the Mutiny involved only the first. Half of its 128,000 Indian soldiers mutinied, a quarter remained loyal, and the rest deserted. Backed by a popular uprising, triggered by a belief that the British wanted to convert all Indians to Christianity, the mutineers in **Meerut** marched to Delhi on 12 May, persuaded Bahadur Shah, the nominal emperor, to become their leader, and swelled their ranks to 40,000. They were defeated by the British at Badliki Serai, 8km from Delhi, on 7 June.

A week later 20,000 rebels encircled Lucknow. At **Kanpur**, a Maratha stronghold, having persuaded Nana Sahib to become their leader, 3000 rebels laid siege to the British garrison, with 300 Britons, half of them women and children. Following their surrender, safe passage downriver to Allahabad was promised to the British civilians. But on hearing that **Colonel M. Neill** had executed mutineers at Allahabad, the rebels massacred their captives. Taking over from Neill, **Sir Henry Havelock** relieved Kanpur in mid-July. Between September and the following June, the British recaptured Delhi, Lucknow and Jhansi.

The rebels' butchery in Kanpur and Jhansi, where fifty Britons were slaughtered, was matched by Neill's barbarism, the massacre of 237 Indian troopers in **Ajnalam**, Panjab, and the bloodbath in **Delhi**. The victorious British often razed villages,

observe the religious taboo about touching or eating beef – as well as Muslim troops with a similar religious injunction regarding pork. The ammunition is thus seen as a ploy to convert them to Christianity – all the more so when at Barrackpore Colonel Wheeler publicly preaches the Gospel to his troops. Other missionary colonels follow suit.

The massacre at Jhansi, as portrayed in an unashamedly partisan 19th-century engraving

killing indiscriminately. The Uprising failed through lack of coordination, ineffective leadership, scarcity of arms and ammunition, poor intelligence, and the mutineers' inability to transform popular support into military strength. The Indians were divided. Of the 11,200 soldiers besieging Delhi, 7900 were Indian. Among them Sikhs, fearful of the Mughal revival, fought valiantly for the British.

In January Indian soldiers at Calcutta's Dum Dum garrison refuse the Enfield rifles and greased cartridges, but the mutiny is suppressed.

On 9 May, 85 Indians are court-martialled in **Meerut**, where the next day a **general mutiny** breaks out. It spreads throughout Oudh and its adjoining areas, affecting garrisons in Delhi, Lucknow, Kanpur, Bareilly, Fatehpur, Faizabad, Jaunpur, Allahabad, Jhansi, Indore and Gwaliar, and is often accompanied by a general rebellion in which both Hindu and Muslim civilians participate.

After **Delhi** is recaptured by the British in September, Lt. William Hodson, a British intelligence officer, murders two sons and a grandson of Emperor Bahadur Shah Zafar in cold blood, to ensure 'the total extinction' of the **Mughal dynasty**, which he describes as 'the most significant the world has ever seen'.

In the same year Lord Canning establishes universities at Bombay, Calcutta and Madras.

1858 By end March/early April the British have regained most of the areas seized earlier by rebels. Following his court martial in Delhi in March, Bahadur Shah Zafar is deposed and banished to a jail in Rangoon, Burma.

In May the British recapture Bareilly, and on 20 June re-take Gwaliar after its seizure three weeks earlier by rebel leaders Tantiya Topi and Rani of Jhansi, effectively ending the thirteen-month-old **Great Uprising**. But the days of the East India Company are numbered when Parliament in London passes the **Act for the Better Government of India**. The Company's directors hold their last meeting on 1 September and offer to the British Crown the Indian empire – with an estimated population of 200 million, of whom only 100,000 are British.

On 1 November this transfer is announced by Viceroy and Governor- General Viscount Canning to the princes and people of India at Allahabad. He restores lands to those *taluqdars* in Oudh who can prove their non-participation in the uprising.

British rule 1859–1919

Notwithstanding that Hindu soldiers had objected as much as Muslims to handling new Enfield cartridges, and that the Marathas had been at the centre of the fighting and had been responsible for the massacre of British civilians at **Kanpur**, the British held Muslim aristocrats more accountable for the **Great Uprising** than Hindus. In particular, they were incensed by **Bahadur Shah Zafar**'s proclamation of the restored Mughal throne. Upper-class Muslims had already lost out as administrators, landlords and military commanders, with most of their estates having been confiscated by the British or mortgaged to Hindu money-lenders. Now they found themselves excluded altogether from Britain's Indian army.

Following the **Uprising**, the British built some 170 cantonments on the edges of cities and towns across their Indian empire, connected by road, rail and, later, telegraph. Each cantonment contained segregated Indian and British sections, with the latter subdivided into military quarters and a civil sector, where civilian officials and other notables lived in bungalows along wide, treelined roads that could be easily protected, with a Europeans-only club at the core. Along with this went a way of life pioneered by privately educated Britons recruited into the Indian Civil Service or Army officer corps. They dressed for dinner, remained unruffled in crisis, and had wives – called *memsahibs* ('madame sahibs') – who were even more disdainful of Indians. They were complemented by business managers, generically called 'boxwallahs', after the boxes containing samples of the British-ware carried by their trading predecessors.

Social and housing segregation went hand in hand with greater economic exploitation of India for the wellbeing of

Britain's steam-powered industry, especially **textiles**, where the colony was both a primary source of cotton and a captive market for British fabrics. To ship raw cotton from Gujarat and Maharashtra to northwest England to be machine-spun and woven into cloth to be exported to India – a sea voyage of some 24,000km – made sense, if at all, only in the context of imperial Britain exercising political control over India for the welfare of its textile industry.

The introduction of modern means of communcation in South Asia primarily served the interests of Britain. Railways ensured rapid transport of cotton and tea from the hinterlands to the respective ports of **Bombay** and **Calcutta**. Postal and telegraphic services enabled the British to consolidate their civil and military authority. That these technologies also benefitted the indigenous people was incidental.

Politically, having discovered deep divisions between Hindus and Muslims – with the former being three times more numerous than the latter – Britain found it expedient to ensure continued Hindu-Muslim antipathy as a means to maintaining its hold over the subcontinent. Conveniently for London, a section of the Muslim upper crust was by now ready to end its sulk, learn English and other modern subjects, and thus catch up with the literate Hindu middle class. It followed the lead of **Sir Sayyid Ahmad Khan** who, during the Great Uprising, had remained loyal to the British. With imperial Britain introducing a semblance of representative government in India, following petitions by upper crust Indians, this section of the Muslim leadership would play an increasingly important role, if only often as a spoiler.

When, during the first decade of the 20th century, discussions were held on extending the franchise for council elections to individual Indians with taxable incomes or university degrees, Muslim leaders like **Sir Sayyid** argued that such a franchise on a common electoral role would result in

Muslims, generally poorer and less well educated, being swamped by Hindus. They demanded therefore, separate constituencies for Muslim voters.

Britain responded positively. The 1909 **India Councils Act** prescribed lesser criteria, materially and educationally, for the Muslim franchise and allowed qualified Muslims to vote in general as well as Muslim constituencies. Ensuring an ongoing political separation of Hindus and Muslims, this electoral system would culminate in the partition of the sub-continent into India and Pakistan.

Meanwhile, there were brief periods when the two communities joined forces to demand emancipation from their British overlords. An example was the **Rowlatt-Khilafat protest** immediately after the 1914–18 World War, but it lasted barely three years. No inter-communal alliance materialized thereafter.

1859 Viceroy Canning abrogates the **Doctrine of Lapse**, thus leaving intact 362 native states and 239 estates – collectively called the **Princely States** – ranging in area from a few square kilometres to the size of France. The aggregate strength of the Bengal, Madras and Bombay armies is reduced from 283,000 before the Great Uprising to 205,000, and the ratio between Indian and British soldiers is reduced from 5:1 to 2:1. The recruitment area for local troops is to be switched from Oudh and Bihar to Panjab, Garhwal and Rajputana. The army headquarters remains at **Simla**, the imperial summer capital.

1861 The **Society for the Promotion of National Feeling** among the literate of Bengal is formed in Calcutta. It invites Bengalis to shun the English language and customs and return to indigenous culture and practices.

The first Indian is accepted into the Indian Civil Service.

The outbreak of the American Civil War (1861–65) disrupts American cotton supplies to British textile mills. As a result Indian cotton exports to Britain double over the next four years to a total worth £81 million.

1862 Bahadur Shah Zafar dies, unhonoured, in Rangoon. The **8th Earl of Elgin** is appointed Viceroy of India.

The Indian Penal Code is enacted.

1864 Following the death of Lord Elgin, **Sir John Lawrence** becomes Viceroy.

1865 The first telegram is sent from London to Calcutta via Persia/Iran.

1866 Famine strikes India's eastern coast. In Orissa alone one million people die.

1869 Lord Mayo, an Irishman, becomes Viceroy.

The opening of the 160-kilometre **Suez Canal**, linking the Mediterranean and Red seas, reduces the journey time between Britain and India from a month to three weeks.

1870 Railway track in India is now 6400km long.

The first cotton textile mill, owned by a local Parsi, opens in Bombay. Its Parsi proprietor has to pay an excise duty while British cotton imports are admitted duty-free.

1872 Viceroy Mayo is murdered by a convict during a visit to a penal colony in the Andaman Islands in the Bay of Bengal. He is succeeded by the autocratic **Lord Northbrook**.

1873 There is an outbreak of famine in Bihar.

1874 The East India Company is formally dissolved.

1875 The Muhammadan Anglo-Oriental College is founded in Aligarh by **Sir Sayyid Ahmad Khan** (1817–98), a descendant of the finance minister of Emperor Akbar Shah

II and author of *Essay on the Causes of the Indian Revolt* (1858) – in which he disputes the view that the Revolt was the handiwork of Muslims – and *The Loyal Muhammadans of India* (1860).

Swami Dayanada Sarswati, a Gujarati brahmin, founds the **Arya Samaj**, a Hindu reform organization.

1876 **Lord Lytton**, the newly arrived Viceroy, shocks British high society in Calcutta and Simla by smoking between courses at dinner. Britain occupies Quetta, a strategic city in Baluchistan with the consent of the Khan of Kalat, thus securing the road to Kandahar and gaining full control over the **Bolan Pass**.

The founding of the **Indian Association** in Calcutta under the presidency of Surendranath Banerjea, unjustly dismissed from the Indian Civil Service, is the latest attempt by Indians to grapple with problems of national importance.

In the far south and Deccan a two-year famine begins that will claim 5.5 million lives, goading Viceroy Lytton to devise fresh means of famine control.

Arya Samaj

The **Arya Samaj (Society of Aryans)**, a voluntary body formed by **Swami Dayanad Sarswati**, played a leading part in the Hindu reform movement pioneered by Ram Mohun Roy (see p.238). It was established at a time when Indology was fashionable in Western academia, and there was much interest in the pan-Aryan studies of **Fredrich Max Muller** (1823–1900), the German-born philologist and Professor of Sanskrit at Oxford University.

In India, after completing a thorough study of the *Vedas*, perceived as the original source of Aryan ideology and culture, Sarswati critically examined current **Hindu practices**. He rejected most of these, including the caste system, idolatry, polygamy, child marriage and the ostracizing of widows. In their place, he advocated return to the rituals of the Indo-Aryans, centred on fire ceremony and congregational worship. This appealed to those who felt weighed down by the complex accretions of later Hinduism. The Arya Samaj spread rapidly in the **United Province** (formerly Oudh) and **Panjab**. While it was not overtly political, it inspired patriotism. Among its early proponents in Panjab was **Lala Lajpat Rai**, an eminent leader of the Indian National Congress. Later, however, its fundamentalist tenets made it intolerant of Muslims and Christians, and it became involved in alliances with ultra-orthodox Hindu groups.

1877 Queen Victoria is proclaimed the Empress of India.

Lytton convenes a *durbar* (imperial assembly) in a gigantic tented enclosure around the ridge from where the British troops had regained Delhi in 1858. It is attended by 84,000 people, including 363 princes and title-holders.

The Indian Association demands that the entrance examination to the Indian Civil Service be held simultaneously in London and Calcutta.

Queen Victoria as Empress of India, in a photograph by Bassamo

1878 Viceroy Lytton promulgates the **Vernacular Press Act**, empowering him to confiscate the press and paper of a local language newspaper publishing 'seditious material'. This results in public outcry in Calcutta, led by the Indian Association.

The Indian **silver rupee** collapses to half its value against the British pound (backed by the gold standard) when the value of the metal falls due to the discovery of vast silver mines in North America.

1879 The first All-India conference of the Indian Association, coinciding with an industrial exhibition in Calcutta, demands the repeal of excise duty on Indian textiles.

1880 In April the newly elected Liberal government in Britain, led by W. E. Gladstone, makes a fresh start in policies towards India.

Lord Ripon, the new Viceroy of India, introduces fully nominated Rural and Municipal Boards, the first step towards creating representative government in the subcontinent.

1881 The first **general census** in India puts the **population** at 253 million. There are over 3100 Hindus but only 60 Muslims with university degrees. 37,000 Hindus are enrolled at English high schools compared to only 370 Muslims.

The first **telephone exchange** opens in Calcutta within five years of the telephone's invention by the American Alexander Bell.

1882 Ripon repeals the Vernacular Press Act.

1884 Many Indians travel to Bombay to give a warm send-off to Lord Ripon who is succeeded as Viceroy by **Lord Dufferin**.

1885 At the initiative of **Allan Octavian Hume** – a retired high-ranking British official who has sent letters to all Indian university graduates – 72 Indians, three-quarters of them lawyers or journalists, meet in Bombay to found the Indian National Congress (popularly called **Congress**). They elect Hume secretary, a position he holds until his return to England seven years later. They demand that 'the Government should be widened and that the people should have their proper and legitimate share in it'. The first president is **Womesh C. Bonnerjee**, a Calcutta barrister.

1887 Queen Victoria's Silver Jubilee is celebrated in her Indian empire.

The first modern **steel plant** opens at Kulti.

1888 Lord Lansdowne becomes Viceroy.

1889 India's first commercially viable **oil wells** are sunk at Digboi, Assam.

1891–92 Britain occupies the Hunza and Nagar forts in the Gilgit Valley, commanding access to the passes through the Hindu Kush mountains, and thus closes a gap in India's northwestern defences.

1892 The **India Councils Act** turns the hitherto fully nominated central and provincial Legislative Councils into partly elected chambers. Municipal boards, chambers of commerce, landowner associations and universities are authorized to submit lists of elected nominees from which the Viceroy and Provincial Governors make a final selection of council members. These elected members, forming a minority, have the right to discuss the budget, but not vote on it.

Dadabhai Naoroji, an Indian Parsi businessman, is elected to the British Parliament as Liberal MP for London's Central Finsbury constituency.

1893 The Indian government, switching from silver to gold as the legal tender, fixes the exchange rate at fifteen rupees to £1, which holds for more than half a century.

1894 The **9th Earl of Elgin** becomes Viceroy.

1895 The Bengal, Madras and Bombay armies are amalgamated into the **Indian Army**.

1896 Auguste and Louis Lumière of France present their **silent films** *Bathers in the Sea* and *Arrival and Departure of a Train* at Watson's Hotel in Bombay.

1896–99 Bubonic **plague**, spreading from Bombay to nearby provinces, causes two million deaths.

A **famine** affecting 70 million people in United Province (formerly Oudh), Central Provinces and Bihar, is the most severe yet.

1899 Viscount Curzon of Kedleston becomes Viceroy.

1901 Queen Victoria is succeeded by her son **Edward VII**. The decennial census puts the **population** of the Indian empire at 294 million.

The total British investment in indigo, tea and coffee plantations, in coal, manganese and gold mining; and in jute manufacturing stands at £350 million, against an Indian investment of £15 million.

Lord Curzon transfers responsibility for the trans-Indus region from Panjab Province to the **Northwest Frontier Province** – newly created to act as a buffer zone between India and Afghanistan with tribal levies under British command maintaining peace.

British expeditionary forces, acting in the name of the Maharaja of Jammu and Kashmir, push the Princely State's boundaries to Chinese Xinjiang. By annexing sparsely populated **Ladakh**, Jammu and Kashmir expands from 106,790 to 225,410 sq km.

In Calcutta, Hiralal Sen launches the **Indian film industry.**

1902 Lord Curzon establishes a separate department of agriculture that will increase areas under irrigation by 6.5 million acres. He also founds the **Archaeological Society of India** to discover past treasures and preserve known antiquities, among them the Taj Mahal, Fatehpur Sikri, the Moti Masjid (Pearl Mosque), and the temples of Khajuraho.

Unveiling a marble obelisk to commemorate the 'Black Hole' of Calcutta (see p.214), Curzon states that John Holwell's list of victims contains 'less than 50 names'.

1903 A two-week long imperial *durbar* in Delhi to celebrate the accession of Edward VII, attended by thousands of Indian luminaries swearing fealty to the British Crown, is the climax of Curzon's viceroyalty.

In July Major Francis Younghusband sets out at the head of a military expedition that will cross the Himalayas to extract

> The scheme of partition [of the Bengal Presidency], concocted in the dark and carried out in the face of fiercest opposition that any government measure has encountered in the last half a century, will always stand as a complete illustration of the worst features of bureaucratic rule – its utter contempt for public opinion, its arrogant pretensions to superior wisdom, its reckless disregard of the most cherished feelings of the people, the mockery of an appeal to its sense of justice, its cold preference of [Indian Civil] Service interests to those of the governed.

Bal Gangadhar Tilak, a radical Congress leader, addressing the party session in December 1905

Lord Curzon of Kedleston 1859–1925

A gifted aristocrat, capable administrator and staunch imperialist, **George Curzon** considered becoming Viceroy of India a stepping-stone to his ultimate ambition, premiership of Britain. Even at Oxford, his self-importance was lampooned by fellow-students at Balliol College: 'My name is George Nathaniel Curzon,/I am a most superior person,/My cheeks are pink, my hair is sleek,/ I dine at Blenheim once a week.'

After graduation, he travelled in and wrote about Iran, Afghanistan, Central Asia and the Far East. As the Indian Viceroy, he declared: 'Our aim should be to rivet British rule more firmly on to India and to postpone the longed-for day of emancipation.' He also remarked, 'The Congress is tottering to its fall, and one of my greatest ambitions while in India is to assist it to a peaceful demise.' But, by dividing Bengal, he unwittingly infused new life into it. 'I look upon all Englishmen in this country as engaged in different branches of the same great undertaking,' he told the British Chamber of Commerce. 'My work lies in administration, yours in exploitation, but both are aspects of the same project.'

He established a department of commerce and industry, and extended India's existing 43,000km of railways by another 10,000. A talented writer, he waged war on bureaucratic obfuscation. He dealt successfully with Afghanistan. But in his commander-in-chief, **Lord Kitchener**, he encountered an equally egotistical leader. When Kitchener protested to the Secretary of State for India that while he was only an ex-officio member of Curzon's Executive Council, one of his subordinate officers was the Council's Military Member, the Secretary decided to amalgamate the two offices, thus augmenting Kitchener's status, to the chagrin of Curzon. In his post-viceregal career, Curzon did not rise above British Foreign Secretary.

Lord and Lady Curzon with the first day's bag, in camp near Nedonda, Hyderabad in April 1902

trading concessions from, and assert a British presence in, **Tibet**.

In December Curzon announces the **partition of the Bengal Presidency** (population 79 million, area nearly 500,000 sq km) into Western Bengal, with its capital at Calcutta, and Muslim-majority Eastern Bengal and Assam, with its capital at Dacca, to be implemented in 1905.

1904 The **Universities Act** – seeking to exert more effective control over private colleges largely funded by an official grant system, and to increase the number of government-nominated university administrators – is opposed by India's middle classes.

The Congress-led agitation against the partition of Bengal gathers momentum.

Lord Curzon returns home on six months' leave before beginning a second five-year term as Viceroy.

1905 The Bengal Presidency is partitioned. Soon after, Lord Curzon resigns in protest at the British government's decision to combine the posts of Commander-in-Chief and the Military Member of the Viceroy's Executive Council, arguing that the change reduces civilian power. He is succeeded by Lord Minto II, a great grandson of Lord Minto I.

At Congress's annual convention in December, its President Gopal Krishna Gokhale, a moderate, attacks the partition of Bengal. As before, Muslim delegates are thin on the ground – only 20 out of 756. The party launches a *swadeshi* (literally, of one's own country) movement, and boycotts British textiles and salt, with its followers making bonfires of British goods.

India's commercial leaders hold the first **All India Industrial Conference** to demand official permission to enter industrial manufacturing.

Parsis

To avoid conversion to Islam in the mid-8th century, many Zoroastrians fled Persia by boat and sought sanctuary in the **Sanjan principality** on India's western coast. They kept their religion, but abandoned the Persian language for Gujarati. Some identified themselves by Gujarati Hindu surnames – Gandhi, Mody, Mehta – and others by their calling – Contractor, Ginwalla, Batliwalla. As they had come from Pars, locals called them **Parsis**, a term which stuck. Many became merchants and shipwrights.

When the East India Company arrived in Surat, the Parsis began acting as middlemen between it and local suppliers. Unlike Hindus, they were not restricted by caste or dietary prohibitions in their social intercourse with the British. When the Company moved to Bombay in 1687, many Parsis followed. In time, they came to own most of Bombay's dockyards. Some procured cotton from the hinterland for textile mills in Britain; others became middlemen for British imports and exports.

Having accumulated commercial experience and capital, Parsis pioneered the industrial manufacture of yarn and cloth in Bombay. Among the most enterprising was **Jamshedji Tata** (1839–1904), who diversified into iron and steel, and whose grandson, **Jahangir Ratanji Dadabhoy Tata**, presided over the second richest business house in independent India, with interests ranging from soaps and detergent to trucks and locomotives. Today there are some 80,000 Parsis in India, most of them still based in Bombay or Gujarat.

1906 Encouraged by the British, a delegation of 35 Muslim grandees, headed by **Agha Khan**, the religious leader of Ismailis, meets the Viceroy to demand separate electorates for Muslims under a proposed electoral system.

In December the newly formed **All India Muslim League** – seeking to promote loyalty to the British Crown while advancing Muslims' political rights – elects Agha Khan as its president.

1907 The Tata Iron and Steel Company's factory, built with American expertise, opens at Jamshedpur, Bihar. The company's founders, Jamshedji Tata and his sons, are **Parsis**.

1909 The **India Councils Act** provides for greater (though not majority) representation of Indians in the 21-member Imperial Legislative Council, now tripled in size, and in provincial legislative councils, now doubled in size. New members are provided by chambers of commerce, landholders' associations and universities.

In response to pressure from the Muslim League, the Act allows for separate Muslim electoral constituencies with reduced franchise qualifications.

To qualify as voters, Hindus are required to have a minimum taxable income of Rs 30,000, whereas Muslims need have only Rs 3000. On the education franchise, a Hindu needs to be a university graduate of thirty years standing while a Muslim is required to have graduated only three years prior to an election. Also, qualified Muslim voters are entitled to vote in the general constituencies as well. While Muslims view these provisions as redressing an imbalance created by greater Hindu wealth and educational attainment, Hindus see them as worrying evidence of Britain's pro-Muslim bias. Radical nationalists, contemptuous of legalistic petitioning by mainstream Indian politicians, resort to bombs and assassinations.

1910 **George V** succeeds Edward VII. The 2nd Viscount Hardinge becomes Viceroy of India.

1911 A census puts the population of the Indian empire at 315 million, an increase of 7 percent in ten years, with Muslims forming a quarter of the total.

At his coronation *durbar* in Delhi in December, George V, the first British monarch to visit India, announces the reversal of the partition of Bengal: Assam is returned to the jurisdiction of a chief commissioner, and Bihar-Orissa-Chota Nagpur forms a separate province with its capital at Patna, making restored Bengal a Bengali-speaking province.

1912 Jules Tyck and Baron de Carters give the first public **aeroplane** display in India at Calcutta.

1913 **Rabindranath Tagore** (see p.284) is awarded the Nobel Prize for Literature, an honour accorded to no other Indian before or since.

Raja Harish Chandra, the first full-length Indian silent feature film, directed and produced by Dhundiraj Govind Phalke, is shown in Bombay.

Muhammad Ali Jinnah, a London-trained lawyer and Congress member, joins the Muslim League, there being no bar on membership of both organizations.

In December, as Viceroy Hardinge enters **New Delhi** on an elephant to mark its adoption as capital of the Indian empire based hitherto at Calcutta, a bomb is thrown at his howdah. Hardinge escapes with injuries.

1914 In August **World War I** erupts in Europe. Viceroy Hardinge II announces that India will support the Allies against Germany. His government gives a grant of £100 million to London.

Congress and Muslim League leaders also support the War, which will boost Indian industry. The number of workers employed in some 3000 factories will rise to around a million. Tens of thousands more work at plantations and mines, as well as on the railways. Of the 1,440,000 Indians who will join the Indian army, 62,000 will be killed.

New Delhi

New Delhi, the customized capital of British India built between 1911 and 1925, is the eighth city constructed in the Delhi area since its founding in the mid-730s as Dhillika. It lies between Shahjahanabad (aka Old Delhi, see p.192) to its north and the earlier Delhi of the Rajput-Sultanate period to its south, the whole Old-New Delhi conurbation measuring 20 x 10km. New Delhi's other antecedants are the Qutb Complex (see p.130), Siri, Tughluqabad, Jahanpanah, Ferozabad and Shergarh.

Built on virgin land, it was designed by the principal architect **Sir Edwin Lutyens** to impress Indians with the power and glory of the British Raj. Lutyens' success in doing so has not precluded his buildings from being regarded as among the finest examples of early modernism. He projected a kaleidoscope of broken triangles and hexagons pivoting on roundabouts, with **Kingsway** (now called Raj Path) as its central axis – a broad throughfare, including the impressive **War Memorial Arch** (now India Gate), rising up to the acropolis on the Raisina Hill past the Japiur Column, and ending at the **Viceregal Palace** (now Rashtrapati Bhavan, President's Mansion), with 340 rooms and 2.5km of corridors, all built in red sandstone. The chamber of the **Imperial Legislative Council** (now Parliament) is tucked away in a corner below the hill.

1915 Mohandas Karamchand Gandhi, 46, a British-trained lawyer, returns home from South Africa after many years' political agitation there, and sets up an *ashram* (retreat) along the Sabarmati River near Ahmadabad.

The government in Delhi promulgates the **Defence of India Act**, which gives it draconian powers of arrest.

1916 Viscount Chelmsford becomes Viceroy.

The capital's residential hexagonal grids were divided into sectors of **gazetted officers** (upper class British), **European clerks** (middle class British) and **Indian clerks**, the lowliest ones being the farthest from the Raisana Hill. To maintain New Delhi's social and political superiority, only one thoroughfare was built to link it with Old Delhi.

The President's Residence, New Delhi

At the behest of Jinnah, the Muslim League signs a pact with Congress, demanding immediate steps towards self-rule in recognition of India's participation in the War.

1917 The **Justice Party** is formed in the Madras Presidency (modern Tamil Nadu, coastal Andhra Pradesh and northern Kerala) to promote the interests of its 97 percent non-brahmin majority.

1918 World War I ends in November with victory for the

The Jallianwala Bagh Massacre

The arrest on 10 April 1919 of speakers at a Congress rally in **Amritsar** sparked protests that led to an orgy of arson and violence and left five Europeans dead. Additional troops summoned by Panjab's Lt-Governor **Sir Michael O'Dwyer** arrived under the command of **Brigadier-General Reginald Dyer**. O'Dwyer's ban on further assemblies was poorly announced, and on Sunday 13 April – coinciding with *baisakhi*, a spring festival celebrated by Hindus and Sikhs – thousands gathered in **Jallianwala Bagh**, a park enclosed by high walls with only two gateways.

After persuading Viceroy Chelmsford to declare martial law in Panjab, Dyer, leading ninety Indian and Nepalese soldiers, marched into the park. Without warning, he ordered his men to open fire. Finding the troops blocking the larger exit, the frightened crowd herded toward the narrower one. By the time Dyer ordered a cease-fire, 1650 rounds of ammunition had killed 379 (according to the official report, but unofficially 530) and injured 1200. Dyer then withdrew his force. The following day there was more rioting and arson in Amritsar as Dyer advocated a strategy of 'frightfulness' to quell disturbances. Although he was relieved of his command and returned to Britain on sick leave, he was never disciplined.

In March 1920, when the House of Commons debated the matter, the Conservative *Morning Post* launched a fund for Dyer and raised £26,317. This sum was presented to him along with a gilt sword inscribed 'To the Saviour of the Panjab'. Whereas the Commons condemned Dyer by 230 votes to 129, the House of Lords declared by 129 votes to 86 that he had been treated unjustly. He died in 1927. Thirteen years later, Udham Singh, a Sikh resident of Coventry, England, shot dead Sir Michael O'Dwyer at the Royal Albert Hall, London, and was hanged.

CORBIS

Brigadier-General Dyer, whose cold-blooded actions on 13 April resulted in the deaths of over 500 civilians

Allies, resulting *inter alia* in the dissolution of the Ottoman Turkish empire, the seat of Islam's **caliphate** since 1517.

1919 As the end of the Defence of India Act nears, Lord Chelmsford proposes replacing it with the **Rowlatt Act** – named after Sir Sydney Rowlatt, chairman of the Committee on the Defence of India Act – empowering him to detain or expel any 'suspected terrorist' without any charge or trial. While the Indian minority on the Imperial Legislative Council rejects the bill, the nominated British majority backs it.

The Rowlatt Act is enforced in March. Congress calls for a nationwide strike on 6 April. Four days later, two speakers at a Congress rally in **Amritsar**, Panjab, are arrested. The resulting mass protest culminates in a slaughter of hundreds of Indians at the **Jallianwala Bagh** – a turning point in Indo-British relations. It outrages Indians of all political hues.

Against this background develops the **Khilafat Movement** with the twin aim of preserving the pan-Islamic Caliphate at Istanbul and expelling the British from India.

At a Khilafat conference in Delhi, Mohandas Gandhi urges Muslims to adopt non-cooperation as a means of gaining their objectives, and Hindus to give their support.

> ❝ When a Government takes up arms against its unarmed subjects, then it has forfeited its right to govern. It has admitted that it cannot rule in peace and justice ... Nothing less than the removal of the British and complete self-government could satisfy injured India ... Plassey laid the foundation of the British Empire. Amritsar has shaken it. ❞

Mohandas Gandhi, reacting to the massacre at Jallianwala Bagh

The demise of Britain's Indian empire 1920–1947

Outraged by the Amritsar massacre, the lawyer-dominated **Congress leadership** underwent a sea-change. It became receptive to the radical, though non-violent, tactics of non-cooperation and civil disobedience advocated by **Mohandas Gandhi**.

Yielding to insistent political pressure, in 1928 the British government appointed a commission to review constitutional reform, only to see it boycotted by both Congress and the Muslim League. By the time the newly elected Labour government in London offered to consider dominion status (as accorded then to Canada and Australia) for India, Congress leaders were demanding total independence.

The 1930s were challenging times for the West and for capitalism. In India, the situation became acute for the British. Within Congress there was a renewed surge of radicalism, powerfully articulated by **Jawaharlal Nehru**, who had a strong base in the United province, and by **Subash Chandra Bose** from Bengal. Economic depression, spreading like a contagion throughout the capitalist world and its colonies, reinforced the resentment many politicized Indians harboured against repressive governmental measures.

Disenchantment spilled over into Gandhi's civil disobedience movement, which many now considered ineffectual. The 1930s ended with the outbreak of a world war that lasted six years. It changed the balance of power globally. Alhough Britain was a leading member of the victorious Allies, it emerged from hostilities economically and militarily exhausted.

In contrast to defiant declarations about retaining the empire at any cost by Winston Churchill, Britain's wartime

Conservative Prime Minister, Labour was committed to granting India independence. With its electoral victory in 1945, Indian hopes rose sharply. If Labour premier **Clement Attlee** had any second thoughts on the subject, these were quickly dispelled by disgruntlement in the ranks of the regular British Indian Army at the trials of the commanders of Bose's anti-Allied Indian National Army, formed during the war with Japan's backing. When mutiny broke out in the Royal Indian Navy in 1946, Britain realized it could no longer rely on the ultimate instrument of coercion – the military – and decided to quit India.

It fell upon **Louis Mountbatten** to perform the last rites of the British empire in the Indian subcontinent. While the jewel in the imperial crown was relinquished at the altar of freedom for the indigenous people, it was split into two, reflecting the rivalry between Hindus and Muslims, which now turned violent.

1920 At its annual convention, Congress adopts Gandhi's policy of **non-cooperation** to achieve self-rule either inside or outside of the British Empire, and demands punishment for those guilty of committing the Amritsar massacre. It also calls for the full restoration of the **Turkey-based caliphate**. Jinnah and other moderates, who want to stay firmly within the empire, lose the debate.

Congress, now seeking a fully autonomous Indian Parliament, refuses to endorse the 1919 **Montford reforms** – named after Secretary of State Edwin Montague and Viceroy Chelmsford. According to these, the existing Imperial Legislative Council is to be replaced with an Imperial Legislative Assembly, a majority of whose members will be elected, but only on a franchise that extends to a mere million out of India's 150 million adults.

The first session of the **All India Trade Union Congress**, claiming affiliation of 107 unions, is held under the chairmanship of **Lajpat Rai**, president of Congress.

1921 Lord Reading becomes Viceroy.

In November Congress calls on Indians to ignore a royal tour about to be undertaken by the **Prince of Wales** (later King George VI). In Bombay, the Prince's first port-of-call, the streets are empty, prompting the Viceroy to imprison most Congress leaders.

In Amritsar, the protest against the Golden Temple's government-nominated manangement committee's decision to

Edward, Prince of Wales visiting Calcutta, from a photograph printed in *Die Nachkinegszeit*

honour General Dyer results in the formation of the popularly elected Shiramoni Gurdwara Prabandhak (Sacred Temples Management) Committee.

The latest census puts India's population at 304 million.

1922 With urban Indians taking up Mohandas Gandhi's call for a tax boycott, Rabindranath Tagore calls him **Mahatma** (Great Soul), a sobriquet that quickly catches on.

The Khilafat Movement has captured the imagination of Muslim masses.

1923 The first Labour government in Britain under Ramsay MacDonald assumes office in November but lasts only nine months. Labour is opposed to imperialism, at least in principle.

1924 Turkey's secular leader Mustafa Kemal Ataturk abolishes the caliphate.

Conservatives form a new government in Britain.

1925 Gandhi switches to furthering such social reform among Hindus as abolishing Untouchability (see p.16).

The lower classes in towns have been seriously affected by the non-cooperation movement. In certain areas, the peasantry have been affected ... The [Sikh] Akali [Party's] agitation had penetrated to the rural Sikhs. The Muhammadan population throughout the country is embittered and sullen.

Lord Reading, reporting to the Secretary of State for India in 1922

Sarojini Naidu becomes the first woman president of Congress.

The **Communist Party of India** is founded in Bombay.

The British Labour Party conference accepts India's right to Dominion Status, defined as common allegiance to the Crown within the free association of the British Commonwealth.

Dr K. B. Hedgewar forms the *Rashtriya Swayamsevak Sangh* (National Volunteer Union), a militant Hindu organization in Nagpur, central India.

1926 Lord Irwin is appointed Viceroy.

Muslim League membership falls to 1330.

The Trade Unions Act grants legal status to registered unions.

1927 The **Indian Broadcasting Company**, a private firm, launches public radio broadcasts in Calcutta and Bombay.

The London-based **Imperial Airways** introduces regular flights between Britain and India.

1928 An all-British, seven-member Commission, chaired by Sir John Simon, arrives from London to assess the Montford Reforms. Congress boycotts it and demands total self-rule. Guided by Jinnah, the Muslim League narrowly follows suit, causing a split in the party.

1929 In Britain a minority Labour government, backed by Liberals and led by Ramsay MacDonald, assumes office. It offers to discuss Dominion Status for India at an all-party conference.

1930 In Lahore, at the stroke of midnight on 31 December 1929/1 January 1930, the annual conference of Congress passes a resolution, moved by Jawaharlal Nehru, demanding **total independence** from Britain, and adopts a tricolour flag for an independent India. Gandhi's call for civil disobedience, involving non-payment of taxes and commercial shutdowns, leads to 92,000 arrests country-wide.

> " My bent is not political but religious, and I take part in politics because I feel that there is no department of life which can be divorced from religion.
>
> It is better in prayer to have a heart without words than words without a heart.
>
> Joy comes not out of infliction of pain on others, but out of pain voluntarily borne by oneself.
>
> Sex urge is a fine and noble thing. There is nothing to be ashamed of in it. But it is meant only for the act of creation. Any other use of it is a sin against God and humanity.
>
> Industrialization on a mass scale will necessarily lead to passive or active exploitation of the villagers as the problems of competition and marketing come in. Therefore we have to concentrate on the village being self-contained, manufacturing mainly for [its own] use.
>
> The conflict between moneyed classes and labourers is merely seeming. When labour is intelligent enough to organize itself and learns to act as one man, it will have the same weight as money if not much greater. The conflict is really between intelligence and unintelligence. "
>
> some thoughts of Mahatma Gandhi

In an address to a poorly attended Muslim League conference in December, President **Muhammad Iqbal** refers to a North-Western State as 'the destiny of the [Indian] Muslims'.

The Indian Broadcasting Company is taken over by the **Indian State Broadcasting Service** established by the Imperial Government.

The first Indian talking film *Alam Ara*, produced and directed by Ardeshir Irani of the Imperial Film Company of Bombay, is released.

1931 In March Viceroy Irwin agrees to release all political prisoners and return the confiscated lands of Congress protesters in exchange for the party's participation at the **London Round Table Conference** on India's future.

In August Ramsay MacDonald's Labour government in Britain falls, and in the election two months later Labour loses heavily.

The **Marquess of Willingdon** becomes Viceroy of India, which now has a population of 338 million.

1932 The Indian government's **Communal Award**, confirming separate electorates for Muslims, Sikhs and Christians, is criticized by Congress.

Tata Airlines, the first indigenous Indian company of its kind, is founded.

1933 India's first major sound-film studio, Bombay Talkies, is established.

In a short pamphlet, *Now or Never*, published in Cambridge, four Indian Muslim students, led by Rahmat Ali, call the Muslim 'fatherland' they are seeking **Pakistan** (Land of the Pure), with P standing for Panjab, A for Afghania, K for Kashmir and S for Sind.

> **❝** The British government in India has not only deprived the Indian people of their freedom but has based itself on the exploitation of the masses, and has ruined India economically, politically, culturally and spiritually. We believe, therefore, that India must sever the British connection and attain *purna swaraj* or complete independence. **❞**
>
> Resolution adopted by Congress, 1 January 1930

> **❝** I would like to see the Panjab, the North-West Frontier Province, Sind and Baluchistan amalgamated into a single State. Self-government within the British Empire or without the British Empire, the formation of a consolidated North-West Indian Muslim State appears to me to be the destiny of the Muslims, at least of North-West India. **❞**
>
> Sir Muhammad Iqbal, addressing the Muslim League's annual conference in 1930

1935 A new **Government of India Act** specifies a parliamentary administration and stipulates as its goals Dominion Status for India and a federal framework, to be applied to both British India and the Princely States. Its stress is on provincial autonomy. Burma is to be separated from the Indian Empire (in 1937), Sind from the Bombay Presidency (in 1936), and Orissa from Bihar (in 1936), thus creating eleven provinces in British India. The franchise, still based on ownership of property and/or education, is to be enlarged from 7 to 35 million – covering only about a sixth of the adult population.

1936 Lord Linlithgow becomes Viceroy, charged with implementing the 1935 Act.

Jawaharlal Nehru is elected president of Congress, which decides to contest the forthcoming elections.

George VI becomes king following Edward VIII's abdication.

The Indian State Broadcasting Service is renamed **All India Radio** (AIR).

1937 In the country-wide poll at the provincial level, **Congress** secures 70 percent of the popular vote in elections on a limited franchise, and despite separate electorates for Muslims and non-Muslims, nearly half the seats. It captures seven provinces, including the Muslim-majority North-West Frontier province (NWFP).

Outside the NWFP, however, it wins only eleven of the 58 reserved seats for Muslims it contests. But the **Muslim League** gains barely 6 percent of the vote. The Muslim-majority Bengal is won by Fazl al Haq's radical **Peasants' People Party** and the Muslim-majority Panjab by Sir Sikandar Hayat Khan's pro-landlord **Unionist Party**.

Nehru, elected Congress president for the second one-year term, refuses the Muslim League's offer of a coalition in the most populous United province.

1938 Jinnah develops the Muslim League as the opposition party in the Congress-ruled provincial assemblies. It opens 170 new branches countrywide.

The Justice Party in Madras elects E. V. Ramaswamy Naicker, a Tamil nationalist, as its president.

1939 When **World War II** erupts in Europe in September, Viceroy Linlithgow declares that India is at war with Germany without bothering to consult Indian leaders, and promulgates the draconian **Defence of India Act**.

When all seven Congress provincial ministries resign in protest, he imposes direct rule on these provinces – a move welcomed by the Muslim League as 'Deliverance Day from the oppression of the Congress rule'.

Muhammad Iqbal 1873–1938

A leading Muslim thinker and poet, **Muhammad Iqbal** formulated the political theory that led to the creation of Pakistan in 1947. Born in Sialkot, Panjab, and educated at Government College, Lahore, he went to Cambridge in 1905, and then to the University of Munich, to study philosophy and law. After qualifying as a barrister in London he returned to Lahore in 1908.

A poet of outstanding quality and power, he published eleven volumes of verse in Persian and Urdu. His style changed from romantic lyricism to the elucidation of a social philosophy as his study of Western philosophy strengthened his belief in Islam, the religion adopted by his Kasmiri Hindu ancestors. Believing that Islam was flexible enough to adapt to the modern age, he interpreted the message of the *Quran* in his poetry. His study of Western civilization led him to reject its materialism but accept its values of freedom and individualism. While stressing the superiority of Islamic spiritualism, he urged Muslims to seek freedom and self-development. In *Asrar-e Khudi* ('Secrets of Self', 1915), a long narrative poem in Persian that established his reputation as a poet-philosopher, he argues that the proper development of the self is best achieved by the individual placing himself at the service of his community.

Regarding Indian Muslims as a distinct community, he proposed a separate homeland for them in 1930 when he was the Muslim League's acting president. In *Reconstruction of Muslim Thought in Islam* (1934), he differentiated between religion, which is timeless, and the science of religion – that is, the thoughts of religion, which are defined by time and place – a thesis that would be adopted by reformists in the Islamic Republic of Iran in the late 1990s.

1940 A resolution, adopted by the Muslim League's annual conference, says that since Muslims are 'a nation by any definition', the League demands a constitution whereby 'the areas in which Muslims are numerically in a majority, as in the North-Western and Eastern zones of India, should be grouped to constitute Independent States in which the constituent units shall be autonomous and sovereign.' In the Madras Presidency, the Justice Party demands an independent **Tamil Nadu**.

As World War II rages, the Indian Army expands from 175,000 to 2 million by the end of the war six years later.

Subash Chandra Bose, a militant nationalist and former Congress president, escapes from house arrest in Calcutta to Afghanistan and then to Moscow and Berlin.

1941 The World War II results in an expansion of Indian industry, from textiles to cement to steel.

At 388 million, India's population is 11 percent higher than two decades earlier, but the area under cultivation remains static.

Rabindranath Tagore dies.

1942 In February, following the fall of British Hong Kong, Malaya and Singapore to the Japanese, a British delegation led by **Sir Stafford Cripps** arrives in Delhi. Cripps promises a **Constituent Assembly**, elected by Provincial Assemblies, to draft a British Dominion constitution for India after the War. Congress rejects the plan, demanding an immediate all-Indian Viceroy's Council with the full powers of a Dominion cabinet.

In August 7500 delegates attending the Congress party's annual conference demand an immediate end to British rule, triggering the **Quit India** movement. The Viceroy arrests all Congress leaders, including Gandhi, and imposes

Rabindranath Tagore 1861–1941

A poet, novelist, dramatist, essayist, composer, painter and educationalist, who also combined classical Indian art forms with folk traditions and encouraged cultural exchange between the East and the West, **Rabindranath Tagore** was a latter-day Renaissance man who dominated the cultural life of Bengal during the early 20th century. By releasing Bengali prose from traditional forms of Sanskrit, he made literary Bengali accessible to the masses; and by devising new metres he enriched Bengali poetry. He also introduced the short story and opera to Indian audiences.

Born in Calcutta to a rich landlord family, he was tutored at home and became proficient in Bengali, Sanskrit and English. At sixteen, he was sent to England to study law, a subject that bored him. Following his marriage to Mrinalini Debi in 1884, he left Calcutta to manage the family estate at Silaidaha. After seventeen years he moved to Santiniketan, the family retreat 160km north of Calcutta. There he founded an experimental school for boys which twenty years later blossomed into an international university, **Visvabharati**.

He published his first volume of poetry at 18, inspired by close contact with Bengal's enchanting landscape. Similarly, insights into peasant life gained as an estate manager underpinned his fiction. His genius found its fullest expression in *Gitanjali* (**'Song Offerings'**), published in Bengali in 1910, and translated into English in 1912. This won him the Nobel Prize for Literature. In 1915 he gained his knighthood. While on lecture tours of America, Europe, China, Japan and Southeast Asia, he advocated blending the East's ancient spiritual heritage with the West's material achievements. Although he did not participate in India's independence struggle, he renounced his knighthood in protest at the Jallianwala Bagh massacre (see p.270). Independent India honoured him by adopting one of his songs, *Jan Gan Man* ('Mind of the People'), as the national anthem.

Rabindrath Tagore and attendants

censorship. British Prime Minister Sir Winston Churchill declares, 'I have not become the King's First Minister to preside over liquidation of the British empire.'

In the first week of the Quit India agitation, militant Indian nationalists attack 500 post offices, 250 railway stations, 150 police stations and derail 60 trains. By the end of September, the authorities have arrested 60,000 agitators, and shot dead about a thousand.

1943 A year-long famine begins in Bengal, killing an estimated 3 million people.

In July Subash Chandra Bose arrives in Japanese-occupied Singapore following two meetings in Tokyo with Japanese Prime Minister Hideki Tojo. He forms a Provisional Government of Independent India with its own **Indian National Army**, composed of 25,000 volunteers (a third of them Sikhs) from 60,000 Indian POWs held by Japan.

In October India has a new Viceroy, **Lord Wavell**, who, as the supreme commander of Allied forces in the Southwest Pacific since December 1941, has overseen the Allied withdrawal from Southeast Asia.

The home-based imperial Indian Army becomes part of General William Slim's 14th Army, a component of the

I am engaged here in meeting the most serious rebellion since that of 1857, the gravity and extent of which we have so far concealed from the world for reasons of military security.

Viceroy Linlithgo to British Prime Minister Winston Churchill, 31 August 1942

South East Asia Command (SEAC) now under Admiral **Louis Mountbatten.**

1944 Early in the year, the Indian Army halts a Japanese advance into Assam at **Kohima** (capital of modern Nagaland). It later participates in General Slim's recapture of **Burma.**

In May the government releases Gandhi on account of his failing health. His initiative to reach a compromise with Jinnah on India's future fails, and this enhances Jinnah's status and makes him more intransigent.

In the south, the Justice Party changes its name to **Dravida Kazhagam** (Dravida Federation).

1945 World War II ends in Europe in May. In June India becomes one of fifty Allied nations to sign the **United Nations Charter** in San Francisco.

At a conference of Indian leaders, Wavell proposes transforming his Executive Council into a national cabinet. The conference fails when Jinnah insists on the Muslim League nominating all Muslim members of the Council, and Congress President Maulana Abul Kalam Azad, a Muslim, refuses to give up his party's right to include a Muslim in its list.

In July the Labour Party wins two-thirds of the British parliamentary seats in a general election, and **Clement Attlee** forms the new government.

The war with Japan ends in August.

1946 The government's decision to put 6000 Indian POWs belonging to Chandra Bose's Indian National Army on trial engenders widespread civilian protest and restiveness in the regular army.

In February a **mutiny** by Indian ratings at *HMS Talwar*, an on-shore signals school, spreads to the Royal Indian Navy's

Muhammad Ali Jinnah 1875–1948

Muhammad Ali Jinnah was the architect of Pakistan. The only son of Jinnahbhai Poonja, an affluent, Karachi-based Ismaili Muslim importer-exporter, and Mithi Bai, he was apprenticed to Sir Frederick Croft, a British businessman, at 16. While serving his apprenticeship in London, he acquired a new surname by shortening his father's first name. He studied law and was called to the bar in 1896. On his return to India, he enrolled as a barrister in Bombay's High Court, where he came under the influence of **Justice Badruddin Tyabji**, a former Congress president. At the 1904 conference of Congress, he met and worked with **Gopal Krishna Gokhale**, a moderate. In 1910 he was elected to the Imperial Legislative Council, and nine years later became president of the Muslim League. He condemned the Jallianwala Bagh massacre but, when Congress voted to adopt extra-constitutional means to achieve its objectives, he resigned his membership. Under his leadership, the Muslim League in 1924 demanded a federal union of autonomous provinces with separate electorates.

When he travelled to London in 1930 to attend the **Round Table Conference** on India's future, he stayed on until he was persuaded to return home in 1934 to revive the moribund League. On the eve of the 1937 elections, the League formed a power-sharing alliance with Congress in the United Province. But when Congress won 135 of 228 seats, Jawaharlal Nehru demanded the League's merger into Congress before its members could be included in a ministry. This turned Jinnah bitterly against

78 ships and 20 shore establishments. In Bombay the mutiny on 22 ships is backed by workers' strikes and commercial shutdowns. Suppression of the mutiny results in 228 deaths.

In fresh **elections** to the 102-member Imperial Legislative Council, Congress wins 57 seats and the Muslim League

Congress, whose decision to oppose Britain during World War II strengthened his hand. The League's impressive performance in the 1946 elections paved the way for the creation of Pakistan. Possessing a strong will, steely nerves and extraordinary tactical skills, Jinnah marshalled the adversarial skills acquired as a lawyer against his political opponents to lethal effect.

Muhammad Al Jinnah (right) with Nehru in 1946 at Viceregal Lodge, Simla

30. Congress also secures majorities in eight provinces, including Assam and the North-West Frontier Province, the provinces to be included in the Pakistan being demanded by the League. Although the League gains 442 of 509 Muslim seats in the provinces, it is able to form governments only in Sind and Bengal.

Five months of intense negotiations by a three-member British cabinet mission, initiated in March, convince Congress leaders that London is sincere about transferring power. The League's 'Direct action to achieve Pakistan', commencing on 16 August, leads to three days of Hindu-Muslim riots in Calcutta, which leave 3500 dead.

Congress agrees to join the interim government in September, with Nehru becoming Foreign Minister, and his right-wing Congress colleague **Vallabh Bhai Patel** Home Minister.

In October the League's Liaqat Ali Khan becomes Finance Minister, even though this means acceptance of Asaf Ali, a Congress leader of Muslim faith, as a fellow cabinet member.

1947 Facing civil disobedience by League activists, the coalition government in Panjab collapses, and the governor imposes direct rule.

In February Clement Attlee promises the end of British rule in India by June 1948.

In March Lord Mountbatten takes over as Viceroy.

In June he publishes a plan to **partition the Indian empire** into the dominions of India and Pakistan, effective from 15 August, with the Princely States being free to join either India or Pakistan. Panjab and Bengal are to be divided into Muslim and non-Muslim-majority sectors.

On 14 August the Dominion of Pakistan is established with Jinnah as its Governor-General and Liaqat Ali Khan as its Prime Minister. **West Pakistan** comprises Baluchistan, the NWFP, Panjab and Sind; and **East Pakistan** East Bengal and the Sylhet district of Assam.

On 15 August the **Dominion of India** is inaugurated, with Lord Mountbatten as Governor-General and Nehru as its Prime Minister.

The demarcation of Panjab into Muslim majority West Panjab and Hindu-Sikh-majority East Panjab is announced on 17 August. Large-scale inter-communal killings and looting follow, resulting in some 500,000 deaths. Between 4 to 5.5 million people cross the newly created international frontier in Panjab in each direction to seek refuge among their co-religionists. In addition, nearly half a million Sindhi Hindus migrate to India, and about an equal number of Muslims migrate from Bombay and the United Provinces to Pakistan. Almost a million Hindus from East Pakistan migrate to India's West Bengal. In the end, 9 million Hindus remain in East Pakistan, and 40 million Muslims in India.

Concerning the **Princely States**, each ruler chooses between India and Pakistan in accordance with the majority religious affiliation of his subjects. The exceptions are Muslim-majority Jammu and Kashmir, ruled by Maharaja Hari Singh, a Hindu; and Hindu-majority Hyderabad, ruled by a Muslim Nizam, Sir Osman Ali Khan.

> **"** Long years ago we made a tryst with destiny, and now the time comes when we shall redeem our pledge, not wholly or in full measure but very substantially. At the stroke of the midnight hour, when the world sleeps, India will awake to life and freedom. A moment comes, which comes but rarely in history, when we step from the old to the new, when an age ends, and when the soul of a nation, long suppressed, finds utterance. It is fitting that at this solemn moment we take the pledge of dedication to the service of India and her people and to the still larger cause of humanity. **"**

Radio broadcast by Jawaharlal Nehru on the eve of Indian independence on 15 August 1947

Earl Mountbatten 1900–79

The last Viceroy of India was born Louis Francis Albert Victor Nicholas to Prince Louis of Battenberg and Princess Victoria of Hesse, a grand-daughter of Queen Victoria. Throughout his career he succeeded as much by his royal connections as by his brilliance, energy and diplomatic flair. Vain and over-ambitious, he frequently tailored or invented facts to glorify his accomplishments. He first went to India at 21 as a companion to the Prince of Wales. The following year, he married Edwina Ashley, a society millionairess, and joined the Royal Navy. In 1942 Churchill appointed him Chief of Combined Operations in the southwest Pacific. A year later, he was promoted Supreme Allied Commander, Southeast Asia.

To distance himself from two British field-marshals – Sir Archibald Wavell and Sir Claude Auchinleck – Moutbatten set up his headquarters in Kandy, Sri Lanka. Even though Burma was recaptured from the Japanese by generals William Slim and Sir Oliver Leese, operating under Auchinleck, Mountbatten never baulked at calling himself Mountbatten of Burma. Clement Attlee chose him as Viceroy partly because he had no preconceived ideas about India, and partly because Attlee trusted his boldness and ingenuity. The appointment of the king's cousin also reassured Indian leaders that the British government was sincere about quitting the subcontinent. At his first meeting with Nehru, Mountbatten reputedly said, 'Mr Nehru, I want you to regard me not as the last viceroy winding up the British Raj, but as the first to lead the way to a new India.' His disarming charm played an important role in ending two centuries of British exploitation in a milieu of genuine *bonhomie*.

While Hari Singh agonizes between joining one or the other Dominion, and declaring independence, on 22 October truck-loads of armed tribals from neighbouring Pakistan rush to the Kashmiri capital Srinagar along the only road to the Kashmir Valley. Three days later the

Maharaja signs an accession instrument with India, with Mountbatten adding a proviso to determine the popular wish once peace has been restored. Delhi airlifts troops to Srinagar. Fighting between Indian regulars and Pakistani irregulars and then Pakistani regulars escalates.

In the south, Dravida Kazhagam leader Naicker instructs party members to boycott Indian independence celebrations since independence will not end 'Hindi imperialism'.

10
Independent India

1947–2002

Since independence, India has made impressive gains in economic development and investment and, the **1975–77 emergency** apart, maintained a multi-party democratic system with a free press and independent judiciary. The life expectancy of Indians has more than doubled, from 32 years to 68, and the literacy rate has risen to 66 percent from a base of 18 percent.

Since the mid-1980s, India has also been self-sufficient in food. In the 1990s it emerged as an important centre of information technology linked closely to Silicon Valley in the United States of America. Today, it produces a wide array of advanced industrial goods and military hardware. In 1998 it became the seventh nation to possess the nuclear bomb – after the United States, Russia, Britain, France, China and Israel.

Yet the country still faces daunting problems. Nearly four-fifths of Indians continue to live in villages which often lack basic amenities; and 70 percent of them depend on **agriculture**, which contributes only 25 percent of the GDP. About a quarter, living below the poverty line – as defined by the government – are unable to afford an adequate diet. Although a vigorously implemented family planning programme has brought the annual population growth to below 2 percent, the current density of 337 persons per sq km remains too high for an underdeveloped economy.

Socially, **caste consciousness** among rural **Hindus** remains strong. And violence between majority Hindus and minority **Muslims** erupts periodically. In the northeastern region, bordering Myanmar/Burma and China, tribal people of Mongoloid stock and Christian faith feel alienated from the Hindu-dominated mainstream. India's dispute with the Islamic Republic of **Pakistan** over **Kashmir**, rooted in religion and differing founding ideologies, remains a grave international problem. With both countries now armed with nuclear weapons, future wars over Kashmir carry the risk of turning nuclear.

Unlike Pakistan, India remains a secular state. Of its eleven presidents so far, three have been Muslim and one Sikh. Its secularism owes much to the leadership of **Jawaharlal Nehru**, an enlightened intellectual, who shaped the new nation during its formative period. Nehru's uninterrupted premiership of seventeen years was followed shortly afterward by that of his daughter **Indira Gandhi**, wife of Feroze Gandhi, a Parsi. Her interrupted premiership lasted a decade and a half. She was folllowed by her son **Rajiv**, who led the country for five years. Thus the Nehru-Gandhi family dominated Indian politics for nearly four decades. But the domination of their Congress Party had begun declining soon after Nehru's death in 1964, with regional opposition parties gaining at its expense. By the 1990s, coalition politics, well established in the provinces – now called Union States, or just States – became the norm in Delhi.

While India's political complexion has changed, its administrative structure, outlined in its constitution of 1950, remains unaltered. A fairly strong central government exercises national sovereignty – defence, foreign affairs, currency and communications – while State governments manage law and order, education and public health. The head of the Republic is the President, elected for a five-year term by an electoral college consisting of lawmakers at the national and

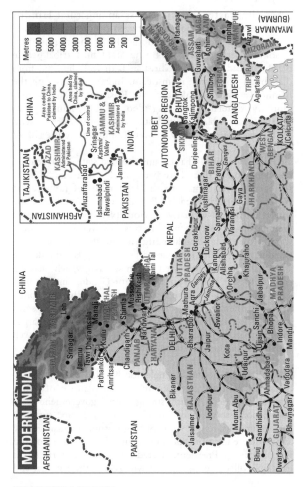

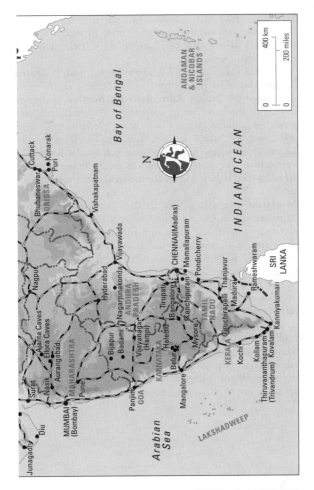

State levels. Each State is headed by a governor appointed by the President on the advice of the Prime Minister. In addition, there are directly ruled union territories, including metropolitan Delhi.

In 2002 there were **27 Union States** and **7 Union Territories**. The pre-independence Indian Civil Service, now called the **Indian Administrative Service**, continues to provide the backbone of government at Central and State levels. As required by the Constitution, elections to Central and States legislatures are held regularly. The leader of the largest group in the legislature is invited by the Republic's President or the State's governor to form the government, which is then required to secure the legislature's vote of confidence. The head of a State government is called **Chief Minister**, and that of the Central government **Prime Minister**. If the Central administration determines that law and order has broken down in a particular State, it has the authority to dismiss the local government and institute Presidential Rule for six months at a time, subject to the Central Parliament's approval.

The bicameral **Central Parliament** (*Sansad*, in Hindi) consists of a directly elected **People's Assembly (*Lok Sabha*)** and the **Council of States (*Rajya Sabha*)** whose members are elected by State Legislative Assemblies. It is the leader of the largest group in the *Lok Sabha* who is invited to form the Central government and who, as Prime Minister, administers India. In the 542-member *Lok Sabha*, a typical deputy represents a constituency of over a million voters, an apt reflection of India's over-population.

India under Nehru (1947–64)

After the deaths, between 1948–50, of Mahatma Gandhi and Vallabh Bhai Patel, Jawaharlal Nehru became the nation's sole surviving founding father. He had the charisma to hold together a polyglot republic during its fledgling years. The masses revered him because he was a fair-skinned brahmin, while the middle classes admired him for his British education, his honesty and integrity, and his socially progressive views.

Nehru, therefore, had a free hand to forge the key characteristics of the **Republic of India**: democracy and secularism at home, and a foreign policy of non-alignment with either the US-led capitalist bloc or the Soviet Union-led Marxist-socialist bloc. Indeed, while launching the **First Five-Year Plan**, he described it as a unique combination of economic planning – a concept commonly associated with Marxist-socialist regimes – and Western-style democracy.

During his tour of China in 1954, Nehru was impressed by the discipline and enthusiasm with which the Chinese, under the newly triumphant Communist regime, were building their economy. Under his guidance, the **Congress Party** resolved to create 'a socialist pattern of society' in India. The **Industrial Policy Resolution** adopted by Parliament in 1956 stated that industries of basic and strategic importance should be in the public sector, which should also include industries requiring large-scale investment: coal, iron and steel, aircraft manufacturing, shipbuilding, and oil extraction and other mining. Industries like machine tools, heavy chemicals and fertilizers were assigned to the mixed public-private sector; and the rest to the private sector. The overall strategy was to lay a solid foundation for the next stage of industrialization: consumer goods and light industry.

Nehru's advocacy of non-alignment with the two international power blocs proved popular with other newly independent nations in Asia and Africa, and became institutionalized in the **Non-Aligned Movement** established in 1955. Seven years later, however, in the war with China that Nehru brought upon India, he panicked and secretly appealed to Washington for military intervention.

1948 In January **Mahatma Gandhi** is assassinated in Delhi by Nathu Ram Godse, a member of the militant Hindu group *Rashtriya Swayamsevak Sangh* ('National Volunteer Union').

In May Lord Mountbatten is succeeded by **Chakravarti Rajgopalacharya** as Governor-General.

In Pakistan, Muhammad Ali Jinnah dies of cancer.

In August, as fighting between India and Pakistan in **Kashmir** continues, the United Nations Security Council adopts a three-part resolution calling for an immediate ceasefire, the withdrawal of both regular and tribal Pakistani troops from all of Jammu and Kashmir, including the area under Pakistani control, and a plebiscite to determine whether voters wish to join India or Pakistan.

Following the march of Indian troops into his territory, Nizam Sir Osman Ali Khan of **Hyderabad** (212,400 sq km; population 17 million) signs an accession agreement with Delhii.

1949 On 1 January a UN-brokered ceasefire takes effect in Kashmir along a Line of Control, with Pakistan holding 82,880 out of 225,410 sq km.

In December India recognizes the **People's Republic of China**, founded by the Communist leader Mao Zedong (Mao Tse-tung) two months earlier.

In the south, a split within the Dravida Kazhagam leads to the formation of the **Dravida Munnetra Kazhagam** (Dravida Progressive Federation) under the leadership of C. N. Annadurai. Although committed to establishing an independent **Tamil Nadu**, the DMK is less vehement in its rhetoric than the DK.

1950 In January India adopts a secular, republican **Constitution** which provides universal adult suffrage for a population that is 82 percent illiterate, and a voting system based on the first-past-the-post model used by Britain.

When Britain discards the rule that a Commonwealth member must accept the British sovereign as its head of state, the door is open for the **Republic of India** (*Bharat*, in Hindi) to join the British Commonwealth, which it does.

India's first President, elected by an electoral college of State and Central legislators, is **Rajendra Prasad**. Article

> **"** On the 26th of January 1950, we are going to enter a life of contradictions. In politics we will have equality and in social and economic life we will have inequality. In politics we will be recognising the principle of one man one vote and one vote one value. In our social and economic life, we shall, by reason of our social and economic structure, continue to deny the principle of one man one value ... If we continue to deny it for long, we do so only by putting our political democracy in peril. **"**
>
> Bhim Rao Ambedkar, Law Minister of India and a principal architect of the Indian Constitution, in a speech to the Indian Constituent Assembly, 25 November 1949

(Mahatma) Mohandas Karamchand Gandhi
1869–1948

A politician, saint, social reformer, and an originator of *satyagraha* (literally force born out of truth), **Mohandas Gandhi** has left a lasting imprint on India's political culture, where the practice of *satyagraha* continues. Son of Karamchand, the trading caste chief minister of Porbandar princely state, and of Putli Bai, Mohandas went to London at 18 to study law. He joined the Vegetarian Society, whose members included playwright George Bernard Shaw, who introduced him to the works of Leo Tolstoy and David Thoreau. These books shaped Gandhi's vision of creating small, self-sufficient communities in India.

After an unsuccessful legal practice in India, he went to Durban, South Africa, in 1893 as a clerk with an Indian legal firm. In his fight for Indian settlers' rights, he synthesized the Hindu concept of *dharna* (literally steadying; in practice, squatting in front of a house or office) with the central idea of Thoreau's essay 'Civil Disobedience', and came up with *satyagraha*, combining passive resistance against, and non-cooperation with, unjust authority. Yielding to Gandhi's sustained agitation against racist laws, South Africa's government compromised.

Following his return to India in 1915, and the Amritsar massacre of 1919, he became the unelected, yet supreme, leader of Congress. During an anti-Untouchability campaign from the mid-1920s, he performed menial tasks associated with Untouchables. Although he ceased to be a Congress member from 1934, he remained hugely influential. During World War II he argued that if the Allies were really fighting for democracy and freedom, then Britain should set India free so that it could then join the anti-Nazi war as an independent nation. When Britain rejected this demand, he launched the Quit India movement in 1942. He lived to see India attain independence, but fell victim to the fanaticism of a militant Hindu who considered him pro-Pakistan. Whereas his political opponents considered him a shrewd negotiator and adept at self-dramatization, the masses revered him as a Mahatma, Great Soul.

Mahatma Gandhi and admirers

370 of the Constitution declares that the powers of the Union Parliament are limited to defence, foreign affairs, communications and currency.

Vallabh Bhai Patel, the right-wing Home Minister, who oversees the integration of Princely States into the Union, dies.

The **United States of America** provides aid to India, including food under its Public Law 480, which allows Delhi to pay for it in Indian rupees, which are then given back to India as grants and loans for development projects.

1951 India's **population** reaches 362 million.

The **Bharatiya Jana Sangh** (Indian People's Union), a Hindu nationalist party, is formed by Shyam Prasad Mookerji.

1952 In the first general election – in which political parties are represented by **symbols on ballots** to aid the largely illiterate electorate – Congress wins 45 percent of the popular vote and over 75 percent of the seats in the Union Parliament.

Nehru continues as Prime Minister. The first **Five Year Plan**, a blueprint for economic development, is launched.

1953 A **States Reorganization Commission** is appointed.

At Delhi's request, the head of Kashmir State, Karan Singh, imprisons the chief executive Shaikh Muhammad Abdullah.

Vijay Lakshmi Pandit, Nehru's sister, becomes president of the UN General Assembly for a year.

Bimal Roy's realist *Do Bigha Zamin* ('Two Acres of Land'), an emotive story of a Bengali peasant's struggle to retain a small plot of land, breaks new ground in Indian cinema, hitherto dominated by mythological, historical and social melodramas.

1954 Nehru's tour of Communist China leaves him impressed with the energetic discipline with which the Chinese are pursuing the task of national reconstruction.

In April Delhi and Beijing sign an agreement on 'Trade and Intercourse between the Tibet Region of China and India' which in its preamble includes the *Panchsheel* (Five Principles) – 'Mutual respect for each other's territorial integrity and sovereignty; Mutual non-aggression; Mutual non-interference in each other's internal affairs; Equality and mutual benefit; Peaceful co-existence.'

1955 Congress Party's annual conference at Avadi near Madras adopts the goal of establishing **'a socialistic pattern of society'**.

During a state visit to India, Soviet premier **Nikolai Bulganin** and Communist Party First Secretary **Nikita Khrushchev** declare that Kashmir is an integral part of India, which starts receiving economic aid from Moscow.

At a conference of independent Asian and African states in Bandung, Indonesia, the **Non-Aligned Movement** is founded under the leadership of Nehru and Indonesian President Ahmad Sukarno.

1956 The boundaries of the **Union States** and former **Princely States** are reorganized along linguistic lines – except for Hindi, the mother tongue of some 40 percent of Indians, inhabiting reconstituted Uttar Pradesh, Bihar, Madhya Pradesh and Rajasthan. Other exceptions are bilingual (Gujarati and Marathi) Bombay State, which is retained intact, and the amalgamation of East Panjab and PEPSU (Patiala and East Panjab States Union) into Panjab (Hindi and Panjabi). Among the new Union States in the south is Tamil Nadu.

Indian cinema

Movie-making, originating in 1913, became India's seventh largest industry six decades later, with an annual output of 400 feature films in a dozen languages.

Following the tradition of popular entertainments based on dramatizations of the *Ramayana* and *Mahabharata*, the first **Indian film** told the story of Raja Harish Chandra's renunciation of his kingdom. For the next two decades historical-mythological scenarios were standard fare. Only later did directors turn to such topics as Untouchability, child labour and the abuse of women.

Nowadays, most Indian movies are contemporary social melodramas, where a villain, who is a lying, gambling crook, and a handsome hero, a paragon of virtue, vie for an attractive young woman, the daughter of a mill owner or rich barrister. Through highly improbable situations, the film maker sharpens this conflict, bringing it to a climax in a fight between the two, followed or preceded by a hot chase. It is *de rigueur* that the film has a birthday party scene, a death-bed scene, a stage show, a duet, a chase, a fist fight and a cabaret performance. The function of the cabaret is to provide vicarious satisfaction for sex-starved audiences in cities where men outnumber women two to one.

In the mid-1950s, however, first **Bimal Roy**, and then **Satyajit Ray**, both influenced by the Italian director Vittorio de Sica's *Bicycle Thieves*, introduced realism into Indian cinema. In the universally acclaimed **Apu trilogy** – *Pather Panchali*, *Aparajito* ('Invincible') and *Apur Sansar* ('Apu's World') – about the growing up of Apu, a village boy – Ray combined humanism with superb cinematic technique, transforming the story of daily struggles of life dominated by poverty and domestic strife into an engrossing, lyrical poetry on celluloid. Among those who have followed Ray's pioneering path are Mrinal Sen, Shyam Benegal, Girish Karnad and Mani Kaul.

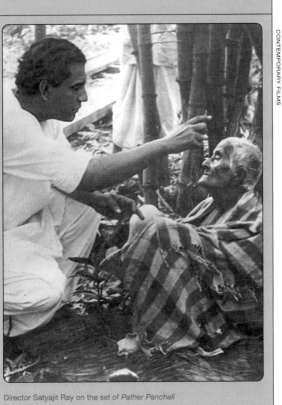

Director Satyajit Ray on the set of *Pather Panchali*

> **❝** I know we make musicals. It is one way of making films. I have made two movies out of 16 without songs. But otherwise you mix song and dance in mathematical proportion. An Indian film is like a mathematical cauldron: bit of story, bit of song and dance, bit of fighting. Actually story is incidental. The excuse for the story is to hang some songs and dances around, to have some fights and to make the boy and the girl meet a number of times. **❞**
>
> Baldev Raj Chopra, a Bombay film producer, in *Observer Magazine*, 10 November 1972

India's first **nuclear reactor** is commissioned.

India imports 12.1 million tonnes of food in the five years up to 1956.

Bengali film director **Satyajit Ray**'s *Pather Panchali* ('Ballad of the Road') wins the Golden Lion Award for the best film prize at the Venice Film Festival.

1957 In the second General Election, Congress gains 45 percent of the popular vote and 371 of the 494 parliamentary seats. Nehru is confirmed as Prime Minister. In the States Legislative Assemblies, Congress wins some 2000 seats out of 3100 and assumes office in all states except **Kerala**.

In Kerala, the capture of power by the **Communist Party of India** through peaceful means is the first such instance in history, excepting tiny San Marino on the Italian peninsula. It forms a State government under E. M. S. Namboodripad.

India sets up the Atomic Energy Establishment near Bombay.

1958 In Pakistan General Ayub Khan suspends the Constitution and imposes military dictatorship.

1959 At the instigation of her father, Nehru, **Indira Gandhi** is elected president of Congress. Prodded by her, Nehru dismisses the Communist government in Kerala and imposes the President's rule.

As Beijing consolidates its control of Tibet, its Buddhist leader, Tenzin Gyasto, the **14th Dalai Lama**, flees to India, which gives him refuge. This creates tension between Delhi and Beijing.

Dwight Eisenhower makes the first state visit to India by an American president. Total US aid to India since its independence now amounts to approximately US$2 billion.

1960 Yielding to mounting popular pressure, Nehru partitions Bombay State into Gujarati-speaking **Gujarat** (capital Ahmadabad) and Marathi-speaking **Maharashtra** (capital Bombay). As stipulated in the Constitution, **Hindi** is declared the official language of India along with English.

Moscow starts supplying India with heavy transport planes and helicopters – which will further Delhi's strategy of establishing forward positions along the Sino-Indian border – and agrees to sell it MiG fighter aircraft.

1961 At 439 million, the **population** of India registers a 21 percent increase on the 1951 census. Life expectancy rises from 32 to 45 years. During 1956–61 **food imports** are put at 19.1 million tonnes, up 7 million tonnes from the previous five-year period.

The first homemade supersonic jet-fighter, the HF-24, is unveiled.

In Washington, President John F. Kennedy promises Nehru increased economic aid during a state visit.

Soon Nehru violates his own doctrine that force should not be used to resolve international disputes when he forcibly ejects **Portugal** from Goa, Daman and Diu.

Indian army scouts discover that the **Chinese military** has constructed a road across the Aksai Chin, an uninhabited salient of the Ladakh region of Jammu and Kashmir, to facilitate troop movement between Tibet and Xinjiang province.

1962 In the third General Election, Congress retains its share of the popular vote and parliamentary seats, and Nehru the premiership.

The India-China War of 1962

Despite the provision of non-interference in each other's internal affairs in the 1954 Delhi-Beijing accord on trade between **Tibet** and **India**, the **Central Intelligence Bureau of India**, run by Nehru, provided assistance to **Gaylo Thondup**, the anti-Communist brother of the Dalai Lama, and other Tibetan activists in **Kalimpong** on the Indo-Sikkimese border. By 1956 Kalimpong-based American and Taiwanese intelligence agents, working with their Indian and Soviet counterparts, were recruiting cadres to foment a separatist rebellion in Tibet. This began modestly in the east, and then spread west to the capital **Lhasa** in early 1959, with the **Dalai Lama** siding with the rebels. Beijing retaliated and regained full control. The Dalai Lama fled to India which gave him refuge.

Such was the background to the border dispute between India and China. In August 1959 the two sides exchanged fire at **Langju** in the eastern sector. In October, in a western sector skirmish, nine Indian policemen were killed. This incensed Delhi. Two years later, Nehru established forward posts in the disputed frontier areas from which China had unilaterally withdrawn its patrols by 20km. In April 1962 Beijing informed

In August and September India commits forces to forward positions on the eastern and western sectors of its borders with China. On 19–20 October hostilities erupt. Within a month, the Chinese overrun Indian border posts and in the east march into Assam. But, just as Nehru makes a secret appeal to the USA for military intervention, Beijing declares a unilateral truce and withdraws to the frontier. Nonetheless, Delhi receives a squadron of large transport planes from Washington. Special American and British military missions lay the ground work for US–UK military assistance worth $120 million over three years.

Delhi that it was resuming border patrols in the western sector, adding that if India persisted in its 'forward policy', it would resume patrols all along the frontier. In September Delhi pressed forward in the western sector. In the third week of October, war broke out in both zones. Within a month China gained the upper hand, and began advancing into **Assam**. On 20 November Nehru secretly appealed to Washington to deploy fifteen bomber and fighter squadrons against the Chinese. President Kennedy ordered a Pacific-based American aircraft carrier to sail to the Bay of Bengal. But the crisis passed the next day when Beijing declared a unilateral ceasefire and began withdrawing its troops.

> We thought it was a sort of game. They would stick up a post and we would stick up a post, and we did not think it would come to much more.

An Indian Army officer cited in the *New York Times*, 11 November 1962.

Jawaharlal Nehru 1890–1964

The only child of **Motilal Nehru**, an aristocratic lawyer and Congress leader in Allahabad, **Jawaharlal** was taught at home by English tutors. After two years at Harrow public school, London, he enrolled at Trinity College, Cambridge, to read chemistry, botany and geology. He then studied law, qualified at 23, and returned home. At 26 he married Kamala Kaul, and a year later they had their only child, **Indira**. Incensed by the 1919 Amritsar massacre, Jawaharlal joined the radical wing of **Congress** and participated in **Gandhi's civil disobedience movement**, courting arrest several times.

Between 1926–27 he travelled to Europe, made many Western contacts, and attended the International Congress against Colonial Oppression and Imperialism in Brussels. He became **President of Congress** in 1937, when the party won power in seven provinces. Though reluctant to undermine Britain during World War II, he supported Mahatma Gandhi's 1942 **Quit India campaign**, again courting arrest. Released in 1945, he was treated as Congress's foremost leader, eventually moving on to become independent India's first **Prime Minister**, a position he held until his death.

Impulsive by nature, he was a poor debater, prone to delivering soliloquies in Parliament. His self-righteousness alienated such diverse personalities as President Kennedy and Chinese premier Zhou Enlai. His 'forward policy' along the India-China border proved disastrous, with the Indian forces suffering a humiliating defeat by the Chinese – a setback that hastened his death 18 months later. However, since he failed to inform even his closest cabinet colleagues of his secret request to Kennedy for military intervention, his cherished non-aligned foreign policy stance remained, publicly, intact.

1963 Parliament passes the **Official Languages Act**, allowing the use of English for all official purposes of the Union beyond January 1965 (the expiry date specified in the Constitution), as well as the use of English as an additional official language in the States until *all* State assemblies and Parliament decide otherwise. A constitutional amendment makes it illegal to demand **secession** from the Indian Union.

To maintain its legality, the Dravida Munnetra Kazhagam lowers its original separatist aim to greater autonomy for Tamil Nadu.

To revitalize Congress – whose membership has plummeted from ten to two million over five years – Nehru drafts Union and State Congress ministers into party work.

India launches its first two-stage rocket.

Delhi's **debt to the USA** reaches $2.32 billion – more than half the total of Indian money in circulation.

1964 To resolve the Kashmiri dispute, **Shaikh Muhammad Abdullah**, released from captivity, holds talks with Nehru in April, then travels to meet General Ayub Khan in May. While he is in Pakistan, Nehru dies of a stroke.

Lal Bahadur Shastri becomes India's second Prime Minister after defeating his rival Morarji Desai for the leadership of the Congress party's parliamentary group. He appoints Indira Gandhi as minister of information and broadcasting.

A faction of the pro-Soviet Communist Party of India forms the **Communist Party of India (Marxist)**, which attracts more followers than its parent. China detonates an atomic bomb in Xinjiang province.

India from 1964

Nehru's death marked the end of the unchallenged suprema-
cy of the Congress party at the centre and most of the
Union States, and the beginning of the rise of **regional
parties** throughout the republic. In the south, besides Tamil
Nadu, a traditional bastion of Dravidian nationalism,
Andhra Pradesh gave rise to **Telugu Desam** (literally
Land of Telugu Speakers), which triumphed in the 1983
polls; and in **Kerala**, the **Communist Party of India**
(Marxist) – nominally an all-Indian formation, but in reality
a regional entity – exercised power intermittently. This trend
then spread to the north, where opposition groups tried to
garner electoral support, often successfully, on the basis of
caste, an important fact of life to Hindus, forming four-fifths
of the national electorate.

The end-result has been political instability in the Union
States and increased intervention by the Central government.
Between 1950–1966, direct Presidential rule was imposed on
States ten times, whereas between 1967 and 1987 this hap-
pened seventy times.

At the national level, within five years of Nehru's demise,
the Congress party split into two: **Congress (R)** (meaning
Requisition – of the All India Congress Committee to elect
a new party president); and **Congress (S)** (meaning
Syndicate – of old, conservative leaders). Both lacked internal democracy. And the majority Congress-S Party, under
the leadership of **Indira Gandhi**, became essentially an electoral machine, open to opportunists.

From State capitals, political instability spread to **Delhi**
where in the late 1960s, Indira Gandhi, as the head of a
minority group in Parliament, governed with the backing of
Communist MPs. Alhough Congress (S) – renamed

Congress (I) (Indira) – was returned to power with a convincing majority in the 1971 general election, the imposition of an **Emergency**, essentially to preserve Indira Gandhi's leadership, stained the democratic history of India.

Indira Gandhi reversed her decision nineteen months later when private polls conducted by the leading intelligence service indicated that her party would win an electoral contest. But in the poll that followed in March 1977, victory went to the **Janata Party** (People's Party), in theory an amalgam of disparate groups, but in practice an uneasy coalition. This inaugurated an era of coalition governments at the Centre, reflecting India's complex linguistic, ethnic, religious and caste realities.

Underneath the ever-shifting alliances and horse-tradings that have become a hallmark of Indian politics, there has been a steady penetration of the roots of democracy into Indian soil, as ordinary voters have grasped the might of their vote, and politicians the meaning of accountability.

In terms of **caste**, power seeped down from brahmins and *kshatriyas* to middle and lower castes. The case of **Bihar**, the second most populous state after Uttar Pradesh, is illustrative. Three-quarters of the population is lower caste, outcaste or tribal. Yet, following the 1962 state elections, only 7 percent of the members of the **Legislative Assembly** (MLAs) were lower caste whereas 60 percent of them were either brahmin or *kshatriya*. By the late 1990s, however, the tables had turned. The lower castes claimed 53 percent of the seats while the upper castes' share shrank to 10 percent, almost in line with their proportion in the population.

Through all these changes, India's foreign policy of nonalignment remained constant. To the United States and the Soviet Union, India was too important to be ignored. Over time, the superpowers tacitly accepted their complimentariness, not competition, vis-à-vis Delhi. They became the top two trading partners of India.

Moscow cooperated actively with Delhi to build India's military industry, a sore point with Washington. In the 1980s, the US co-opted **Pakistan**, a rival of India, into its successful, multi-faceted campaign to oust the Soviets from Afghanistan, which they had entered in 1979. Consequently, India and America, the world's largest democracies, remained wary of each other.

It was several years after the collapse of the Soviet Union in 1991 that US president **Bill Clinton** grasped the importance of India as a multi-party, secular democracy which deserved to be courted. This revised perception of India broadly coincided with the **information technology revolution**, which transformed American society, and to which India contributed by exporting tens of thousands of its computer engineers to the US.

1965 The **Green Revolution**, involving the planting of High Yield Variety (HYV) wheat and rice seeds, is launched.

On 1 September Pakistan launches an attack on Indian-administered **Kashmir** aimed at capturing a strategic road linking Jammu with the Kashmir Valley, but is repulsed. India retaliates with a three-prong assault on Pakistan across the international boundary. Neither side penetrates more than 8km into enemy territory. Both accept a UN-mediated ceasefire on 24 September. During the conflict Washington suspends military supplies to both sides, preventing the repair of US-made hardware. India begins to further integrate Kashmir into the Union.

1966 In January, at Soviet-sponsored talks in Tashkent, India and Pakistan formalize a ceasefire and restore the *status quo ante*.

In Tashkent, Lal Bahadur Shastri dies of a heart attack, and **Indira Gandhi** becomes Prime Minister after defeating her challenger Morarji Desai. She meets US President Lyndon Johnson in Washington, and praises him as a 'man of peace' despite his escalation of American involvement in Vietnam.

Johnson persuades US Congress to provide India with 3.5 million tonnes of food once Indira Gandhi agrees to devalue the Indian currency by 58 percent, as demanded by the **International Monetary Fund**.

Facing sustained agitation by **Sikhs** for a *Panjabi Suba*, Panjabi-speaking state, Gandhi agrees to separate a Hindi-majority area (Haryana) from Panjab, leaving the rump as a Panjabi-speaking state with Sikhs making up 56 percent of its population.

India signs the **Nuclear Non-Proliferation Treaty**.

1967 Congress Party's share of the vote in **parliamentary elections** drops to 40.7 percent and the number of its MPs from 371 to 281, with 150 seats won by a margin of 500 votes or less, in constituencies with an average electorate of 500,000. Congress also loses control of nine major states containing two-thirds of India's population.

In **Tamil Nadu** a DMK-led coalition government bans the teaching of Hindi in schools and raises the status of Tamil.

From 1961–66 **food imports**, mainly from America, total 25.4 million tonnes, up 6.3 million tonnes on the previous five years.

1969 In March, facing popular unrest in **Pakistan**, General Ayub Khan steps down as President in favour of his commander-in-chief General Yahya Khan.

India inaugurates its first **nuclear power station**, built by Canada, at Tarapur, Maharashtra. The Soviet Union becomes India's largest supplier of weapons.

Inside **Congress**, a split develops when finance minister **Morarji Desai**, controlling the party machine, advocates strengthening the private sector and forming an alliance with the right-wing Bharatiya Jana Sangh and Swatantra (Independence) parties.

Following the death of India's Muslim President Zakir Hussain, left-of-centre Indira Gandhi backs **V. V. Giri** as presidential candidate while her rightist rivals sponsor Sanjiva Reddy, Speaker of the *Lok Sabha*, Lower House of Parliament.

Giri is elected president after Gandhi nationalizes India's fourteen largest banks and forces Desai to resign as finance minister. Consequently, Congress splits, with a majority of its members preferring Gandhi's **(R)** (for 'Requisition') faction against Desai's **(S)** (for Syndicate) faction. Supported by 43 Communists in the *Lok Sabha*, Gandhi continues as Prime Minister.

1970 The area under High Yield Variety seed cultivation reaches 35 million acres out of a national total of 129 million. Where HYV wheat is grown, average annual yields rise from 1385 to 3280 lbs per acre.

1971 In early March Indira Gandhi's Congress (R) Party, renamed **Congress (I)** (Indira), and campaigning under the slogan *Gharibi hatao* (Remove Poverty), wins 351 parliamentary seats out of 520 on a popular vote of 43 percent, while rival Congress-S captures only 16.

The decennial census shows the **literacy rate** at 30 percent, but because of a continuing increase in population, the number of illiterates is up from 298 to 386 million. Official figures show 40–50 percent of Indians living in 'abject poverty'. Food imports for 1966–71 reach 31.4 million tonnes.

In August Delhi signs a Friendship and Cooperation treaty with Moscow that contains a mutual defence clause. By now the Soviet Union is the largest buyer of Indian goods. With Moscow's total military aid to Delhi amounting to $1.1 billion, India is the second highest recipient of such aid in the world.

India supports separatist Bengali guerrillas in **East Pakistan** against the military dictatorship of General Yahya Khan. Following India's defeat of Pakistan in a two-week **war** in December, East Pakistan gains independence as **Bangladesh** with a population of 70 million.

In Pakistan Yahya Khan relinquishes power to Zulfikar Ali Bhutto.

1972 In State elections, Indira Gandhi's Congress (I) wins 70 percent of 2560 seats, while the rival Congress (S) manages only 3 percent.

Following a meeting between Gandhi and Pakistan's Prime Minister Bhutto at Simla, India agrees to release all Pakistani POWs and return 7500 sq km of Pakistani territory in exchange for 150 sq km of Kashmir seized by Pakistan during the 1971 war. Article VI of the **Simla Agreement** declares that the two sides will meet again to discuss *inter alia* a final settlement of the Kashmir dispute.

1973 The second **Richard Nixon** administration cancels $2.2 billion of India's $3.2 billion debt to the United States and ammortizes the remainder to cover future expenses of American embassies, consulates and information centres in India and Nepal.

Delhi's annual trade with Moscow climbs to US$425 million.

1974 Despite the widespread use of HYV seeds for rice and wheat, India's annual foodgrain output stagnates at 80–83 million tonnes, requiring the government to import 5.5 million tonnes to cover the deficit.

The India-Pakistan War of 1971

The India-Pakistan War, resulting in the establishment of **Bangladesh**, benefited India ideologically and strategically. It destroyed the Muslim League's doctrine of Indian Muslims being a nation unto themselves on which Pakistan was founded. Also, for Delhi, the transformaton of East Pakistan, part of a hostile

Indian soldiers advancing along a road, ten miles inside West Pakistan, on 9 December

High **inflation**, caused partly by a surge in oil prices, leads to popular protest. Two-thirds of the 1.35 million employees of the state-owned **railways** strike for higher wages and better working conditions. The Gandhi administration dismisses 30,000 rail workers and uses force to break the strike.

neighbouring state, into a friendly Bangladesh was a strategic boon. In the Pakistani poll in December 1970, the East Pakistan-based **Awami League**, seeking autonomy for provinces, won almost all the regional seats in the Central Assembly and thus an overall majority – with the West Pakistan-based Pakistan People's Party doing well in the western wing (population 60 million versus 70 million in the eastern wing).

To prevent the League from forming a government, Pakistani President **Yahya Khan** delayed convening the Assembly, flew to East Pakistan's capital Dacca, and allowed talks with League leader **Mujibur Rahman** to drag on until troop reinforcements arrived from West Pakistan. On 25 March the army arrested League activists and let loose a reign of terror. Armed resistance, aided and abetted by India, grew. By October, the **Mukti Bahini** (Freedom Regiment) claimed to have killed 20,000 collaborators. On 3 December India's army marched into East Pakistan, and soon Delhi opened a second front on the West Pakistani border. On 16 December Pakistan's army surrendered to India in East Pakistan. The following day Delhi declared a unilateral ceasefire on the western front after capturing 5000 sq km of Pakistani territory in Sind and another 2500 sq km in the Panjab-Kashmir region; and Pakistan reciprocated. **Islamabad** lost half its navy and a quarter of its air force. India lost 40 aircraft, 66 tanks and one warship. While Moscow supported Delhi, thus keeping China out of the conflict, Washington did little to help Islamabad.

During the industrial dispute, the government explodes a **'nuclear device'** near Pokharan in the Rajasthan desert, claiming that it is for 'peaceful purposes'.

Delhi and Washington agree to form joint commissions on economic, commercial, scientific, technological, educational and cultural cooperation.

The Emergency of 1975–77

High inflation and scarcity of essential goods prompted widespread protest in 1974. Using a Presidential Ordinance, **Indira Gandhi**'s government froze wages without controlling prices. In November five major opposition parties formed the **National Coordination Committee** to coordinate anti-government protests. The following March, **Jaya Prakash Narayan**, a non-party opposition leader, led a procession of hundreds of thousands in Delhi against Congress corruption and misrule. In May Congress lost in elections in Uttar Pradesh and Gujarat.

Following a judicial verdict against Indira Gandhi, opposition leaders announced rallies on 29 June to compel her to step down. In a pre-dawn swoop, her government arrested hundreds of her opponents and imposed censorship. President Fakhuruddin Ali Ahmed declared a state of emergency, suspending Constitutional articles guaranteeing protection of life and liberty. Claiming that 'forces of disintegration [are] in full swing', Gandhi asserted that the purposes of the emergency were to improve civil administration, curb inflation and improve the economy. By late 1975 those jailed without trial totalled 100,000.

Freed from democratic accountability, police resorted to arbitrary arrests and became more venal than before. Industrialists sacked about half a million workers. Under the guise of urban beautification, people were forcibly ejected from cities, and a programme of compulsory family planning by vasectomy was introduced under the supervision of Indira Gandhi's son Sanjay. However, non-Congress ministries in **Tamil Nadu, Gujarat** and **Kashmir** refused to toe Delhi's line. The dismissal of Tamil Nadu's DMK government in January 1976 led to 16,000 arrests. Protest on the first anniversary of the emergency in June resulted in 35,000 detentions. The statistic of 125,000 political prisoners was twice the figure during the 1942 Quit India movement. In the absence of an uncensored press, intelligence services became the chief agents of government news-gathering. It was the prime intelligence agency's finding that Congress (I) would win a general election that persuaded Gandhi to end the emergency.

> **❝** The closest parallel to the emergency provisions of the Indian can be found in the Weimar Constitution of the Third Republic. Compared to Article 48 of the Weimar Constitution, the provisions of the Indian Constitution are actually more drastic. **❞**
>
> Mohan Ram, in *Economic and Political Weekly* (Bombay), 29 March 1975

1975 An Indian **space satellite** with US-supplied components is launched on a Soviet rocket from the Baikonur Space Centre in Kazhakstan.

Fakhuruddin Ali Ahmed becomes the sixth president of India.

In June the High Court in Allahabad upholds charges of electoral malpractice in 1971 brought against Indira Gandhi by her chief rival, socialist Raj Narain. Although this should automatically disqualify Gandhi from holding office, she secures a three-week deferment of the court order to enable her Congress (I) party to elect a new leader, then persuades President Ahmed to declare a **national emergency**, thereby suspending the Constitution. Gandhi continues as prime minister as her government detains thousands without charge.

In November *Heat and Dust* by Delhi-based Ruth Prawer Jhabvala wins the Booker Prize in London, awarded annually for the best novel published in English in the British Commonwealth.

1977 In January Indira Gandhi lifts the nineteen-month emergency and calls the sixth General Election in mid-

Indira Gandhi 1917–84

Jawarharlal Nehru's daughter **Indira Priyadarshani** became India's first, and the world's second, woman prime minister. She was educated at schools in Switzerland to be near her tuberculosis-infected mother Kamala Kaul, and at Visvabharati University in Bengal. She enrolled at Somerville College, Oxford University, but failed to graduate. In 1938 she married Feroze Gandhi, a leftist Parsi. She was imprisoned during the Quit India movement.

Following the breakdown of her marriage after the births of her sons **Rajiv** (1944) and **Sanjay** (1946), she lived with her father at the prime minister's residence until his death in 1964. By 1960, when Feroze Gandhi died of a heart attack, she had become Congress president and was later granted a cabinet post by Nehru's sucessor, **Shastri**. In the 1966 prime ministerial contest, she beat her rival Morarji Desai by 2:1. Once in power, the manipulative ruthlessness she had first exercised as Congress president in destabilizing Kerala's Communist government became more pronounced.

Following the poor performance of Congress in the 1967 poll, she outflanked her rightist rivals. Consolidating her position in the party's parliamentary wing, she requisitioned a session of the 750-strong **All India Congress Committee**. The 441 members who turned up expelled Congress President S. Nijalangappa from the party. When the split in the party's parliamentary wing in 1969 deprived her of a majority in the *Lok Sabha*, she managed to survive by courting Communist MPs. In the mid-term general election in 1971 – the first of its kind – she won a comfortable majority but the euphoria generated by her success and the break-up of Pakistan later that year, did not last.

During the 1975–77 emergency she turned Congress into her personal handmaiden, personalized politics and flagrantly advanced the ambitions first of her thuggish son, Sanjay, and then of his none-too-bright elder sibling, Rajiv.

March. Opposed by an amalgam of five opposition parties – including the Bharatiya Jana Sangh, led by **Atal Bihari Vajpayee** – called the **Janata Party**, Congress (I) fails to win a single seat in northern India, and its defeated candidates include Indira Gandhi and her son Sanjay.

With the Janata securing a majority of seats, **Morarji Desai** becomes Prime Minister.

In West Bengal, a coalition led by the Communist Party of India (Marxist) assumes power.

1978 Desai's government appoints a commission under **B. P. Mandal**, a former Chief Minister of Bihar, to recommend ways of improving conditions for India's **backward or lower castes.** The ruling Janata Party, composed of factions with different agendas united only in their opposition to Indira Gandhi, begins to fragment.

1979 Jaya Prakash Narayan, a senior non-partisan figure highly esteemed by all Janata factions, dies. The Janata splits, and the government falls. A minority government is formed by **Charan Singh**, leader of a Uttar Pradesh-based faction.

1980 Sanjay Gandhi is killed in an aeroplane crash while performing aerobatics over Delhi. Indira Gandhi then drafts her elder son **Rajiv Gandhi**, an airline pilot, into politics.

The failure of Prime Minister Charan Singh to present his cabinet for a parliamentary vote of confidence leads to his dismissal by the President and the calling of the seventh General Election.

The **Bharatiya Janata Party** (BJP) – a Hindu nationalist party, and virtual successor to the Bhartiya Jana Sangh, albeit open to non-Hindus – is founded under the leadership of Atal Bihari Vajpayee. Congress (I) wins a majority of seats, and Rajiv Gandhi is elected an MP. Indira Gandhi

The Sikh Golden Temple at Amritsar, stormed by Indian troops in June 1984

returns as Prime Minister. The Mandal Commission's Report, recommending 49.5 percent reservations for backward (or lower) castes in government jobs, is quietly ignored.

1981 A meeting of **Sikhs** in New York, chaired by Gurcharan Singh Tohra, president of the (Indian) Shiramoni Gurdwara Prabadhak (Sacred Temples Management) Committee, passes a resolution declaring that Sikhs are a separate nation, and so signals the start of a movement for a sovereign **Khalistan** (Land of Khalsa Sikhs).

1982 In Britain, a four-month **Festival of India** exposes Western audiences to the full range of the arts of India.

Shaikh Muhammad Abdullah of Kashmir dies, and his son Farooq Abdullah becomes chief minister.

1983 The movement for Khalistan gathers momentum in **Panjab**. With law and order deteriorating rapidly, the state is placed under the direct rule of India's President **Zail Singh**.

At a triennial conference of the Non-Aligned Movement held in Delhi Indira Gandhi is elected NAM president until the next such conference.

In Hollywood, British director Richard Attenborough's *Gandhi*, a biopic of Mahatma Gandhi, wins an Oscar for the best film. A Hindi version, released in India, proves popular.

At the Lords cricket ground in London, India defeats the West Indies to win the (Prudential) World Cup when the competition is inaugurated.

1984 As tension between the agitators for Khalistan and the government mounts, in June Indian troops attack the **Sikh Golden Temple** in Amritsar, killing many, including the movement's leader Jarnail Singh Bhindaranwale.

Cricket in India

Cricket was brought to the Indian subcontinent by the **British** in the 18th century. Now cricket is to urban Indians what football is to Britons and baseball to Americans. Administered by the **Board of Control for Cricket** in India, in the mid-1980s the Indian cricket team chalked up impressive victories. In its games with England, the home of cricket, India has performed better in One Day Internationals than in Test Series, each series consisting of three five-day matches. Since Indians learned cricket from the English, there is much interest in how Indian teams perform against their English rivals. In 36 One Day Internationals with England played during 1974–2000, India won sixteen and lost nineteen matches with one match declared 'No Rating'. But in the 84 Test matches with England until 2000, India won only 14 and lost 32, with the rest being drawn.

Because of the historic India-Pakistan rivalry, matches between their respective teams frequently turn into surrogate wars. When Delhi-Islamabad tensions are high, the two sides refrain from playing against each other – or at least not on Indian or Pakistani soil.

In 2000 the integrity of cricket came under a shadow in India – as well as Pakistan and South Africa – amidst allegations that players had been bribed to rig matches and that captains had provided information for money to bookmakers about pitch conditions and team selection. India's Central Bureau of Investigation named **Captain Muhammad Azharuddin** and three other players for their involvement in the scam. Following a Board of Control inquiry, Azharuddin and **Ajay Sharma** were banned for life, and two other players were suspended from cricket for five years.

In October Indira Gandhi is shot dead by two Sikh body-guards, sub-inspector Beant Singh and constable Satwant Singh.

Rajiv Gandhi, a junior MP, is sworn in as Prime Minister by President Zail Singh, and then elected leader of the ruling Congress (I).

In Delhi anti-Sikh violence leaves 10,000–20,000 dead, although officially only 3000 are killed.

In the eighth General Election held in the aftermath of Indira Gandhi's assassination, Congress (I) wins a majority of seats. Rajiv Gandhi's main campaign slogan – 'The nation is in danger' – has undertones of Hindu nationalism. He is re-elected Prime Minister.

1985 Under Prime Minister Rajiv Gandhi there is less interference in state politics than under his mother, Indira.

1986–87 Rajiv Gandhi's image as a 'Mr Clean' is tarnished when a scandal breaks in which it is alleged that he is implicated in kickbacks deriving from India's purchase of self-propelled **Bofors artillery guns** from their Swedish manufacturer. This is all the more damaging to his Congress (I), since he possesses neither the cunning of his mother nor the intellect of his maternal grandfather, Jawaharlal Nehru. Nonetheless, he concludes that the central government has become too interventionist in the economy and starts to liberalize.

1987 Responding to a request by Sri Lanka, facing armed insurgency by its Tamil minority in the northeast, Rajiv Gandhi dispatches Indian troops to Sri Lanka, ostensibly for peacekeeping – a step condemned by the separatist Liberation Tigers of Tamil Elam, popularly known as Tamil Tigers.

The government passes a law making glorification of *sati/suttee* (see p.242) a criminal offence.

Modern Literature in India

India has been a treasury of tales – folk, classical, romantic and fantastic. Stories from the *Panchtantra* (c.500 AD) resurfaced in the Arab world and Europe, making the tale-within-a-tale a popular literary device. In modern times, the first known novel was **Bankam Chandra Chatterji**'s *Anandmath* ('Seminary of Bliss', 1882), written in Bengali. Set during the decline of Muslim power in Bengal, it depicts Anandmath members struggling against the ruler's tyranny and misrule. Bengalis remained foremost in vernacular literature, producing such writers as **Rabindranath Tagore** (see p.284) and **Bibhutibhushan Banerji**, author of *Pather Panchali* (1929).

Among Hindi writers, the most eminent was **Munshi Prem Chand** (1880–1936) whose *Godaan* ('Gift of a Cow'), a story of the struggles of a poor peasant, is a classic. As a short-story writer, he was much influenced by Anton Chekov and Ivan Turgenev. **Urdu literature** is particularly strong in poetry, which is often both lyrical and muscular. In this field, **Faiz Ahmad Faiz** was foremost, and his poetry has been translated into English by V. G. Keirnan. As an all-rounder, **Amrita Pritam**, poet, short-story writer and novelist is pre-eminent in **Panjabi** letters. **Marathi literature** is especially rich in drama, much performed in Bombay, the base of highly talented **Vijay Tendulkar**. With its almost universal literacy, **Kerala** is home to many novelists in Malayalam, the best-known being **M. T. Vasudevan Nair** and **Kamala Das** (real name Madhavi Kutti). Madras-born **R. K. Narayan** was India's greatest fiction writer in English. Between 1935, when *Swami and Friends* appeared, and his death in 2001, he published fifteen novels and scores of short stories.

Other celebrated fiction-writers in English include **Mulk Raj Anand**, noted for such socially committed novels as *Untouchable* (1935), **Ruth Prawer Jhabvala**, **Vikram Seth** and **Arundhati Roy**.

1988 **Economic liberalization** gathers pace.

The state-run television channel begins broadcasting a 96-episode serialization of the *Mahabharata* (see p.24), scripted by Moonis Reza, a Muslim.

1989 Free market reform turns the Bombay stock market bullish, inflation drops to single digits, and Western multi-nationals, so far kept out of India, start moving in.

The **Vishwa Hindu Parishad** (World Hindu Council) conducts a sacred rites ceremony outside the **Babri Mosque** in Ayodhya, Uttar Pradesh, claiming the mosque – built on Emperor Babur's orders to celebrate his 1527 victory at Ghaghara (see p.169) – replaced a Hindu temple marking the birthplace of Lord Rama. The Council vows to rebuild the Rama Temple there.

As the Bofors guns scandal snowballs, Rajiv Gandhi's Congress (I) loses the ninth General Election to the **National Front** – an alliance centred on the Janata Dal (People's Front). The new Prime Minister is **Vishwanath Pratap Singh** of Uttar Pradesh. The BJP gains 89 seats.

In Kashmir, terrorist activities by pro-Pakistani militants begin.

1990 V. P. Singh, a progressive *kshatriya*, decides to implement the Mandal Commission's recommendations on job reservations for backward/lower castes, and so incurs the anger of middle and upper castes. By November he has lost his parliamentary following due to the defection of middle and upper caste MPs, and is replaced as Prime Minister, briefly, by **Chandra Shekhar**, another Janata Dal leader.

Lal Krishna Advani, a BJP leader, starts *ratha yatra* (travel by chariot) at the southern tip of India on a nine-month journey northwards to highlight the story of the *Ramayana* and the issue of the Babri Mosque in Ayodhya.

India's annual economic growth rate in the 1980s is 5.8 percent against a population increase of 2.2 percent.

1991 During the election campaign for the tenth Parliament, Rajiv Gandhi is killed in Madras (aka Chennai) by a woman Tamil Tiger suicide-bomber as retribution for Indian troops' anti-Tamil intervention in Sri Lanka. In the poll, Congress (I) wins most seats, with the BJP, at 113, emerging as the second largest group. Congress (I)'s parliamentary leader, Andhra Pradesh-born **Pamulaparti Venkata Narasimha Rao** becomes the first Prime Minister from the south.

> **"** It's been happening a long time.
> Time bribed
> And bought
> Pages of history without its knowing,
> Changed some lines,
> Rubbed off others
> Wherever it wanted.
> History felt mad and depressed
> But forgave the historians.
>
> But today it's sad.
> A hand unfolds its cover,
> Tears off a few pages
> And tapes fake ones in their place.
> History looks,
> Quietly comes out of the pages
> And stands under a tree
> Smoking a cigarette. **"**

Amrita Pritam, 'Resigned', trans. from Panjabi by Mahendra Kulasrestha

The Hong Kong-based satellite network Star TV, which includes BBC World Service Television and MTV Asia, begins beaming into India, thus ending the monopoly of state-run television.

1992 Before his death in hospital, Satyajit Ray receives a Hollywood Oscar for life-time achievement in cinema.

In December 200,000 Hindu militants, led by the Vishwa Hindu Parishad, storm barricades erected around the Babri Mosque and demolish it with pickaxes, ropes and sledge-hammers in four hours. Muslims throughout India protest and are assaulted.

1993 In January there is week-long violence against Muslims in Bombay, orchestrated by the fanatical **Shiv Sena** (Army of Shivaji). Some 40,000 Hindu zealots, operating in mobile hit-squads with the tacit support of an almost wholly Hindu police force, hunt down their victims, setting fire to their homes and killing them in the streets.

Delhi-based Vikram Seth publishes *A Suitable Boy*, probably the longest novel in English in the 20th century.

1995 India becomes a founder member of the Geneva-based **World Trade Organization**, established to oversee an international trading system, replacing the earlier General Agreement on Tariffs and Trade (GATT).

1996 In the eleventh General Election, the Bhartiya Janata Party increases its parliamentary seats to 161. As the largest group, its leader, **Atal Bihari Vajpayee**, forms a government which falls when it fails to win a parliamentary vote of confidence. He is succeeded as prime minister by the leader of the United Front – an alliance of mainly regional parties – **Haradanahalli Devegowda Deve Gowda**, a middle-caste farmer from Karnataka belonging to the Janata Party.

1997 Deve Gowda is replaced as prime minister by **Inder Kumar Gujral**, a member of the Janata Dal (United) faction, a constituent of the ruling United Front alliance.

Kerala-born **Kicheril Raman Narayanan** becomes the first *dalit* (Untouchable) President of the Republic.

Atal Bihari Vajpayee b.1924

With four consecutive years in office as the chief executive, **Atal Bihari Vajpayee** has emerged as the longest-serving non-Congress prime minister. Son of Krishna Bihari Vajpayee, a school teacher in Gwaliar, he joined the *Rashtriya Swayamsevak Sangh*, a

Atal Bihari Vajpayee on parade

India hosts the Miss World television beauty contest.

Delhi-based Arundhati Roy wins the Booker Prize with her novel *God of Small Things*.

1998 In the twelfth General Election, the BJP secures 179 seats out of 542. Its leader, Atal Bihari Vajpayee, becomes

militant Hindu group, in 1941. The following year, he was imprisoned for participating in the Congress-sponsored **Quit India** agitation.

After gaining a post-graduate degree in political science, he worked as a journalist in Lucknow and became a founder member of the **Bharatiya Jana Sangh**. On entering the Lower House in 1957, he was elected leader of the BJS's parliamentary wing, a position he held until the party's absorption into the Janata Party twenty years later, when he became Foreign Minister in the Janata government.

During the 1980s he was president of the **Bharatiya Janata Party (BJP)** and leader of its parliamentary wing. Following his stint as leader of the opposition in the Lower House from 1993 onwards, he became the prime minister briefly in May 1996. His second chance came in March 1998 at the head of an unwieldy alliance. Two months later, he ordered the detonation of an atomic bomb. His third chance of high office followed in 1999 when he headed a multi-party coalition, the **National Democratic Alliance**. Considered a moderate within the BJP, during a visit to Iran he declared, 'There may be occasional aberrations, but neither the state nor civil society [in India] would ever weaken its bond with secular values inherent in our civilizational and cultural inheritance.' He strengthened ties with Washington and continued economic liberalization initiated by his Congress (I) predecessors.

The Kashmir Dispute

Since the Indian subcontinent's partition in mid-1947, the State of **Jammu** and **Kashmir** – or Kashmir, for short – has been a bone of contention between India and Pakistan. Established in 1901 within its present (legal) boundaries, this Princely State, with 77 percent Muslim population, was ruled by a Hindu king. Sharing common borders with Pakistan and India, **Maharaja Hari Singh** had the choice to join either country. To pre-empt his options, the predominantly Muslim inhabitants of the Poonch-Mirpur region established an independent government, and sought help from neighbouring Pakistan to liberate the rest of the state. On 25 October 1947 – as armed Pakistani tribals approached the state capital, Srinagar – Hari Singh acceded to India. Delhi complained against Pakistan at the UN Security Council. Fighting continued until January 1949 when a UN-brokered ceasefire came into effect, leaving Pakistan with 37 percent of the territory.

Hari Singh abdicated in favour of his son, **Karan Singh**, while Shaikh Muhammad Abdullah, leader of the secular National Conference, became the state's popularly elected executive head. A special provision in the Indian Constitution accorded Kashmir the right to have its own constitution. The popularly elected

the Prime Minister, heading an unstable coalition of many parties.

In May India tests a **nuclear bomb** at Pokharan, Rajasthan. Pakistan follows suit with its own nuclear test.

Sonia Gandhi, the Italian–born widow of Rajiv Gandhi, is elected president of Congress (I).

1999 In February Vajpayee has a cordial meeting with his Pakistani counterpart, **Muhammad Nawaz Sharif**, in Lahore.

Constituent Assembly began drafting it. When pro-Indian elements insisted on India's right to impose Presidential rule if the need arose, tensions mounted. Karan Singh arrested Abdullah in 1953 and kept him imprisoned for eleven years. In 1963, the then chief executive **Ghulam Muhammad Sadiq** cooperated with Delhi by agreeing to dilute Kashmir's autonomy. Following the 1965 Indo-Pakistan War, the National Conference was dissolved and resurrected as the state unit of Congress. Abdullah was re-arrested. The 1967 and 1972 polls were rigged. Then, following negotiations with Gandhi, Abdullah became Kashmir's chief executive in 1975. His National Conference fairly won a majority of seats in the 1977 poll. Following his death in 1982, his lacklustre son Farouq took over his mantle.

In 1989, when Soviet troops' withdrawal from Afghanistan signalled the victory of local Islamic fundamentalists, pro-Pakistan groups in Kashmir were inspired to take up arms against India. In counter-insurgency operations, 400,000-strong Indian security forces killed 30–40,000 Kashmiris in twelve years. Delhi accuses Islamabad of training Kashmiri separatists and infiltrating them into the Indian-administered Kashmir, while Pakistan denies complicity.

In May intense fighting between Indian and Pakistani troops in the Kargil region of Indian-administered **Kashmir** raises the spectre of all-out war between nuclear-armed neighbours. Pressured by US President **Bill Clinton** during their meeting in Washington, Nawaz Sharif orders the withdrawal of Pakistani forces without consulting his military commanders in Islamabad.

In October General **Pervez Musharraf** overthrows the civilian government in Pakistan and imposes martial law. Following the passage of a no-confidence motion in Parliament against Vajpayee's government, the thirteenth General Election is called. The BJP-led National Democratic Alliance of 14 parties wins 304 of the 543 seats, and forms the government, again under Vajpayee.

An estimated 3.9 million Indians are infected with the **HIV/AIDS** virus.

2000 President Clinton is warmly received during a state visit to India.

P. V. Narasimah Rao, former Congress (I) Prime Minister, is found guilty of bribing non-Congress (I) MPs on the eve of a no-confidence vote against his government.

In the 1990s India's **annual economic growth** has been 6.4 percent against a population increase of 2 percent, but its share of **world trade** has fallen from 2 percent in 1950 to 0.8 percent.

2001 In January and February an estimated 70 million Hindus bathe at the confluence of the Ganges and the Jamuna at Allahabad during the six-week **Maha Kumbh Mela** (Fair of the Great Pitcher [of elixir]), held every twelve years, with 24 million bathing on the first day – the world's largest gathering of humans in one place.

In state elections in May, the Communist Party of India (Marxist)-led alliance is **returned to power** in West Bengal for an unprecedented sixth time.

In Pakistan, General Musharraf compels President Farouq Tara to resign and then assumes the presidency for himself. His summit with Vajpayee at Agra in July fails when he seeks a joint declaration naming Kashmir as the core problem between the two nations, while Vajpayee wants to focus on cross-border terrorism being aided by Pakistan.

Three months after the September **terrorist attacks** on New York and Washington, an attempt by five armed Kashmiri terrorists to storm the Indian Parliament in Delhi and kill senior politicians is foiled. India blames Pakistan, which denies any involvement.

The **decennial census** puts India's population at 1.1 billion, its adult literacy rate at 66 percent and life expectancy at 68 years.

2002 Following an **attack** by Kashmiri terrorists on a military residential quarters near **Jammu** in which 37 people are killed, India puts its armed forces on the highest alert. Pakistan does likewise, and more than a million soldiers face one another across the international border. While Delhi says it will not be the first to use nuclear arms, Pakistan fails to reciprocate. It takes many weeks of active diplomacy by America to persuade the two neighbours to pull back from the brink of war.

Dr Avul Pakir Jainalabdeen Abdul Kalam is elected India's third Muslim President in July.

books

books

Whenever a book is in print, the UK publisher is given first in each listing, followed by the publisher in the US – unless the title is available in one country only, in which case we have specified which country, or is published by the same company in both territories, in which case only the publisher is specified.

General history

HM Elliot and J Dowson (eds) *The History of India as Told by its Own Historians* (Low Price; South Asia Books). These eight volumes comprise selections from major chroniclers writing in Sanskrit, Arabic and Persian, and also some later writers.

Gordon Johnson, CA Bayly and John F Richards (eds) *The New Cambridge History of India* (Cambridge University Press). Begun in 1987, this mammoth project – still unfinished – is the single most important project of its kind. The 21 volumes published to date cover not only the political, economic, social and military history of the sub-continent but also the history of Indian art, architecture, science and technology, as well as secular and religious ideologies.

John Keay *India, a History* (HarperCollins; Grove). A comprehensive and immensely readable account; probably the first book to buy if this guide has kindled a deep interest in the subject.

Jawaharlal Nehru *The Discovery of India* (Oxford University Press). Written during his imprisonment in 1942–45, this historical narrative illustrates Nehru's diverse interests – science, drama, history, international politics – as well as the elegance with which he handled the English language.

NK Sinha and Nitish R Ray *A History of India* (Sangam, UK). Authored by Indian academics, this is a more than serviceable textbook which deals with certain aspects of Indian history that are often overlooked by Western historians.

Vincent A Smith (ed. Percival Spear) *The Oxford History of India* (Oxford University Press). Originally published in 1919 by Vincent Smith, a British administrator in India who later turned to historical research, and revised in the 1950s by Percival Spear, a British academic, this account is fascinating in large part for the insights it gives into the perspectives and prejudices of the British civil service in India.

Romila Thapar *A History of India: Volume 1* (Penguin; Viking). The doyen of Indian historians condenses a lot of information and insight into a brief book, which ends with the arrival of the Mughals in India. Volume 2 is by Percival Spear, a British specialist on India, who covers the post-Delhi Sultanates period up to the late 1970s.

Stanley A Wolpert *A New History of India* (Oxford University Press; University of California). Originally published in 1982, now in its sixth edition, this highly readable one-volume history of India from ancient times to the present day is a fair portrait of the country, outlining both the illustrious achievements of India's civilization as well as its persistent socio-economic inequalities and political-administrative corruption.

Prehistory and ancient India (c.3000 BC–400 BC)

DD Kosambi *The Culture and Civilisation of Ancient India in Historical Outline* (Vikas, o/p). Published originally in 1950, this book – by a pre-eminent authority on ancient India – is a must for all those interested in the period.

RE Mortimer Wheeler *The Indus Civilisation* (Cambridge University Press, o/p). Originally published in 1953, this book by the famous British archeologist put the civilization of the Indus Valley firmly in the same league as other ancient civilizations.

Classical period (c.400 BC–700 AD)

The Travels of Fa-Hien (Dover). The journals kept by Fa-Hien, a Chinese monk who travelled through India around 400 AD, have proved indispensable to historians of both India and China, but are of far more than academic interest.

Romila Thapar *Asoka and the Decline of the Mauryas* (Oxford University Press, India; South Asia Books). This study of Emperor Ashoka and the subsequent Maurya rulers by a pre-eminent Indian historian remains a standard work on the subject.

From the Muslim incursions to 1806

Al-Beruni *India* (Low Price, UK). Reissued in 2000, this account of India in the 12th century by the Arab scholar Al-Beruni, translated by Edward Sachau in 1914, is packed with fascinating detail.

Babur *Baburnama* (Oxford University Press). Wheeler M Thackston's translation of *Baburnama*, the memoirs of the first Great Mughal of India, is a unique document – part history, part intimate diary.

Ibn Battuta *The Travels of Ibn Battuta* (Picador). Tim Mackintosh-Smith's translation of Ibn Battuta's extensive travels is the most recent version of this classic text, which records a 29-year, 120,000-kilometre journey from the Volga to Zanzibar.

Abraham Eraly *The Great Mughals* (Penguin, India). An engagingly written history of the Mughal rulers, from Babur to Aurangzeb.

Bamber Gascoigne *A Brief History of the Great Moghuls* (Constable Robinson, UK). A fluent, accessible survey of India's most extravagant rulers and their achievements in art, architecture, science, religion and statecraft.

Stewart Gordon *The Marathas 1600–1818* (Cambridge University Press). Part of the *New Cambridge History of India*, this book on the Marathas is a definitive work, unlikely to be surpassed in the near future.

John Keay *The Honourable Company: A History of the English East India Company* (HarperCollins). Keay strikes the right balance between those who regard the East India Company as a rapacious institution with malevolent intentions and others who present its acquisition of the Indian empire as an unintended, almost accidental process.

Jadunath Sarkar *Fall of the Mughal Empire* (Sangam; South Asia Books). This four-volume history, first published in 1950 in Calcutta, is an outstanding piece of scholarship by an eminent Indian expert on the later Mughal period.

The British Raj

Charles Allen *Plain Tales from the Raj* (Abacus; Henry Holt, o/p). First-hand accounts from erstwhile sahibs and memsahibs of everyday British India, organized thematically.

CA Bayly *Indian Society and the Making of the British Empire* (Cambridge University Press). Forming part of the magnificent *New Cambridge History of India*, the book deals with the 18th century and the onset of British imperialism in the subcontinent, and for that reason is essential reading if you want to understand modern India.

Ian Copland *The Princes of India in the Endgame of Empire, 1917–47* (Cambridge University Press). A history of the Princely States, which constituted nearly a third of the British empire in the Indian subcontinent.

R Palme Dutt *India Today* (Gollancz, o/p). Written in the late 1930s by the long-time general secretary of the Communist Party of Great Britain, this is the only analysis of British rule in India to present a Marxist viewpoint on the subject.

Patrick French *Liberty or Death – India's Journey to Independence and Division* (Flamingo; Trafalgar Square). The definitive account (and a damning indictment) of the last years of the British Raj. Material from hitherto unreleased intelligence files shows how Churchill's 'florid incompetence' and Atlee's 'feeble incomprehension' contributed to the debacle that was Partition.

Christopher Hibbert *The Great Mutiny: India 1857* (Penguin, o/p). Hibbert's account shows a degree of objectivity not often found among his predecessors.

Lawrence James *Raj: The Making and Unmaking of British India* (Little, Brown; St Martin's Press). A door-stopping 700-page history of British rule in India, drawing on recently released official papers and private memoirs. The most up-to-date, erudite survey of its kind, and unlikely to be bettered as a general introduction.

James Mill *History of British India* (University of Chicago Press). A two-volume abridgement, edited by William Thomas, of Mill's ten-volume original, which dates from 1817. An indispensable guide to the early period of the British in India, providing fascinating insights into the ideology that shaped the 19th-century imperialist rule and practice.

Geoffrey Moorehouse *India Britannica* (HarperCollins; Academy Chicago). A balanced, sharply written survey of the British in India by a British journalist who spent much time travelling around the country in the 1970s.

Anil Seal *The Emergence of Indian Nationalism: Competition and Collaboration in the later Nineteenth Century* (Cambridge University Press, o/p). Seal unravels the tortuous processes whereby Indian nationalists constructed support at national level by acting as power brokers at local and provincial levels.

Surendra Nath Sen *Eighteen Fifty-Seven* (Publications Division, Government of India). A scholarly and judicious account of the most controversial event in the last two centuries of Indian history.

Independent India (1947 to the present)

Jad Adams and Phillip Whitehead *The Dynasty: The Nehru-Gandhi Story* (Penguin, o/p; Diane). A brilliant and intriguing account of India's most famous – or infamous – family, and the way its various personalities have shaped post-Independence India.

Paul Brass *The Politics of India since Independence* (Cambridge University Press). This general survey by an American academic is a good introduction to modern Indian politics.

Judith M Brown *Modern India: the Origins of an Asian Democracy* (Oxford University Press). A socialist perspective on modern India, which stresses social history more than political.

Bipan Chandra *Communalism in Modern India* (Vikas; South Asia Books). A balanced and insightful analysis of India's most sensitive subject – relations between the Hindu majority and the Muslim minority. This book provides an illuminating account of the historic tension between the two communities.

Sumit Ganguly *The Crisis in Kashmir: Portents of War, Hopes of Peace* (Cambridge University Press). In this 1999 account Indian academic Ganguly focuses on the Muslim separatist insurgency in Indian-administered Kashmir, and reveals a disjunction between Delhi's stifling of political dissent and its drive to expand education and exposure to the mass media.

Dilip Hiro *Inside India Today* (Routledge & Kegan Paul, o/p; Monthly Review Press). Based on scores of field interviews, this is a trenchant critique of the Congress rule in India up to and including the 1976–77 emergency.

Sunil Khilnani *The Idea of India* (Hamish Hamilton, o/p; Farrar Straus & Giroux). A thoughtful long essay in political theory, published on the fiftieth anniversary of Indian independence. Only for those already familiar with India and its recent history.

Ross Mallick *Indian Communism: Opposition, Collaboration and Institutionalization* (Oxford University Press, India). Mallick's study provides a well-researched study of the Indian Communist movement from its inception in the early 1920s, when it was treated as a severe threat by the British Raj, to the 1990s, by which time it had become an accepted part of India's political mainstream.

Robert G Wirsing *India, Pakistan and the Kashmir Dispute* (Palgrave). An American specialist on South Asia dispassionately unravels the tangled origins and the current tensions underlying this long-running dispute, and discusses its impact on the domestic politics of India and Pakistan. Published in 1994, the book is balanced and well-documented.

Religion, philosophy and society

Sri Chinmoy *Commentaries on the Vedas, the Upanishads and the Bhagavad Gita: The Three Branches of India's Life-Tree* (Blue Beyond; Aum). Invaluable commentaries on the Indo-Aryan scripture and philosophy.

TW Rhys Davids *Buddhist India* (Motilal Banarsidass). The reissuing of this book more than 80 years after its first publication in 1903, is sufficient evidence of its importance as the most comprehensive portrait of India during the period when Buddhism was in the ascendant.

Geraldine Forbes *Women in Modern India* (Cambridge University Press). Part of the *New Cambridge History of India*, this survey draws on copious first-hand accounts to construct an all-encompassing picture of the role of women in India's economy, culture and political life during the last two centuries.

Dilip Hiro *The Untouchables of India* (Minority Rights Group, UK). A well-documented monograph which combines a brief history of the caste system with a study of the discrimination suffered by outcaste Hindus in contemporary India.

John H Hutton *Caste in India* (Oxford University Press, o/p). This pioneering survey of the evolution of caste, first published in 1946, remains essential reading on the subject.

Pramila Jayapal *Pilgrimage to India: A Woman Revisits her Homeland* (Seal). Sensitive account of diverse social situations and problems in far-flung parts of India by Jayapal, an academic and development expert. Also provides insight into the experience of a Westernized Indian returning after most of her life abroad.

Sarvepalli Radhakrishnan *Indian Philosophy* (Oxford University Press, India). This eminent Indian scholar-philosopher, who later became his country's vice-president, offers a two-volume standard work on Indian philosophy, first published in 1923.

Kshitimohan M Sen *Hinduism* (Penguin, US). Originally published in 1961, Sen's work on India's principal religion remains definitive.

Khushwant Singh *History of the Sikhs* (Oxford University Press, India). Originally published in 1963, this is a scholarly two-volume work by a well-known Indian writer and journalist. It's the only book of its kind, but unfortunately the first volume is currently out of print.

MN Srinivas *Caste in Modern India* (Asia Publishing House, India). An authoritative study by one of India's leading experts on caste, indispensable to those seeking an understanding of this uniquely Indian phenomenon.

Mark Tully *No Full Stops in India* (Penguin; South Asia Books). Earnest but highly readable dissection of contemporary India by the former BBC correspondent, incorporating anecdotes and first-hand accounts of political events over the past twenty years.

Max Weber *Religion of India: The Sociology of Hinduism and Buddhism* (South Asia Books). By attempting to relate religion to its adherents and their society, the great German sociologist Max Weber raises some provocative questions.

Classics in translation

Chankaya Kautilya *The Arthasastra* (Penguin, India). This classic by Chankaya, after whom the diplomatic enclave in New Delhi is named, is competently translated by LN Rangrajan. Currently unavailable in the UK and US, but likely to be reissued before long.

Hindu Myths (Penguin). Wendy O'Flaherty's translations of key myths from the original Sanskrit texts provide an indispensible insight into the foundations of Hinduism.

Mahabharata: The World's Greatest Spiritual Epic of All Time (Torchlight). The hyped-up subtitle notwithstanding, this translation of the Indian epic is as good as any. The same publishers also produce an abridged version, which is one-third the length of the unabridged text.

The Ramayana of Valmiki (Princeton University Press, o/p). Hari Prasad Shastri's multi-volume translation of the Indian epic is the most authoritative version, but it's very hard to track down; a good introduction is offered by RK Narayan's prose account (published by Penguin) of the episodes dealing with Prince Rama's courtship of Sita, their exile, Sita's abduction by Ravana and the great battle between Rama and Ravana.

The Rig Veda (Penguin). Translator Wendy O'Flaherty has selected some 108 pieces from the thousand Sanskrit hymns that comprise the vigorous, life-affirmative scripture of the *Rig Veda*.

Sacred Books and Early Literature of the East (Kessinger). For anyone with a passionate interest in the sacred literature of India, this fifty-volume set, first published between 1878 and 1901, is a great point of reference, featuring excellent translations of *The Upanishads*, *The Sacred Laws of the Aryas*, *The Bhagvad Gita*, *The Dhammapada*, *The Laws of Manu*, *Vedic Hymns* and *The Vedanta Sutras*. Less committed students could get hold of *Sacred Books of the East* (South Asia Books), which includes excerpts from *The Upanishads*, *The Dhammapada* and the *Vedic Hymns*.

Thirteen Principal Upanishads (Oxford University Press, US & India). Robert E Hume's translation of the thirteen principal *Upanishads*, first published a century ago, is a classic translation of these seminal works. Accompanied by a concise summary of the underlying philosophy of the Sanskrit texts, this edition offers a fine introduction to classical Indian thought.

Mallanaga Vatsyayana *Kama Sutra* (Oxford University Press). The OUP translation, by Wendy O'Flaherty and Sudhir Kakar, is the most recent English version of this much-misunderstood treatise, which addresses far wider issues of social behaviour than its reputation as a sex manual might lead you to believe. This edition also includes the earliest Sanskrit commentary on the *Kama Sutra*, plus a twentieth-century Hindi commentary and explanatory notes.Of earlier translations, the most renowned and enjoyable is the pioneering work by Richard F Burton, available from Modern Classics.

Biography and autobiography

Tariq Ali *The Nehrus and the Gandhis: An Indian Dynasty* (Picador; Pan). Published originally in 1985 after the assassination of Indira Gandhi, this fine book was updated to include Rajiv Gandhi's assassination in 1991, thus providing a complete story of the Nehru-Gandhi dynasty.

Nirad C Chaudhuri *Autobiography of an Unknown Indian* (New York Review of Books). Reissued half a century after its publication in 1951, this moving, evocative, self-effacing autobiography of a man who was born in present-day Bangladesh in 1900 is a modern-day classic.

Nirad C Chaudhuri *Clive of India: A Political and Psychological Essay* (Barrie & Jenkins; South Asia Books). A benign biography of Clive by Nirad Chaudhuri, an Indian writer who specialized in challenging established orthodoxies among his fellow-citizens.

Louis Fischer *The Life of Mahatma Gandhi* (HarperCollins). First published in 1950, this biography has been reissued several times since, and quite rightly – veteran American journalist Louis Fischer knew his subject personally, and his book provides an engaging account of Gandhi as a man, politician and propagandist.

Katherine Frank *Indira: A Life of Indira Nehru Gandhi* (HarperCollins; Houghton Mifflin). A well-researched biography that presents a rounded portrait of her subject, including an interesting account of Indira's husband, Feroze Gandhi.

Mohandas Karamachand Gandhi *An Autobiography, or The Story of my Experiments with Truth* (Penguin; Beacon). First published in Gujarati in two volumes in 1927 and 1929, this is Gandhi's fascinating account of his spiritual and moral development, his changing relationship with the British government in India and his gradual emergence into the fore of politics.

David Gilmour *Curzon* (Macmillan, o/p). A highly readable description of the life and times of Lord Curzon, a colourful British politician who left a deep mark on India.

VP Menon *Transfer of Power in India* (Sangam, UK). This account of the transfer of power in India in 1947 by a senior Indian civil servant combines insider knowledge with a personal touch.

Jawaharlal Nehru *An Autobiography: with musings on recent events in India* (Oxford University Press, India). Written in prison in 1934–35, this narrative is more than a personal document – immensely wide-ranging in scope, it fully demonstrates the profound erudition of its author.

Bhikhu Parekh *Gandhi: A Very Short Introduction* (Oxford University Press). A perceptive, concise and very balanced monograph which illuminates both the strengths and the weaknesses of Gandhi's thought.

Culture, art and architecture

Benoy K Behl and others *Ajanta Caves: Artistic Wonder of Ancient Buddhist India* (Thames & Hudson; Abrams). A well-informed, beautifully produced illustrated study of the Ajanta murals.

AL Basham *The Wonder That Was India: A Survey of the History and Culture of the Indian Subcontinent before the Coming of the Muslims* (Sidgwick & Jackson). A veritable encyclopedia by India's foremost authority on his country's ancient history. Every page of this masterpiece bristles with the author's erudition and scholarship. A companion volume, by SA Rizvi, brings it up to the arrival of the British.

AL Basham (ed.) *A Cultural History of India* (Oxford University Press, US & India). An unrivalled history of India's multifarious culture, which extends its analysis beyond the country's borders to consider the global influence of Indian civilization.

Percy Brown *Indian Painting under the Mughals* (Cosmo; Asia Book Corp). This painstakingly researched and well-illustrated account was first published in 1924 and retains its standing as the benchmark study.

Roy Craven *Indian Art* (Thames & Hudson). Concise general introduction to Indian art, from Harappan seals to Moghul miniatures, with lots of illustrations.

JC Harle *The Art and Architecture of the Indian Subcontinent* (Yale University Press). Harle's book, first published in 1986, is a highly readable and meticulously illustrated survey of the subcontinent's art and architecture.

George Michell *The Hindu Temple* (University of Chicago Press). A fine primer, introducing Hindu temples, their significance, and architectural development.

Shobita Punja *Divine Ecstasy: The Story of Khajuraho* (Viking, o/p). Punja provides a thorough description of the awe-inspiring cave temples.

Stuart Cary Welch *India: Art and Culture 1300–1900* (Prestel; Holt Rinehart). Originally produced for an exhibition at New York's Metropolitan museum, this exquisitely illustrated and accessibly written tome covers every aspect of India's rich and varied culture. Highly recommended.

glossary

glossary

aam general, public

adhikari royal official

adi original

aditi infinity

advaita second to none

Agni Fire god

Agni-kula Family of Fire

ahinsa lit. non-hurting of living objects; fig. non-violence

ain institutions

akali eternal

akbar great

al the

alam universe

anand bliss

an-Arya/an-Aryan non-Aryan, ignoble

aparajito invincible

aphabhramsa falling away

arak alcoholic spirit (distilled from aniseed)

aram dharma, duty

artha lit. land, property, welfare; fig. polity

Arya/aryan lit. kinsman; fig. noble

ashram retreat

asi are

asna posture

asrar secrets

atharva knowledge of magic formulas

atimiya spiritual

atman soul

ayurveda knowledge of life

azm great

babur lion

bahadur brave

bahia bay

Bhagvad Lord

bhakti devotion

bhang hemp, hashish

Bharat India

Bharatiya Indian

bigha half an acre

bin son

bodhisattva Buddha-to-be

bom good

Brahamans Prayers

Brahma lit. God of expansion; one of the three prime divinities of Hinduism

brahmin priest

Brahmo of Brahma

buddha awakened

buland lofty

chaitya prayer hall

chandravamisha lunar

charita life

Daivaputra Son of Heaven

dakshina south

daro mound

darpan mirror

darshan viewing

darwaza gateway

dasa lit. destroyer; fig. servant, slave

Dassera Tenth Day

dawla dominion, realm

dev/deva god, deity

devanampiya beloved of gods

devdasi maid of god

devi goddess

dharma law, condition, duty

dharna steadying (of the mind)

digambara lit. sky-robed; fig. naked

din faith

Dipavali/Divali row of lights (festival)

dvija twice born

Dyas-putra Father of Sky

-e of

emir commander

fatwa religious decree

gharibi poverty

ghazi warrior (in Islam)

gita song

gitanjli song offerings

godaan gift of a cow

granth book of scripture (Sikh)

guru teacher

hatao remove

hath force

Hind India

Hindoostan/Hindustan India

hinyana small, lesser (Buddhist)

hum in

-i of

Illahi Divine

Indra God of atmosphere/weather

inham love

iqbal lucky

itimad trust

jahan world

jalal glory

jan/jana people

janata people, public

jataka folk tale

jihad effort, holy war (in Islam)

jina victor

jizya Islamic tax on noncombatants

jo of

kachha underpants

kali black

kama sex, love

kanga comb

kara bangle

karma action, deed

kaur princess

kazhagam federation

kess hair

khalifa caliph

Khalistan Land of Khalsa (Sikhs)

khalsa pure

khas special, private

khilafat caliphate

khums one-fifth (of booty or income)

khurram joyous

koh mountain

kottam group of districts

krishna black

kshtra nobility

kshatriya warrior

kul all

kumbhar potter

kural couplets

kurram collective of villages

maan (weight) 82 lbs

madressa theological college (of Islam)

madya wine

Mahabharata Great Bharata Dynasty

Mahadeva Great god (applied to Lord Shiva)

mahal palace

maharaja great raja/ruler

maharajatiraja king of kings, emperor

mahasabha great assembly

mahavir great hero

mahayana great vehicle (Buddhist)

malfuzat memoirs

mamsa flesh

man mind

mandapa hall

mani is (Buddhist)

mansa story

mansabdar office holder

mantra formula comprising words or sounds possessing magical/divine powers

masjid mosque

math monastery (Hindu)

matsya fish

mayon black

meru mountain

mihirgula sunflower

mihr light

minar minaret

misqal Indian weight for precious stones

mithuna sexual intercourse

moen dead

moti pearl

mudra foodgrain

muhtasib guardian (of public morals)

mukti freedom

muminin faithful

mumtaz favourite

munnetra progressive

nabob *see* nawab

nadu district

nag serpent

nai barber

na'ib deputy

nasiri victorious

nawab (nabob) deputy ruler, viceroy

nisa women

noor/nur light

om a sacred syllable regarded by some as the seed of all mantras

padma lotus

padmapani lotus bearer

pahul baptism rite of Sikhs

panchama fifth class; outcastes

pancheli ballad

panch-janah fifth people; outcastes

panj-ab five waters (ie rivers)

panth order, brotherhood

parva life

pather road

porul land, property

prajapati lord of living beings

Prakrit lit. made of natural process; fig. derivative

pratihara gate-keeper

Prithvi Earth goddess

priyadarshi of gracious mien

purohita chief priest

Purush Primordial person

qutb pivot

quwwat victory

raj rule, royal

raja ruler, king

rajanya nobility

Rajasthan Land of Rajputs

rajputra son of raja, prince

rana raja, ruler

rashtra nation

rashtriya national

ratha chariot

rig verse

rihala travels

sabha council

sadhana pathway

samachar news

samadhi concentration

samaj society, order

samiti assembly

samrat ruler

samsara transmigration

sangh union

sangha order; society (Buddhist)

sansar world

Sanskrit lit. cultivated

satyagraha force born out of truth

savtir luminous (term for the Sun)

sayyid lit. prince; title accorded to a male descendant of Prophet Muhammad

sena army

senani commander

shaikh lit. old man; fig. wise man

Shaiva follower of Shiva

shah ruler, king

shakti power

shan-en-shah king of kings, emperor

shastra instruction

shikara pyramid top (of a temple)

shilappadikaram ankle bracelet, jeweled anklet

Shiva one of the three prime divinities of Hinduism; lit. propitious

shloka metre consisting of two lines of 16 syllables each/double octosyllable couplet

shudra menial, serf

siddhartha aim achieved

sing/singh lion

siraj mirror

sita furrow

sitar string musical instrument

soma hallucinogenic drink of Indo-Aryans

smiriti remembered

sonar goldsmith

sruti heard

stupa lit. funeral tumulus; fig. mound commemorating the Buddha's death

sufi follower of Islamic mysticism

sulh tolerance, acceptance

sultan ruler, king

sultanate kingdom

Surya the Sun

suryavamisha solar

sutra manual

suttee self-immolation by widows

svetambara white-robed

swadeshi of one's own country

swayamsevak volunteer

tahqiq description, narrative

taj crown

takht throne

takhta coffin

taluqdar landowner

Tamilkam Tamil land

tarikh history

tat that

tauhahd monotheism

teli oil presser

tiru sacred

tuzuk memoirs

twam thou, you

ulema religious-legal scholars (of Islam)

Upanishad lit. One seated near the teacher; fig. treatise

Urdu lit. military camp

Ushas Goddess of Dawn

Vaishnavaa follower of Lord Vishnu

vaishya lit. common people; fig. peasants and traders

vajra thunderbolt

vajrapani thunderbolt bearer

vallabha lover

vana forest

varaha boar

varna colour, social class

Varuna God of water

veda knowledge

Vedanta lit. end of Vedas; fig. complete knowledge of Vedas

veena lute

vihara monastery (Buddhist)

Vishnu one of the three prime divinities of Hinduism; lit. One who prevails

ya or

yajur sacrifice

yama self-control

yamin deputy

yantra mystical diagram or symbol with magical powers

yatra travel

yoga lit. yoke; fig. spiritual discipline

yojna 7.2 kilometres

zakat lit. purifier; fig. alms tax in Islam

zamin land

zamindar lit. landowner; fig. land revenue collector

index

Entries in **colour** represent feature boxes

f

g

h

t

u

Yoga 56–7
Yoga Sutra 55
Younghusband, Francis 261

Z

zamindari 220, 223
Zoroastrianism 70, 73

around the world

Alaska ★ Algarve ★ Amsterdam ★ Andalucía ★ Antigua & Barbuda ★
Argentina ★ Auckland Restaurants ★ Australia ★ Austria ★ Bahamas ★
Bali & Lombok ★ Bangkok ★ Barbados ★ Barcelona ★ Beijing ★ Belgium &
Luxembourg ★ Belize ★ Berlin ★ Big Island of Hawaii ★ Bolivia ★ Boston
★ Brazil ★ Britain ★ Brittany & Normandy ★ Bruges & Ghent ★ Brussels ★
Budapest ★ Bulgaria ★ California ★ Cambodia ★ Canada ★ Cape Town ★
The Caribbean ★ Central America ★ Chile ★ China ★ Copenhagen ★
Corsica ★ Costa Brava ★ Costa Rica ★ Crete ★ Croatia ★ Cuba ★ Cyprus ★
Czech & Slovak Republics ★ Devon & Cornwall ★ Dodecanese & East
Aegean ★ Dominican Republic ★ The Dordogne & the Lot ★ Dublin ★
Ecuador ★ Edinburgh ★ Egypt ★ England ★ Europe ★ First-time Asia ★
First-time Europe ★ Florence ★ Florida ★ France ★ French Hotels &
Restaurants ★ Gay & Lesbian Australia ★ Germany ★ Goa ★ Greece ★
Greek Islands ★ Guatemala ★ Hawaii ★ Holland ★ Hong Kong & Macau ★
Honolulu ★ Hungary ★ Ibiza & Formentera ★ Iceland ★ India ★ Indonesia
★ Ionian Islands ★ Ireland ★ Israel & the Palestinian Territories ★ Italy ★
Jamaica ★ Japan ★ Jerusalem ★ Jordan ★ Kenya ★ The Lake District ★
Languedoc & Roussillon ★ Laos ★ Las Vegas ★ Lisbon ★ London ★

in twenty years

London Mini Guide ★ London Restaurants ★ Los Angeles ★ Madeira ★ Madrid ★ Malaysia, Singapore & Brunei ★ Mallorca ★ Malta & Gozo ★ Maui ★ Maya World ★ Melbourne ★ Menorca ★ Mexico ★ Miami & the Florida Keys ★ Montréal ★ Morocco ★ Moscow ★ Nepal ★ New England ★ New Orleans ★ New York City ★ New York Mini Guide ★ New York Restaurants ★ New Zealand ★ Norway ★ Pacific Northwest ★ Paris ★ Paris Mini Guide ★ Peru ★ Poland ★ Portugal ★ Prague ★ Provence & the Côte d'Azur ★ Pyrenees ★ The Rocky Mountains ★ Romania ★ Rome ★ San Francisco ★ San Francisco Restaurants ★ Sardinia ★ Scandinavia ★ Scotland ★ Scottish Highlands & Islands ★ Seattle ★ Sicily ★ Singapore ★ South Africa, Lesotho & Swaziland ★ South India ★ Southeast Asia ★ Southwest USA ★ Spain ★ St Lucia ★ St Petersburg ★ Sweden ★ Switzerland ★ Sydney ★ Syria ★ Tanzania ★ Tenerife and La Gomera ★ Thailand ★ Thailand's Beaches & Islands ★ Tokyo ★ Toronto ★ Travel Health ★ Trinidad & Tobago ★ Tunisia ★ Turkey ★ Tuscany & Umbria ★ USA ★ Vancouver ★ Venice & the Veneto ★ Vienna ★ Vietnam ★ Wales ★ Washington DC ★ West Africa ★ Women Travel ★ Yosemite ★ Zanzibar ★ Zimbabwe

also look out for our maps, phrasebooks, music guides and reference books